THE ONLY WAY IS WEST

A Once In A Lifetime Adventure Walking 500 Miles On Spain's Camino De Santiago

Bradley Chermside

COPYRIGHT © BRADLEY CHERMSIDE

TABLE OF CONTENTS

1. DATE WITH THE DEVIL

Two years before I walked the Camino de Santiago, I was partying in a packed nightclub on the Greek holiday island of Corfu. I hadn't even heard of the Camino, but was about to unwittingly trigger a series of extraordinary coincidences that would guide me down the fabled pilgrim path and change my life.

The first of those coincidences occurred when I bought a drink in the club and the barman handed me a €20 note in my change. Scribbled on that €20 bill was an email address. Tightening the note between my fingers, I held it up to the lights and tried to focus as a drunk guy holding beer bottles in both hands barged past.

Natalix_666@*********.com

Why would anyone write their email address on a banknote? Was it someone in the club wanting to chat me up? A quick scope of the dance floor didn't reveal any alluring looks. Did the account belong to a girl called Natalie? Was she a Satan worshipper? A fan of death-metal music? A devil between the sheets?

Then the fog of irrational thought cleared and a smile of realisation flashed across my face – so this was why every attempt to impress the ladies that night had failed miserably. In a desperate bid to catch a roving eye, I'd spent the evening dancing half-heartedly to music I hated and asking women for cigarettes even though I wasn't a smoker. I'd plunged to a new low when I'd scored a smoke from some girls and tried sparking up while holding it like a pen between my shaky fingers, nowhere near my mouth. The girls had walked away, ridiculing me, and I'd felt very silly indeed.

Desperate times called for desperate measures. Resorting to using the lame chat-up line that I was a singer in a rock band got the reply it deserved. 'What's your band called – Crap Street Boys?' mocked a girl with holiday braids in her hair as she looked me up and down in contempt. If anyone was on form that night, it certainly wasn't me. The reason why, though, was now obvious. Clearly the deities of destiny were guiding me to something and someone much more exciting: the email address of a mysterious girl.

Bolting through the doors of the club and out into the humid Greek summer night, I made for the nearest twenty-four-hour internet café. Being out all evening had drained my mobile's battery and it was the quickest way to get in contact. A sour-faced insomniac at the front desk with greasy hair, stubble, and storm clouds under his eyes snatched my €2 coin for an hour online. Once logged on, I shot Natalix_666 a message. Time was of the essence. I explained how and where I'd found her email address, asked if she was still in Corfu and told her my exact location. Signing off, I popped the big question: would she like to meet... tonight?

I dreamt of a happy ending to my ego-crushing evening. Maybe she was in that very internet café, my email would pop up on her screen, she'd leap from her seat, come running into my arms and we'd skip hand in hand back to the club and fall in love doing the Macarena, the conga or even Agadoo.

I sprang out of my chair, bought a Coke from a vending machine and returned to the computer. Great news – the message hadn't bounced back. The email address was real and surely a reply was just minutes away. I stared at the screen, my fists clenched in hope. I tapped my fingers on the table. I sifted through my junk mail in case her reply had got lost somewhere among the offers of Viagra, Thai brides and surgery to enhance my lance. I searched for her email address on the web, hoping for a lead to a phone number or social-media profile but uncovered nothing. I worried that the police might burst in and arrest me for stalking (I mean Greek law enforcement, not Sting and his bandmates). I got bored and disheartened.

My glass drained to half empty. Sobriety soon came marching

around the corner with her party-pooper friend realism. What if 'she' was actually a 'he'? Natalix could be a six-foot-four rugby player called Nathan who was about to come storming in and tackle me to the ground for disturbing him in the middle of the night. Or what if she was female but thousands of miles away and had never even set foot in Corfu? The €20 could have journeyed across countless countries and been brought there by someone else entirely.

When my hour was up, I sighed disappointedly and conceded that my idea was nothing more than an inebriate's insanity and my chances of receiving a reply were extremely slim.

Imagine, then, how my socks were knocked off when, two years later, as I packed my bag to walk the Camino, Natalix_666 unexpectedly dropped back into my life.

***

In that Corfu club, walking the Camino couldn't have been further from my mind. Nevertheless, a year or so later, it was a decision I made because of an entirely freak encounter on the London Underground; a second extraordinary coincidence that would inadvertently make my world collide with Natalix_666.

On a late-summer Sunday afternoon, I was riding a hot and clammy tube train with heavenly cool air blowing through the carriage-door window caressing my flushed face. Somehow, in a dopey daze, I'd taken the wrong train by mistake. Realising my error, I hurried off the train when it screeched to a halt and headed for the opposite platform. Everything seemed back on track until I heard a voice frantically shouting my name. I spun around and couldn't believe my eyes. Waving his arms in a frenzy was someone I hadn't seen in three years. As the hordes of carrier-bag-wielding passengers parted, we ran into each other's arms like long-lost brothers.

After our spontaneous, somewhat clumsy hug, I stood back and took a disbelieving look at German Julian, my old room-mate from university. We were both lost for words.

I broke the silence. 'You've still got that fucking orange T-shirt!' I blurted out. 'What the bloody hell are you doing here?'

It turned out we'd just been on the same train and he'd darted through the closing doors like Indiana Jones when he'd seen me walking past his carriage window.

Twenty minutes later, in a packed beer garden overlooking the barges moored in Camden Lock, Julian filled in the gaps over some cold beers as the sun toasted our shoulders. He'd flown over from Munich for the weekend to go to an art exhibition of some sort. I didn't ask too many questions about it because I was dying to know more about something he'd mentioned earlier.

'Tell me about that trail you said you walked in Spain last month,' I said as wisps of marijuana smoke danced past, leaving me light-headed and boss-eyed.

'Aah!' he said, pulling his chair up to the table like we were finally getting down to business. 'It's a Christian pilgrim route called ze Camino and is taking vun munts valking from souzen France to Santiago in ze norse-vest of Spain.'

Having not seen Julian in three years, it took me a while to decode his loveable Germ-glish. 'So,' I clarified, 'it's a pilgrimage path that starts in southern France, crosses the whole of Spain and finishes in the north-western city of Santiago?'

'Yes!' he confirmed, wiping beer from his moustache and pushing his curtain of hair from his eyes.

'And it takes one month to walk, right?'

'Vun munts valking, yes!'

'And it's called the Camino?'

'Ze Camino de Santiago. Yes. And it's ferry old. More than a zousand years old! You voot luff it. Lots of people from all over ze vorld, not only Christians, are walking ze path. Zere are special cheap pilgrim hostels and such beautiful sceneries and cities,' he said with contagious enthusiasm.

Before I could say I was sold, he carried on.

'I voss looking for your email to tell you to do it. But I didn't find it. I find you instead. Bah! It's a miracle,' he said, looking up to the equally rare phenomenon of a blue London sky. 'Okay! So I tell you now. You must do it!' He stared me square in the eyes before sipping at his beer.

Heading home on the right train that night, reflecting on an extraordinary day, I was convinced I'd met Julian on the wrong train so he could deliver the right message. This was a sign I could not ignore. I told myself that someday, sooner or later, when the time was right, I had to walk el Camino de Santiago – the Road to Santiago.

2. IRRATIONAL FEAR
OF THE NORM

After the decorations had come down the following Christmas and the New Year fireworks had fizzled out, the clock struck the right time. One foggy afternoon under gloomy March skies, the decision was made while having a kick-about over the park with my brother Matt.

A few hours earlier, I'd attended an induction for a job I'd been offered that coming summer. A full-time contract to manage five soccer schools in holiday resorts across the Mediterranean had my name on it. This would be the culmination of a decade's hard work. Even more importantly, the generous monthly salary would end the money worries of running my own football coaching business. The frequent, pushy phone calls from my franchisor telling me I had to expand, grow and earn more money would become a thing of the past. I'd be trading sodden, freezing cold, state-school fields peppered with dog downloads for coaching by the sea. It was everything a soccer-mad man who wasn't quite good enough to fulfil his boyhood dream of turning pro could ask for – a full-time job in the game, in the money.

'It's an unbeatable offer,' I said, carefully placing the ball on the edge of the penalty area, setting myself up to shoot at Matt. 'Definitely the best I've ever had. But it just doesn't feel right to take it.'

I stepped up to sky a right-foot rocket over the bar.

'Well maybe that's because you've been coaching for so long and this just feels like the same old thing,' Matt suggested as he craned his neck and watched the ball fly over the bar and into the trees behind him. 'You've been going on about the Camino since you bumped into Julian last year. Why don't you do that instead?'

He raced off to retrieve the ball from the woods behind the goal.

Matt was right. Ever since the serendipitous reunion with Julian on the London Underground, I hadn't shut up about walking the Camino de Santiago.

The idea of walking for 'vun munts', where every step would take me to a new place and a new face, made me smile. It made me pull funny faces in the mirror and do a stupid little Riverdance. It felt right.

Accepting the Mediterranean coaching job, on the other hand, would take me a step closer to the lifestyle I was most afraid of – mortgage, marriage, and saving up to retire and die. 'An irrational fear of the norm' was how Matt had always diagnosed my neurosis. A mortgage meant obligations, commitment and my freedom compromised. Marriage was an institution of which I'd always been suspicious. My parents had fought constant vicious verbal battles until they eventually divorced when I was eighteen. To me as an innocent young bystander, marriage seemed like nothing more than a declaration of domestic warfare. Rarely did they lay a finger on each other, but their toxic war of words fanned the flames of my irrational fear of the norm. I was determined that my future kids wouldn't witness the sort of upsetting scenes Matt and I had seen.

I'll always revere my mum for her tough love and moral grounding and for working the night shift as a nurse in our local hospital to make sure we never wanted for anything. She toiled all the hours available to make up for my dad's inability to work after he injured his back in an accident on the Ford assembly line. Just like I looked up to Mum, I longed to idolise my dad, the alpha male, but sadly we never saw eye to eye. In their heated disagreements, I always stood up for Mum. Dad and I feuded bitterly about my meddling. He thought I was just a kid who should stay out of matters that weren't my concern. My view was very different. Seeing Mum, my best friend, upset was definitely my concern and I never thought twice about joining their fights on her side.

The forced period of reflection after their divorce softened us both. The hurtful and regrettable insults Dad and I spewed at each other down the years stopped. Though relations were still strained, we'd both backed down and slowly began rebuilding our kinship. I was able to see how alike we were and many reasons to be grateful to him. As well as driving me to football every Sunday for ten years, I had Dad to thank for my sense of humour, clown personality and soft, soppy centre.

In the game of life, however, I was still lacking strong guidance from a father figure. Someone to challenge me with the big, soul-searching question that had been bobbing about in the sea of my subconscious for some time: had I designed my life around an unrealistic, unattainable ambition? Was it ridiculous to continue dreaming of becoming the singer for the biggest band in the world, a band so big, that I'd knock my hero, Bono from U2, off his perch? I'm well aware that after that last sentence you may be wondering if I'm off my medication, but this was my big dream. My moonshot. My 'if I could do anything...'. Writing songs was the only pursuit I enjoyed more than scratching my back with my mum's hairbrush. My intentions were well-meaning too. I've always said musicians can have a positive influence on more people than politicians. I wanted to pen lyrics that inspired, gave hope and pulled people through bad times, just as my most cherished favourite songwriters had done for me.

That said, had the time come for me to face my irrational fear of the norm? Instead of trying to better Bono, was I now meant to focus on developing my career, settling down and finding my Yoko Ono?

There and then, as Matt emerged from the woods and threw the ball back to me, I trapped it under my foot and made it public. I told him I was going to turn down the Mediterranean job, take a summer sabbatical from my football-coaching career, and walk eight hundred kilometres on the Road to Santiago.

**

Having committed to taking on the Camino, I devised a long to-do list that would enable me to close down my coaching business for the summer. The most important item on that list was informing kids' parents, head teachers, school PE coordinators and my franchise director - who was fuming with me - that I'd be out the office for the summer holidays. As my departure date drew nearer, I thought I should let friends and family know of my travel plans too. Since I planned to abstain from using my mobile phone and social media for the duration of the trip, the easiest and quickest way to do that was to send an email to everyone in my address book.

> *>To: All Contacts*
>
> *>From: Brad Chermside*
>
> *>Subject: My Spanish Summer*
>
> *Hi there my friends, family and best buddies!*
>
> *Some of you will not have heard from me in a while, so I thought I'd update you all.*
>
> *I've made a big and bold decision to take a summer sabbatical in Spain and walk the Camino de Santiago. It's a trail that starts in the French Pyrenees and goes on for 804 kilometres until the city of Santiago in north-west Spain.*
>
> *I'll be disconnecting from all mobile devices and on a social-media detox, so my only means of contact while I'm away will be email. My smartphone will be switched off and used only in emergencies. I'll endeavour to write once a week to let you all know that I'm alive and well.*
>
> *I do appreciate that some of you may not want to keep receiving my travelogue, so if you'd prefer I take you off this list, let me know. I won't be offended but will sneak into your house at night and put chilli powder in your underwear.*

Brad:)

Love and Peace (or else!)

I saved the message into my drafts folder because there were three important people I had to tell face to face before I could press send – my fellow bandmates. Having left it until one month before leaving, I was dreading telling them. We were enjoying a very productive spell and I was petrified of breaking the news that they'd have to cancel our summer gigs, postpone rehearsals and abandon songwriting sessions. I knew that the friendliest and most laidback member of our four piece, James Nash, the bass player, would be the safest person to start with. He was so nice, I wanted to award him a medal engraved with the words 'Nicest Bloke Called James in the World Ever'. It was surely only a matter of time before he'd be invited to hobnob with the Queen at a garden party and receive said accolade. When he was not making love to his 5-string, he was rustling up snacks to share with us in rehearsals, cooking for his Dad or volunteering to work with disabled people. Since he lived in the same town as the other lads, I messaged him and asked that he get everyone together down their local pub. When his reply came through soon after, I thought he'd gone too far with all this nice bloke business.

Hello sexy! Wanna come round and watch me play bass naked?

I read it once. I read it twice and then thrice, but it still said the same thing. I knew my answer was 'Please God, no!', but while trying to think of a way to break it more gently, another message buzzed.

Fuck shit! Ignore that – it was meant for Clare! We'll see you down the pub Friday at 8. Wearing clothes.

Clare – his girlfriend. Phew!

Not only was the Nash man stupid nice, with a penchant for playing bass naked, he was also full of interesting but utterly useless facts. Facts so interesting and useless that I rarely remembered them. Except for this one: the average person spends five years of their life on the bog.

Five years was also the amount of time the band had been together. Half a decade in which we'd paid more in parking and speeding tickets getting to our gigs than we'd made selling tickets for them. And though our greatest success to date had been getting barred from a venue because James stripped off and played a song wearing only his birthday suit one very messy night, things were looking up. We'd just recorded our first full album, and after years of juggling, I finally had my soccer-coaching business set up perfectly around nightly rehearsals and weekend gig commitments. We'd even won a competition to open for The Cure at an invitation-only show in London and had rubbed shoulders with their famous singer Robert Smith backstage. Or, should I say, we got off on the wrong foot when we helped ourselves to what we didn't know was The Cure's private buffet. We thought it was for all the artistes, not just the superstars.

Thankfully Robert Smith saw the funny side. 'Help yourselves, lads,' he said, waving us on with a bemused smile. Though he looked like a dark alley monster, dolled up in full Gothic stage make-up and with electric-chair hair, he was actually a very approachable, humble and lovely man. So lovely that we had the temerity to thrust a single from our new album into his hands. On the front cover was a quote from an independent record label that had recently featured the song on their *Best of Unsigned UK* compilation album: 'An earth-shaking shot of straight, hard-hitting rock,' it said. 'No chaser!'

Also emblazoned on the front of the single was our band's name, which had been inspired by a paragraph from Paulo Coelho's book *The Alchemist*. At a pivotal moment in the story the protagonist stands at the Straits of Gibraltar about to cross into Africa. He fantasises about realising his ambition to get to the pyramids in Egypt, where his dream lover awaits him. In a moment of self-doubt, the fangs of fear take a bite from his bravery and he turns back. But then the wind picks up and carries the smell of the desert of his dreams, and a kiss from the woman awaiting him nestles on his lips. The freedom of the wind prompts the revelation that nothing can hold him back and he plucks up the courage to cross the straits and venture into Africa. Our band was named after the very same wind, the one that roused him into chasing his dreams and kept me determined to carry on chasing mine: Levanter.

Considering the timing of my decision, the lads took the news well. They said they would work hard in the studio while I was away, finish mixing our album and start sending demos to record companies. They also promised to draft a press release to inform our five ardent followers – Dave Galpin and his girlfriend Gemma; two Aussie girls called Jodie and Carly; and a sixteen-year-old with long ginger hair down to his bottom, called Seejay – of our summer hiatus. I thanked them for their support and they wished me well.

With the blessing of my bandmates and a weight off my shoulders, I went home and pressed send on the email I'd drafted earlier to all my contacts. The next time I opened my inbox, I was inundated with well-wishing replies, but one in particular hit me between the eyes – a message from Natalix_666.

3. BITTER ORANGES

I'd forgotten Natalix_666 even existed. Since I'd sent that message on a drunken whim in Corfu two years earlier, I hadn't heard a whisper. But now her unexpected reply brought a glimmer of hope after a long run of disheartening romantic rendezvous.

It was five years since I'd parted from my first love, Jane. We split after I took up the chance to do the final year of my sports-coaching degree on a student-exchange programme in Florida. Though I was madly in love with her, it was a once-in-a-lifetime offer and one I'd regret forever if I didn't take it. Jane, my blue-eyed English rose, whose Sunflower perfume will always stir up such sweet memories whenever I catch the scent, was the perfect girlfriend. So much so that she gave me her blessing to go and promised to wait for me. But I didn't want her to endure the heartache a long-distance love cruelly inflicts. It wouldn't have been fair of me to have my own big slice of American Pie and eat it while she faithfully waited for me at home. Jane had been talking excitedly of post-graduation jobs, saving up for a house, and potential baby names. She deserved a more mature, committed and thoughtful Tarzan when all I could think of was monkeying around across the pond.

As heart-wrenching as it was to break up, I knew letting her move on was the right thing to do after four years together. She cried her heart dry and her body convulsed with anguish in my arms when we said our last goodbye. I walked the nine miles home that evening instead of taking my usual bus to ease the tension in my thumping head. I felt terrible for hurting someone I loved so much but reasoned that staying together would do more damage in the long run.

After that, I had relationships with plenty of women who

were girlfriend material. It was my irrational fear of the norm, though, that steered me into a number of more unconventional, edgy and tempestuous amorous entanglements.

There was a Colombian girl in Florida whose ex-boyfriend back home sent a hatchet man to threaten us in the dead of night. I cowered behind the sofa in my Sponge Bob boxer shorts while he hammered on her apartment door warning me that my days were numbered. The next morning I found the passenger window of my car smashed and that was the final move in my dance with Latin America.

After returning home, I had more ill-advised dangerous liaisons. The kind of encounters when your happy-condriac rose-tinted glasses make you blind to all the warnings from your friends and family. There was a Sicilian girl who'd secretly copied the keys to my flat and stormed in as I was about to strike the match with a new flame. There was another unstable Mabel, who will remain anonymous because to this day I still get jumpy when I think of her. She was more of a crime-scene investigator than a girlfriend:

'Why are there two wet towels in the bathroom?'

'You got petrol three days ago, why do you need more already?'

'Whose strand of hair is this?'

'I saw you online this morning. Who were you talking to?'

'Did you want your surfboard? 'Cos I've just smashed it up!'

Just some of the many questions I had to field during her flash cross-examinations over lunch.

I even dated a previous Miss Hungary for a while. Yes, you read that right. Hungary, not hungry. And no, she didn't win her country's beauty pageant in 1880. Fed up with dating self-obsessed models, egotistical Hungarian celebrities and womanising Formula One drivers, she thought she'd try something different: an aspiring but misfiring rock star whose most expensive possession was a green Peugeot 106 that smelled of vinegary football socks from his day job running a soccer school. That didn't last long either because she'd scream at me if I ate a potato after 3pm. 'You're already too fat!' she'd bawl in my face while poking an accusing finger into the porkpie crust hanging over my jeans. She was right. I did have some wobbly love to handle, but what was the world coming to if you couldn't have a spud-u-like every now and again?

All attempts at finding lasting love had ended in a horrible mess of emergency locksmiths, near-death experiences and me crying guilty tears into my jacket potato.

With my search for a soulmate (or 'half orange', as they say in Spain) leaving a bitter taste in my mouth, I sought solace in matters more metaphysical. I had a longing to meet my maker and journeyed far and wide as a spiritual tourist. I barked up the yoga tree and howled with laughter in class one evening when a lady bow-wowed out of her backside in Downward Dog position. After that, my posh classmates stuck their noses in the air at me and I left the group with my tail between my legs.

I went on a weekend meditation retreat with Buddhists and battled vegan-cuisine-fuelled flatulence to maintain my fragile vow of noble silence. I volunteered at a Hare Krishna temple and learned to chant and make pea soup. I worked part-time for my local church's youth programme, hoping to find Jesus, but instead I just got tired of listening to the choir trying to find the right note on Friday club nights.

Experimenting with something less conventional, I joined the Karma Army, a network of altruists who performed weekly random acts of kindness for strangers on what they dubbed 'Good Fridays'. I bought a Snickers for the baffled person behind me in the queue at the petrol station; hugged an unsuspecting traffic warden; gifted a surprised, slightly suspicious old lady some flowers at a bus stop. I even gave my favourite *Big Issue* vendor £25 to buy another batch of magazines to replace the ones he'd had stolen. The next day a thoughtful lady from the congregation at the church where I worked gave me £25 in Tesco vouchers. 'What goes around does come around,' I slurred repeatedly to anyone stupid enough to listen to me in the pub that Friday night.

Try as I might, the desperate search to find my spiritual home and my half orange had come up fruitless. Every weekend I would try to fill those gaping holes in my soul in the same sorry way – at another gig, in another bar, with another girl, before nursing another head-banging hangover.

It was a meaningless, empty existence exacerbated by the Monday morning blues. Every week at 9am I'd have sixteen under-fives looking at me with puppy-dog eyes waiting to have their laces tied. Many of them would have their left boot forced onto their right foot and it was often so cold I couldn't even tie my own laces let alone theirs. I knew I'd really miss teaching the little cherubs, by far the most rewarding part of my job. I'd done this for so long though, that I was losing my enthusiasm for it. I needed a new challenge and a break from the pressures of running a money hungry franchise. A change of approach and scenery was badly needed for some clarity and headspace. Leaving for the Camino, a route along whose course many former pilgrims claimed to have found enlightenment, couldn't come quick enough. My career, one I wasn't even sure I wanted to continue with, was being held back by a musical ambition on which I'd made little progress. My dances with the divine just weren't moving my spirit. My love life had become a cycle of one sorry disaster after another. All was not lost though, because as I began preparing for the Camino, I got a glimmer of hope that this particular cycle of disasters might soon be broken. I found it hard to believe, but there it was on the screen in front of me – a reply to my email from Natalix_666!

> *To: Brad Chermside*
> *From: Natalia*
> *Subject: Re: My Spanish Summer*
> *Hello Brad!*
> *¿Remember me? ¡Is Natalia!*

I live in Melide. Here we have el Camino, so when you come to here, if you want that you sleep on my house is no problem.
Here its the number of my movil: 6*********
¡Bye bye!

I couldn't believe what I was reading. Just like that, the identity of the person who'd written their email address on that €20 note had been revealed. I now knew for sure it was a woman and not a man. My guessing at the name Natalie hadn't been far wrong, and in an extraordinary twist of fate she lived just fifty kilometres from Santiago and had invited me to stay 'on her house'. Maybe she'd let me come down from the roof and sleep inside if I promised not to dribble on the pillows?

Courting yet more mystery, she'd attached a teasing photo hiding her face. The image was of a svelte brunette dancing, her long frizzy hair flicked theatrically across her face, her arms thrown into the air flamenco-style. I fantasised about what she might look like under that hairy face.

Hollywood actress Shirley MacLaine in her book *The Camino* puts forward the notion that the Camino chooses you rather than the other way round. She believes this because she received two anonymous letters in the same handwriting beseeching her to walk to Santiago. Was I being chosen too? Was this the reason I'd bumped into Julian on the wrong train on the London Underground twelve months after the €20 note crossed my palm? Had fate intervened so that Natalia and I would meet on one of the world's most famous pilgrim trails instead of in a seedy Corfu nightclub? Was this love moving in its famed mysterious ways?

I recalled another line from Shirley MacLaine's book. 'The Camino offers everyone a love affair,' she promises.

I couldn't wait to get to Melide, just fifty kilometres before the end of my walk, and find out if Natalia would be mine.

4. THE AWKWARD
AU REVOIR

The day before leaving for the Camino, I received a welcome surprise from my best friend Chappers – a good-luck charm. Chappers is possibly the only person on the planet who still reads Teletext, refuses to use a smartphone or social media, and will only go online at his local library because it's free. It was from there that he'd scanned and emailed some words he'd written underneath a picture of my footballing hero, former West Ham United goalkeeper Ludo Miklosko.

> *Bradders!*
>
> *Here is Ludo Miklosko.*
>
> *You will be in safe hands if you keep him stashed away.*
>
> *Bradders, I send you my best wishes for your trip, I think it's a great move you're making.*
>
> *What can I say, don't be dangerous and be safe but create opportunities and take your chances. It will be the making of you, my friend. You will come off your trip a new man.*
>
> *Remember, don't stress. Everything will be fine in the end!*
>
> *I'll be thinking of you roaming & singing your day away.*
>
> *Chappers*

It was the perfect send-off – good wishes from a best mate and a picture of Ludo, the man who'd saved my beloved West Ham on countless occasions. He was now sure to save me too when called upon. I printed off the email and held onto it like china.

Chappers was also the man I'd turned to for assistance when devising a kit list. When it comes to preparing for crazy trips, Paul Laurie Chapman, my best friend and partner in pranks since we were eleven years old, knows more than most. He is the living legend of a 1,800 kilometre bike ride through Africa to Timbuktu; a 2,900 kilometre trip around Europe on roller skates; a 3,900 kilometre BMX ride from Mexico City to Panama City; and, just while you take a moment to catch your breath, 2,250 kilometres on Skikes (these are road skis with wheels on the bottom) from Hong Kong to Shanghai.

I got on the phone and asked him to send some ideas as to what my kit list should include. Two days later, an envelope inscribed with his money-spider-sized handwriting dived through the letterbox. He'd always insisted on writing so small to save ink, paper and money. At first glance, everything appeared quite straightforward:

2 pairs of shorts
3 pairs of socks
3 T-shirts

Reading further on, things were getting technical:

Water-purification system
Rehydration solution
Travel towel

This was turning out to be trickier than I'd ever imagined. What was the difference between a travel towel and a normal one?

Can I fly on it like a magic carpet? I texted him.

It's quick drying, lighter material, you numpty, he replied with a smiley emoji.

Thanks to Chappers' invaluable assistance and some other helpful hints I'd got from past pilgrims on Camino internet forums, I typed out a detailed kit list and divided it into six sections.

1. Clothing: 2 pairs of boxer shorts, 3 pairs of shorts, 1 pair of tracksuit bottoms (for cold nights), 1 sleeveless T-shirt, 1 T-shirt, 1 long-sleeved T-shirt, 2 pairs of hiking socks, 2 pairs of

pants, waterproof jacket, travel towel, bandanna.

2. Essentials & Financials: passport, travel insurance, debit card, credit card, fake wallet containing old bank cards (in case I get mugged), body-belt wallet that slips under clothes.

3. Sentimentals: journal & pen(s), Dictaphone, good-luck cards, Southend-on-Sea fridge magnet for Natalia.

4. Optional Extras: Flip-flops, duct tape (for blisters), needle and thread, nail cutter, Spanish phrasebook, mp3 player, camera, plastic cutlery, roll mat, ground sheet, clothes pegs, batteries, tent, tent pegs, mallet, guy lines, inflatable pillow, bumbag/duffel bag, binoculars, safety pins, mobile phone, (switched off at all times and for use in emergencies only).

5. Security & Survival: samurai sword (only joking!), headlamp, first-aid kit, mini sun-cream, guidebook, mini after-sun, sunhat, mosquito net, Vaseline (for blisters), black plastic bag (to keep clothes dry), sleeping bag, Flexi Flask, water epoxy purification system.

6. Toiletries: toothbrush, toothpaste, roll-on deodorant.

Was it just me, or was that a helluva lot to lump around Spain for a month? Online, I'd read a plethora of accounts from pilgrims who'd ended up ditching a shedload of stuff along the way. I wasn't sure if I was going to use all the things I had on the list. I'd only know when I started walking. So, for now, I was sticking with it.

After seeking help from a best friend, I turned to a distant family member (being 50 per cent Smithsonian thanks to my mum's maiden name), to uncover all the vital Camino information. From his galaxy of stationery, bookshelves and magazine racks, WH Smith presented me with a quite brilliant guidebook: *A Guide to the Ancient Pilgrim Path, Camino de Santiago* by John Brierley. This gem was a treasure chest of key facts on everything I needed to know. Maps, I was pleased to read, were not essential as yellow arrows would show me the way for the entire 804 kilometres. From my chosen starting point in southern France to Santiago, just one hundred kilometres from the Portuguese border, I'd be chasing those yellow arrows all the way.

Reading about the journey in more detail, it became quite clear this was not going to be a walk in the park. The author John Brierley fired a warning: 'About half-way, there is a twenty-one-kilometre stretch where you will encounter no roads, no bridges, no metal signs, no farm, no village, and no houses. There is little shade and the only place to get water will be from a couple of streams that are hard to see and easy to miss.'

This paragraph piqued my interest in the various types of terrain I'd encounter. Studying each stage of the Camino, I made some calculations. I was delighted to discover that just over five hundred kilometres would be on natural paths. For two hundred kilometres I would be bouncing along the bitumen of quiet streets, and for around one hundred kilometres I'd have to put up with walking close to busy roads.

Leafing through the pages brought more revelations.

'The summer months of July and August are bedlam. Expect to share the trail with an estimated 35,000 pilgrims from all over the globe,' John Brierley wrote. Since summer was the only time I could travel, I could look forward to being one of a cosmopolitan cast of thousands.

The Camino hadn't always been so popular. Back in the 1980s, a group of Camino enthusiasts in London founded the Confraternity of St James. Their simple aim was to provide a place for former pilgrims to share stories and future pilgrims to get advice. When they first collated statistics in 1986, only 2,491 arrivals into Santiago were recorded. Compare that to the 301,166 pilgrims who descended on the city in 2017 and you can see the exponential increase in people going walkabout. By 1989, for instance, the 2,491 of 1986 had more than doubled, to 5,760. That could have been because pilgrims wanted their arrival in Santiago to coincide with the Pope's visit there that year. But surely the Proclaimers' song 'I Would Walk Five Hundred Miles', the same distance as the Camino and released that same year, must have inspired a few to go too?

In the following years, figures continued climbing at an

astonishing rate. Though no one can put their finger on exactly why, many cite the rise of the internet, social media and two books by best-selling authors. Paulo Coelho's *The Pilgrimage* (1997) and Shirley MacLaine's *The Camino* (2000) elevated the Camino's profile to new heights and brought it to the attention of their millions of loyal readers. On the Confraternity of St James's online forum I was dismayed to see people ridiculing my suggestion that Forrest Gump's travels on foot across America must have added to the numbers as well. More recently, another film, *The Way* (2010), starring Emilio Estevez and Martin Sheen, has helped to bring the Camino into mainstream consciousness and onto the bucket lists of more people than ever.

Though the earliest pilgrims started out from their dwellings, that more authentic, traditional option wasn't open to me. Wearing walking apparel and carrying a backpack, I wouldn't even make it to the end of my high street without getting mugged or stopped by the police on suspicion of being a fugitive, terrorist or sex pest. Taking the safer option, I followed in the carbon footsteps of most modern-day pilgrims and flew over with Ryanair. On the short flight, I deflected the persistent and grating pleas to buy scratch cards, cheap booze and baguettes that tasted like the soles of my grandad's old army boots and touched down in Biarritz. From there I was only a train ride away from the start of the Camino in St-Jean-Pied-de-Port.

Poked into the foothills of the French Pyrenees, the town is just fifteen kilometres from the Spanish frontier and the official beginning of the Camino Francés. 'The French Way', as it translates, is the most trodden route of the many pilgrim trails leading to Santiago from various starting points throughout France, Spain and Portugal. The pilgrim office in Santiago registered that over 60 per cent of the pilgrims invading the city in 2017 came via the Camino Francés. The biggest pull for me to begin in St-Jean-Pied-de-Port wasn't that it was the most popular starting point. I just couldn't resist the chance to indulge my passion for surfing in nearby Biarritz before going gallivanting.

On the journey over I had my lucky-charm Ludo tucked into

my wallet and another best friend, Luke, by my side. By day we rode waves in blazing sunshine on a sparkling ocean, and by night we blew our supply of beer tokens at a seaside bar. Luke and I had been mates for ten years, but that weekend we got on better than ever. Saying the dreaded goodbye seemed to come way too soon. I am never good at goodbyes. With a girl, my nervous enthusiasm causes me to shake the wrong hand or end up kissing their nose or ears. With a guy, I often fare better and offer a firm handshake or macho pat on the back, before cracking a silence-filling, unfunny joke. This time, though, we both knew this wasn't the standard goodbye sketch. This was the farewell when two old friends don't know when they'll see each other again, or actually if they will, such was the challenge ahead of me.

Standing by a zebra crossing outside a boulangerie piping out the alluring smell of freshly baked bread, we braced ourselves for the awkward au revoir. In a church square across the road, generations of local families and friends waltzed, spun and skipped like morris dancers to French folk music. We stopped to watch the entertainment for a few minutes and bought ourselves some time to figure out how we were going to part ways in as macho a fashion as possible.

'You'd never see this on a Sunday morning in Essex,' I said as a bus roared past, choking us in a toxic cloud of exhaust fumes. 'Everyone would be too smashed from the night before.'

'Not wrong – they'd get egged!' Luke joked, sparking up a cigarette to calm his own nerves about saying goodbye.

With a map in my hand ready to guide me to the train station and Luke looking to hail a taxi to the airport, it was time to say sayonara.

'Luke, you're one of my best mates, you know that?' I said, swallowing the lump in my throat.

Then for some reason, I still don't know why, I held out a clenched fist to him and he reciprocated. There we were on a busy Biarritz street in the middle of the day, knuckle to knuckle like we were about to start a boxing match, with morris dancing music playing in the background. A most unconventional valediction, but we'd got the final farewell out the way.

Although my eyes were welling up with emotion, I felt euphoric as I walked off and left Luke waiting for a taxi by the side of the road. I was treading the first steps of an estimated one million I'd take on the way to Santiago. I now had nothing holding me back – apart from what felt like a dead body in my backpack. How the hell was I going to carry this monster 804 crazy kilometres across Spain?

5. DON'T! CARRY ON CAMPING

The rickety train to St-Jean-Pied-de-Port bumped and ground its way out the station, then lurched, tilted and rattled around the verdant valleys encircling Biarritz. After clearing takeaway coffee cups from the seats and patting dust clouds out of the retro brown upholstery, I spent most of the journey peering enviously out the windows. I longed to emancipate myself from the stuffy carriage, tear off my clothes and go bask with the locals in the mini waterfalls cascading into the white-water rivers dotting the lush landscape. To pass the time and take my mind off the heat, I had no other option than to flick open the pages of my guidebook and get educated about the history of St James and the Camino.

Although St. James or Santiago as the Spanish call him is the country's patron saint, rumour has it that when he was alive he could be quite the sinner too. So much so, he was nicknamed the Son of Thunder because of an explosive temper and tendency to throw his Bible out the pram. The word on the Bethlehem streets is that one evening, whilst out on a jolly in Jerusalem, he begged Jesus to use his superpowers and make hellfire rain down on a hotel refusing them a room. It's not known exactly why they were blacklisted. Whether it was because on previous stays, Jesus had cost them a fortune by turning all the guests' water into wine hasn't been confirmed or denied. In any case, the thunderous son didn't take the knockback well and he's believed to have caused a storm that night.

Despite St Jimmy's fiery temperament, Jesus knew a good egg when he saw one. Eyeing him up as prime messenger material, the Son of God ordered the Son of Thunder to travel the globe spreading the word of the Lord. With Jesus's blessing, he grabbed his Good Book and staff, then set sail for Galicia on the north-west coast of Spain. It's presumed he was sent to the Iberian Peninsula because it was a bastion of pre-Christian spirituality. After a good few years converting sun worshippers into cross worshippers, James went back to Judea and was martyred in AD 41. His disciples are thought to have returned to Galicia later with his body, to an area roughly twenty-five kilometres south of Santiago. However, the sands of time blew over these events and St Jimmy's eventual resting place was shrouded in doubt.

Around the turn of the ninth century, with Spain now under the control of the Muslim Moors and known as Al-Andalus, any talk of St James might have seen your head rolling down the hill. But then the country witnessed the mother of all miracles – the discovery of his tomb. Legend tells that a shepherd called Pelayo played a big part in finding his burial place. On a crystal-clear night he was mysteriously drawn to a field after following a mesmerising star that twinkled more brightly than all the others. Word travelled fast, attracting startled stargazers from far and wide. This chain of events led to the unearthing of St James's remains by a jubilant bishop who duly christened the site 'Santiago de Compostela' – St James of the Star Field.

The miraculous recovery of the relics provided the divine inspiration needed for Spain's Crusaders to revolt against the occupying Moors and reinstall Christianity as the official religion. The overthrow inspired thousands of Christian pilgrims from across Europe to flock to the Star Field and el Camino de Santiago – the Road to Santiago – was born. The reconquering of Spain was supported by French forces, who crossed the Pyrenees to help push the Muslims back to Africa and as far away from France as possible. It was at the foot of those same Pyrenees that my train finally juddered to a halt after two hours of sweaty torture.

I had no idea where to go when I arrived in St-Jean-Pied-de-Port, so having spotted some fellow pilgrims on the train, I decided to follow them. My decision was a good one. After five minutes pursuing strangers hoisting backpacks down handsome streets where crimson roses climbed whitewashed, mahogany-shuttered houses, I came to a Camino information centre. Inside, an old lady whose English took my French to the cleaners called me over to her desk.

'Where are you from?' she asked, lowering her glasses inquisitively.

'England!' I answered with a big smile as I put my backpack on the floor and took a seat.

'Ah, Finland. We have many pilgrims from Finland,' she declared.

'No, no. England. I am English,' I said, and actually sung the melody to 'God Save the Queen' until people around me started staring.

My nationality finally established, the hard-of-hearing old lady then warned me that the first day would be tough going: a twenty-four-kilometre hike up and over the imposing, hazy, forested Pyrenees where I wouldn't find a shop anywhere, only cows, sheep, goats and wild horses. If I didn't fancy eating the livestock, I should buy enough food in St-Jean-Pied-de-Port before heading into the hills. She then gave me the all-important *Credencial* – the pilgrim's passport to more than seventy hostels (*albergues*) scattered conveniently along the Camino. The Credencial, she advised me, would need two stamps per day if I wanted to be granted a Compostela, the coveted Certificate of Completion awarded upon arrival in Santiago. She assured me I'd be able to score the stamps at albergues, cafés and shops along the way.

On my way out the office, I dipped my hand into a basket full of scallop shells, tied one to my rucksack and tossed some euros into a donation box. All paintings, statues and images of St James show him with a scallop shell hanging around his neck. Theories abound about how and why the shell came to be synonymous with the Camino and could be told in the style of a riddle:

Did you hear the one about St James, the knight, the bride and the horse?

All of them are rumoured to have emerged from the Atlantic Ocean covered in scallop shells.

But how did they end up in the sea? Some say the ship sailing from Judea back to Spain was caught in a storm and that St James's remains were lost overboard. Others believe a knight fell off a cliff and the disciples on the ship carrying St James's body pulled him aboard and saved his life. Another myth mentions a horse at a wedding on the shore getting spooked by the sight of the ship and bolting into the brine with the bride still in the saddle.

Whether these stories are fact or fancy and who really did surface from the sea covered in those pesky shells, no one knows. Nevertheless, it's because of those tall tales that modern-day pilgrims hang scallop shells round their necks or, like me, have them swinging on their rucksacks while they walk.

Following directions the hard-of-hearing old lady had outlined on a map of the town, I headed for a camping area she'd recommended. Navigating down the steep, cobbled high street, I passed jewellers, florists and bakeries where shoppers spoke in many languages. I heard German, Spanish and Italian and some old people speaking in an alien dialect I assumed to be the language of the locals – French Basque. At the bottom of the gradient, pigeons perched in a church clocktower dwarfing the rest of town waited for scraps from the people passing under an archway below.

Turning left off the main drag, I skirted a river, then took a right across a wooden footbridge over gushing white water to the campsite gates. I arrived the same time as a young American whose name I can't recall, but I do remember he was from Idaho and looked like a twenty-something Woody Allen. At a log-clad kiosk we both fished up €3 for a pitch then wandered around looking for a suitable place to camp. Woody found a great spot underneath a tree with ample shade and I scored a place by the riverside where the giggling white water making a dash for the freedom of the sea would put me peacefully to sleep.

With great difficulty, I erected my tent while an obese, sun-burnt German gent wearing Speedos of a size more suitable for Barbie's Ken eyed my every move. With bulging love handles engulfing his frightful dick stickers, he sat on a deckchair out-side his caravan, lowered his newspaper and watched with great interest while I tussled with the tent's outer sheet as it snapped out of control in the wind. Frustrated by my pathetic inability to put up a taut tent and irritated by my unwanted audience, I went for a stroll around the campsite.

Among the city of motorhomes, tents and washing lines strung up between the trees, I met a middle-aged couple from the Midlands called George and Mildred. Okay, I admit those weren't their real names, but since I've forgotten them, that's what they'll be known as from here on in. Shamefacedly con-fessing the shortcomings of my tent erection, I told them I was seriously thinking of sending it home. They suggested I talk to an English lady who they'd heard was driving back to Blighty later that night.

'She might be able to take it for you, save you a few euros!' George cleverly suggested.

Sadly, George was unaware that the lady in question actually lived in southern Spain. She sincerely apologised, as all good Brits do, for not being able to help me.

George and Mildred were both sitting reading on their double air mattress when I sauntered back over and disappointed them with the bad news. Again as all good Brits do, George sincerely apologised for not being able to help, but then came up with Plan B. He slammed down his book and with excited eyes looked at Mildred as if to say, 'Are you thinking what I'm think-ing, my dear?'

'You need Dick!' he exclaimed with a finger in the air, as if he'd solved my problems.

Dick, he informed me, was another English camper who was going home and definitely lived in England – Kent, to be precise!

As if by magic, as if by Mildred saying hocus pocus, Dick came from nowhere and George introduced us. He was an effervescent fella whose beaming blue eyes, muscular physique and infectious positivity defied his sixty-five earthling years. He had good news and bad news. The bad news: he couldn't take my tent because he was riding home on a motorbike and wouldn't be able to take more weight. The good news: he'd cycled the Camino a few years ago and informed me that camping opportunities were limited and most pilgrims stayed in the albergues, which were cheap, cheerful and convivial.

He had me at cheap. After setting aside enough money to pay the rent while I was away and cover my travel back to England, the sterling that remained had got me €500. For a month on the Camino, I aimed to live off €16 per day. Dick said that while some privately owned albergues might be more expensive, most were run by church parishes and local councils and cost around €5 to €10 per night. Though they operated on a first-come, first-served basis, they had large capacities, were ubiquitous on the trail and my chances of getting a bed would be high. Weighing up my options, I was confident the money I'd have left every day after paying for an albergue could sustain me. Whenever possible, I'd only drink water at the fountains along the way and get the biggest bang for my buck by procuring food from supermarkets. This would be nothing compared to the hardships of the earliest pilgrims, who walked penniless and dealt with dangers like bandits, wolves and fatal diseases.

'Go to the post office and send the bloody tent home. You don't need it,' he ordered.

Dick had a point. The tent had to go. I would buy it a ticket home and spend an extra night in St-Jean-Pied-de-Port.

Sitting cross-legged with George and Mildred on their inflatable mattress a little later on, I got to find out some more about them. George had quit his high-profile, high-salary job as a banker to study psychology at forty-four years old. Now, three years later, he was about to start a PhD in the same subject.

'We were money rich and time poor,' Mildred said, bringing

their predicament into perfect focus.

When I suggested that George was a very brave man to make such a bold career change, Mildred hit me with another pearl of wisdom.

'Every now and then you have to frighten yourself to feel alive,' she said.

With this one-liner she hit the nail on the head as to how I was feeling about walking the Camino. I was frightened because I didn't know where I would end up staying each night; frightened because I didn't speak the language; absolutely petrified of getting lost and my face ending up on a Missing Persons poster. It was, on the other hand, the most exhilarating feeling I'd had in my life. Any doubts I had about whether taking a break from my business and my band was the right thing to do disappeared there and then. The decision to walk the Camino was the best I'd ever made.

6. THE ENGLISHMAN, THE IRISHMAN AND THE HUNGARIAN

At sunset, after my insightful chat with George and Mildred, I wrote my journal at a restaurant looking out over the silhouetted Pyrenees broadening up and out against the tangerine sky. I wanted to treat myself to one last nice meal before living off tinned tuna, loaves of bread and mayonnaise for the next month.

Friends, families and couples were dining all around me on the packed terrace, but I wasn't sad to be alone. This was the best view I'd ever had from a dinner table and my veins bubbled like champagne with the excitement of knowing that the beginning of my adventure was literally just around the corner.

It wasn't long, though, before my contentment turned to concern. Without warning, quiffs of white clouds turned into bruised tumours, the temperature dropped dramatically and the wind threw a tantrum, tossing my paper tablecloth onto the ground. The words of a wise old lady I once met in Georgia, USA came back to haunt me. 'Are sme-yell ray-ne,' she'd predicted in a Deep South drawl, before sitting bolt upright in her rocking chair and sniffing at the air. Sure enough, within minutes a deluge was duly delivered from what had previously been summer-holiday skies.

With my nostrils now sensing a similar threat, I threw my dinner down my throat, paid the bill and ran back to my tent to prepare for the opening of the French heavens. I shoved all my clothes into a black plastic bag, and put a waterproof cover over my rucksack and placed it in the centre of the tent away from any potential leaks in the outer seals. I was ready for the rain and, after a long day, more than ready to hit the hay.

I lay there for hours trying different tactics in an attempt to get to sleep: with and without a jumper, with and without the sleeping bag. I lay in many different positions: on my back, on my left side, on my right side, on my stomach. No matter how much I tried, I just couldn't get comfortable, and when the rain finally started to hammer down, I found it even harder to settle. I was disturbed further by a worrying rumble, not in the clouds but this time in my stomach, warning me of some pending paperwork. In a panic, I wriggled out of my sleeping bag and ran like mad across the campsite in the slanting rain, using my head-lamp to defeat the darkness. With danger averted but mission incomplete, I shone my headlamp around the dark, damp cu-bicle and found some soggy toilet roll discarded thoughtlessly on the wet floor. Back in my tent, somewhat relieved but totally exhausted, the damp ground swallowed me up for a precious few hours of slumber.

I dozed for about three hours until I was woken by a fresh bout of torrential rain blasting my flaccid tent. Even though I'd had little rest and my sleeping bag was soaked from the damp ground, I didn't let the inclement weather dampen my spirits. I was proud of myself because the precautions I'd taken the night before had ensured that most of my belongings had stayed dry.

'I fought the rain and the rain lost!' I sang defiantly as I pulled down my tent and sprinted to the shower block.

Under cover and out of the rain, I carefully selected what else I could send home with the tent. I couldn't even make it to the shower block with my rucksack weighing so much, let alone Santiago. I was taking no prisoners. The mosquito net was the first casualty. I gave a mallet, twenty pegs, a groundsheet and four guy lines to the grateful owner of the campsite. A pair of tracksuit bottoms, some combat shorts and two pairs of boxer shorts went in the bin. That's right: no room for underwear. I was going commando for the summer.

Under crying, grey skies, I squelched out of the campsite and back into town. With my backpack now seemingly half the weight, I capered up the steep high street like a woman in a tampon commercial. I felt lighter, liberated and more flexible, ready for a game of badminton and a lemon meringue with the girls.

As the Bodyform sanitary-towel theme tune played in my head – 'Woooaah Bodyform, Bodyform for youuuuuu!' – an anonymous saying I'd always remembered interrupted my mental melody: 'The definition of happiness is removing negatives from your life.' It occurred to me that doing to my life back home what I'd just done to my backpack could make me a lot happier. What were the negatives weighing on my shoulders, the life choices holding me back and slowing me down like the unnecessary objects in my rucksack? Did I have too many eggs in the band basket? Was it my weakness for unstable women? My unsatisfying job? My lack of faith in a religion?

All these were big questions that would need answering somewhere along the way. The next question that needed answering was where I'd stay my second night in St-Jean-Pied-de-Port. Luckily, the solution was right in front of my eyes when I arrived at the top of the hilly high street. Propped up outside the arched wooden double doors of an albergue was a walking stick, and by the side of the doorstep were a rucksack and a pair of boots, left on display to attract pilgrims in need.

I pushed open the wooden doors and tiptoed into a living room of antique furniture where two greying old dogs were snoring away to calming classical music playing on a radio. As I waited to be attended to, three cats ran out from underneath some beaded curtains leading to the kitchen and purred around my ankles. From there, the smell of the onion soup I could hear bubbling away on a stove drifted past my nostrils and woke my appetite. I stroked the cats for a short while until a diminutive, ageing woman with olive skin and long brown hair held out her hand, asking €7 for a bed. Upon payment, the gap-toothed lady kindly offered to wash and dry my sodden sleeping bag, which was draped over my backpack. I gratefully accepted and wrote a few words in her guest book to tell the world about how helpful the little old lady had been.

A room for the night secured, I caught up on some sleep, sent the tent and mosquito net home from the post office, then bought some food for the first day's hike. The essentials ticked off, I went out to explore the town and stopped by the pilgrim office to check the online weather report for my first day. If it rained again, the advice was to take the safe option along the country lanes and roads that cut through the flats of the Pyrenees. If the weather was good, however, I could take the route up and over the mountains, which was described in my guidebook as 'long and arduous but beautiful and spectacular'. With a hot and sunny day forecast, I could look forward to a day both beautiful and spectacular.

Being a twenty-first-century boy, I couldn't resist the opportunity to check my emails while connected. I wished I hadn't when I saw this one sticking out of my inbox.

> *To: Brad Chermside*

> *From: Jane W*

> *Subject: Long time – no speak*

Hiya Brad,

Very nice to hear from you!

Seems like you have a challenging summer ahead of you, but fun all the same, I am sure!

I thought I would let you know my recent good news – Berwyn proposed to me last week in Venice and I said yes! I am very excited, although we don't plan on getting married for another two years. There is still a lot to do and to save for!

Anyways, have fun on your adventures, hope you are well,

Jane

This was a shot to the heart. Until I met Jane in my late teens, I was a spotty, mute, nervous wreck around girls. Being with her, though, such a pretty, fun and intelligent young woman, gave me the confidence and self-esteem I so badly needed. Her mum, Dad and two sisters treated me as one of their own and, coming from a broken home, I was so grateful to feel part of a united family for the first time in my life. Even though we'd split five years earlier, I always wondered if one day we might get back together and I frequently dreamt about that.

My stomach sank when I read the words 'getting married'. Who did this bloke called Berwyn think he was, stealing my first love? Berwyn! What kind of a name was that anyway, and how the hell did you even say it? Ber-winn? Ber-wer-yinn? Berrin? Ha! She could have married a Brad but she was marrying a Reggie Berrin! As you can tell, I wasn't bitter at all!

I left the pilgrim office with my head down and my hands in my pockets, looking like a sad, lonely, distraught man. I wondered if I would ever find someone I loved that much again and immediately my thoughts turned to Natalia. Perhaps with Jane gone forever, I was ready to fall head over heels again and Natalia had come along at just the right time. Playing on my mind was the faceless picture she'd sent me. I was dying to see what she looked like underneath all that hair. I fantasised about her having irresistible come-to-bed eyes and a Marilyn Monroe beauty spot bejewelling a Penelope Cruz type pout. I told myself I had to send her a message the next time I got back online, to keep the lines of communication open.

On my way back to the albergue, I passed the campsite and saw Katie and Ryan, a young Kiwi couple I'd met there briefly the night before. They invited me to join them and a vivacious Irishman with a name I could imagine seeing over handprints on Hollywood Boulevard: Hugo Sweeney. I told him he sounded like the Irish James Bond. He told me to 'feck off'! All three were great company and we shared cake and coffee over stimulating conversation. I found out that Katie and Ryan had what could be considered the best job in the world. They spent three months of the year working every day without a break in the wine industry and the rest of it drinking the fruits of their labour and travelling the world. Hugo, who had a mischievous smile and bawdy sense of humour, was roaming France to find peace of mind after a divorce. He loved making fun of my Essex accent and found me particularly amusing when I asked a passing French couple to take a photo of us.

'*Une pictoire, s'il vous plaît?*' I said, handing them my camera, trying to sound all French.

'It's fecking "*photo*", not "*pictoire*", ya fecking cockney idgit!' he said, with a despairing and slightly embarrassed shake of the head.

As the rain clouds finally began to part, Hugo told chilling tales of people getting ambushed by packs of wild dogs on the Camino. His stories watered the weeds of fear already growing in the shadows of my mind from having read about both Paulo Coelho's and Shirley MacLaine's personal horrors with hounds. In *The Pilgrimage*, Coelho gets ravaged by the same wild woofer not once but twice! Weeping wounds to his face, hands and legs meant he had to take some time out from his journey to recuperate. In *The Camino*, Shirley MacLaine writes of the special measures she undertook to survive a so-called 'abandoned village of wild dogs'. If you thought she did this by carrying biscuits, throwing a stick one way then running the other, or by tickling their bellies to the point of incontinence, you'd be wrong. She succeeded, by, in her own words, 'sending a red heart full of love to the barking dogs'.

What would I do if a dog actually jumped out at me? Should I try and psych him out, eyeball to eyeball, until he backed off whining? Should I threaten him with the punishment of no sticks, tennis balls or squeaky toys if he bit me? Should I carry sticky toffees and run for my life while he took an hour to chew them into a bolus? If none of those approaches worked, I was dubious a packet of Shirley MacLaine's Love Hearts could save me from the rabid jaws of death.

Perhaps when Paulo Coelho was set upon he should have repeated one of the many rituals he performed on his pilgrimage as part of his initiation into an exclusive Catholic sect. 'I had become a tree,' he tells the world after one such supernatural ceremony. Maybe if he'd done this when attacked by a dog, it would have been more interested in spraying his stump than sinking its fangs into his flesh.

Wild dogs aside, Shirley Mac's biggest problems on the road were, thankfully, not ones that I was likely to experience. She agonised over whether she should wear a bra – I checked and I still hadn't developed breasts so had nothing to worry about on that front. She had to work out a way to stop the paparazzi from following her all the way – the only thing likely to follow me was the smell of my sweaty boots. Another big question she considered was if a walking stick she found in the woods was male or female. Undoubtedly mine would be a girl and she'd be called Sticky Vicky.

After I'd zoned out and flown off to the scary planet of gurning growlers and Shirley MacLaine's universe of sticks with dicks, Hugo brought me back to earth with a sharp prod in the shoulder and suggested we take a walk now that the rain had finally abated.

St-Jean-Pied-de-Port at dusk was warm and enchanting. The squeals of giddy kids playing out late, rinsing every last minute of fun from a long summer's day, echoed around town. Lone pilgrims meandered among the shops, boutiques and restaurants, lost in thought, far from home. Islands of cloud shadows drifted in slow motion over the wooded mountainsides beyond, where flocks of birds fluttered and fell in perfect formations like Red Arrows. The warm and gentle light of the falling sun kissed my face and glinted in the puddles left by the rain. It was every hypnotist's happy place come to life.

I was soon back in the room when we came to the medieval citadel and tackled the 269 steps to the top. From there we were treated to king-of-the-castle views of the town and beyond. Furthest away, past the terracotta rooftops, rugby posts, fields, hedges, and mists parting to reveal tumbling valleys, were tomorrow's formidable opponents: the sky-scraping Spanish Pyrenees. It was a stark reminder of the challenging first day ahead and the need for an early night.

After a tricky descent down the uneven steps, I said a reluctant farewell to Hugo, Katie and Ryan outside the albergue. I really enjoyed being with them and though I knew it was unlikely, I hoped somehow to see them all again.

Another thing that seemed unlikely was getting a good night's sleep. I'd managed three hours the night before and early signs suggested that I wouldn't do much better that evening. A French guy sleeping in the bunk below me had clearly been shower dodging for a long time and needed to put deodorant at the top of his shopping list. To make matters worse, he snored like a snarling lion having his nipples twisted.

Just before I climbed into my top bunk, I was approached by a small, friendly gentleman with a moustache and receding spiky hair.

'Tomorrow. We go together. It's okay?' he asked in a thick European accent I couldn't quite place.

This was a tricky one. I was determined to walk the trail alone, but in the dark and unpredictable wilderness of the Pyrenees, some company and support could come in handy. If a dog tried any dirty tricks, at least we'd match them for legs.

'In the morning, I wake you. Five o'clock,' I told him, pointing to my five fingers to make sure he understood. I wanted to leave so early because my fears of getting lost were still very much alive and I had visions of being stranded in the mountains come nightfall. The earlier I left, the bigger the margin for error.

'Thank you very much,' he said, slackening more in relief than gratitude.

Maybe I wasn't the only one having four-legged nightmares.

'Your name?' I asked.

He gave me a blank look.

'Me, Brad,' I said, tapping my chest. 'You?' I prompted him with an open hand.

'Ah! Sorry. I. Crazy Frank,' he replied with a hand on his heart and an adorable bow.

Though I was dying to know how this man who looked like Barry Chuckle got the nickname Crazy Frank, it was something I'd have to find out later on. In the morning we'd be climbing for more than twenty kilometres up to an altitude of 1,450 metres. Having to take on a peak taller than Ben Nevis, the highest mountain in the British Isles, was the stuff of first-day nightmares. If only Snore-kasaurus underneath me would shut up so I could get some badly needed sleep.

7. PRAYEROBICS

When my alarm slapped me in the face at 5am, my eyes refused to open and my body played dead, pretending it hadn't heard. Thanks to the nostril tremors shaking the bed, a constant stream of noisy passers-by and a street-cleaning vehicle parked outside our ground-floor window with the diesel engine left panting interminably, I'd had very little sleep again. But I wasn't about to let that get me down. This was the day I was going to start my Camino, my new life, with or without sleep. I peeled open my eyes, unzipped my sleeping bag and climbed carefully down the creaking bunk-bed ladder, trying not to disturb Snore-kasaurus. Waking him could see me eaten up with one flick of his tongue.

Keeping my promise to Crazy Frank, I roused him with a gentle nudge on the shoulder. After a delayed response, he rolled over, opened his big brown eyes, twitched his moustache, then sprang out the bed like a frog off a lily pad. With the rest of the room still snoozing, we forced our sleeping bags into their stuff sacks, strapped them onto the bottom of our backpacks and clicked the dorm door closed.

I was grateful to have Crazy Frank's company when we took our virgin Camino steps on the cold, dark and eerily deserted streets. After marching through town, past shuttered shops, warring cat colonies and fleets of out-of-service buses at the station, we came to the foot of the beastly mountains we'd be clawing our way up for most of the day. Before abandoning the security of civilisation, we filled our flasks at a water fountain and stuck on our woolly hats to keep warm. I dug out some biscuits for us to share on the go.

As we began our ascent, Crazy Frank and I got to know a

little about each other. Using a combination of signs, sound effects and song titles, thanks to his obsession with pop music, I discovered he was a twenty-nine-year-old security guard from Budapest, his favourite band was Depeche Mode and he was doing the Camino for the first time. Considering we didn't speak each other's language, we were getting on great, especially once I'd got the message across that I was from Basildon, the same town as his favourite band.

We'd been trudging up the Pyrenean escalator for an hour or so when the darkness lifted and the sun popped its spiky blond hair over the mountaintops. At every viewpoint where the horizon unfolded we stopped for a moment to take it all in: layer upon layer of jagged peaks stabbing through the belly of clouds sagging over the mountainsides. Birds of prey on dawn patrol gliding gracefully in the crisp blue sky eyed up the cows, sheep and goats grazing precariously on the ridges. On grassy banks flanking the path daisies and yellow lilies nodding in the wind kept time with the cowbells chiming in the valleys.

Whenever Mother Nature's jewels came alive in our eyes, Crazy Frank stopped and communicated his feelings in the only way he knew – with misremembered lyrics from his favourite songs.

'All I ever want it, all I ever need it, is here in my arms,' he sang in full voice.

'Enjoy the silence,' I responded, name-checking the Depeche Mode song to which he had charmingly sung the wrong words.

Even though my legs were twice as long as his, he matched me step for step and we proved to be a good pairing. Maintaining a respectable pace, we overtook many of our fellow pilgrims, always giving them a bubbly '*Bonjour*', accompanied by a smile and a wave. Before the morning was out we'd covered seventeen kilometres on the up and had crossed the Spanish frontier. From then on, my '*Bonjour*'s changed to '*Hola*' or sometimes '*Bonjour* – oops, shit, I mean *hola!*'

I was a little apprehensive as we approached the border, expecting tight patrols by armed guards holding back snarling dogs, helicopters monitoring the land and CCTV hanging from the trees. But my fears did not materialise. The only thing marking these momentous steps was a vertical-coffin-shaped monolith announcing our arrival into the province of Navarre. Luckily, some Italians crossed the border at the same time and duly obliged when I asked them to take a photo of us.

'*Arrivederci*,' I said with a salute as we walked off in search of a suitable lunch spot.

Having worked up a rapacious appetite on the tough climb to the top, we threw down our bags on the next patch of grass we hit, ripped them open and stuffed our faces. I tore into some ham and cheese sandwiches, crisps and a handful of peanuts generously donated by Crazy Frank. I admit that doesn't sound like a Christmas dinner fit for the Queen, but five hours of scaling a mountain can make cat food taste like caviar.

Getting back into our stride after our break proved difficult and worsening weather conditions didn't help. The sky turned from a blissful blue to a grisly grey. A balmy breeze became a gusty gale and the temperature changed from cool and comfortable to bitter and Baltic. For a short while, I wallowed in self-pity. I was freezing cold, my hands had gone numb and my ankles, knees and hips were aching. I asked myself, why the hell did I take the summer off work to put myself through such an ordeal! I wondered if my knee pain was serious and if I'd have to abandon the walk and call Natalia to come pick me up and nurse me back to health with daily bed-baths, night-time stories and hourly foot tickles. I was feeling so weak that for a brief moment I doubted I would even make it that far. Then I had a flashback to a calamitous episode when Chappers and I conquered Mount Snowdon in Wales.

On a bright and sunny spring morning, we pulled up at the base of Snowdon and sat in the car debating whether or not trekking to the top was a good idea. Given that we had bags of belief, a tin of baked beans and great weather conditions, we were both up for it. Everything was going golden, absolutely hunky-dory, until the weather turned, throwing its full box of tricks at us. First our visibility was reduced to a few metres by thick mountain mist. Then we were pelted with a confetti of hailstones the size of cooking apples, soaked to our freezing bones by torrential rain and pinned back by a bullying wind. We thought about turning back but kept going, motivated by talk of getting a hot bevvy in a café we knew awaited us at the peak.

Against all the odds, we got to the summit. Seeing the café in front of us was heaven. Finding the doors locked was hell. To make matters worse, half-way back down, we got lost and had to go all the way to the top again to find the correct trail leading back to our car. It was without doubt the coldest I had ever been in my entire life, so much so that I urinated on my hands to warm them up. I definitely wasn't going to tell Natalia that on our first date, but it did bring some feeling back to my numb hands.

I was praying that I had learned from that disastrous experience and history wasn't about to repeat itself. Wrestling my negative thoughts into submission, I declared it was time to man up and smash through the pain barrier. With my second wind on full force, I got an urge to start running.

'Crazy Brad!' Crazy Frank shouted, tapping his finger on his temple as I left him and overtook four concerned Frenchmen who couldn't believe their eyes. As I ran past with my backpack bouncing up and down, one of them pointed to his knees, warning of the damage I could do. His advice went in one ear and out the other. Determined to get my blood pumping, release some feelgood endorphins and warm up my body, I carried on regardless.

With Crazy Frank far behind and no one else around, I naturally slowed and sang my heart out in delirious happiness down the vertiginous descent tipping me into Roncesvalles. It was only the first day but I was already having the time of my life.

After six and a half hours of huffing and puffing in the Pyrenees, I hung up my boots for the day around 12.30pm. Walking into Roncesvalles was more like striding into a scene from *The Sound of Music* than my first Spanish town. It was a sleepy settlement tucked into a verdurous valley bed of beech, fir and oak forests where clear skies widened to show off an impressive thirteenth-century church imitating the design of Notre Dame Cathedral in Paris. Apart from a monastery, a broad white building of three floors directly opposite the church, there were no dwellings, no apartments, flats or houses to be seen. I guessed that Roncesvalles' population of just twenty-one inhabitants must all belong to the church and live and work in the two small hotels situated either side of the single carriageway bisecting the community.

Arriving at the albergue located in the monastery, I was disappointed to be hit with the news it didn't open until four. With no other option than to use my time wisely, I paid €5 in advance for a bed, rinsed my walking clothes in a nearby stream, hung them out to dry and booked a table for an evening meal in the village's only restaurant.

Crazy Frank got there soon after and came and sat with me to soak up some rays outside the albergue. Like a typical sun-starved Englishman, I ripped off my T-shirt, kicked off my boots and lay back on a patch of grass. Crazy Frank followed suit and as he peeled off his Pyrenean layers, baring his pale pigeon chest, he made me chuckle with another lyric, this time from Right Said Fred.

'I'm so sexy for my shirt,' he sang, drumming his chest Tarzan-style.

Little by little the Crazy was coming out of the Frank.

When the albergue opened late afternoon, I was the first person through the door. This privilege allowed me to choose a good hard bed, take a shower with hot water – I was soon to find this was something of a rarity in an albergue – and grab a power nap. Everything was going so very well, until my slumber was blown apart by a familiar sound and smell. To my horror, lying way too close for comfort, was Snore-kasaurus. To save space, his bed had been pushed so close to mine, we might as well have booked a king-size to share. The night before, I'd slept above him; now we were spooning.

I got out of there quick fast and went out to meet some of the characters rolling down the mountain into town. I got chatting to four likeable Canadians: Alyson and Catrina, two bonny ladies in their mid-twenties; and Bob and Margaret, an older couple who'd taken ten tiring hours to drag themselves over the Pyrenees. The pair of them were in a lot of pain and were hobbling about after their extreme exertions. Being addicted to running and having a job that required me to play football with tireless kids all day, I was lucky. I hadn't had to do any extra training for my long walk. Bob and Margaret, on the other hand, talked of how they'd trained for two years to get in shape for the Camino. Willing them on, I told them I admired their courage, dedication and determination to see their goal through to the end.

When my new maple-leaf mates left me for the albergue, I popped into a tourist shop in a building attached to the church to enquire if they sold earplugs. After rigorously rehearsing a sentence I'd pieced together using my Spanish phrasebook, I strode in with the confidence of a local, flamenco-stamped at the counter, and hit them with it.

'*Las cosas para enchufar aquí* – the things for plugging in here,' I requested, sticking my fingers in my ears.

The señora standing by the till gave me a look of horror like I'd just asked her to pop a spot on my back. Without saying a word, she scurried off and returned with a colleague.

I repeated my request to her co-worker.

'Eeen Eeengleesh, pleese,' she pleaded, equally stumped.

'Earplugs,' I said, sticking my fingers in my ears again.

As the penny finally dropped, she pulled a set off a hook behind the counter and I thanked them for their patience. It was only later on that I found out from Alyson, who spoke fluent Spanish, that I'd actually asked them to electrocute me through my ears. *Tapones*, she informed me, was the magic word that would keep me out of future trouble.

I had no plans to attend Mass in the village church at 8pm, but when invited by Alyson and Catrina, I decided to be sociable, tag along and join the party. Instead of experiencing some sort of union with God, Jesus or the Holy Spirit, what I mostly felt was frustration, impatience and tiredness. The priest, dressed in a shiny green robe, made us continually stand up and sit down throughout his sermon. Doing squats on the pews like we were taking part in a prayerobics session after nigh on thirty kilometres of mountain hiking certainly won't go down as one of my most divine experiences. Staying in bed scratching Snorekasaurus's back might well have been more relaxing.

The evening meal was a much more enjoyable affair for which I made sure my arse remained planted throughout. Crazy Frank and I shared a table with Steffan and Sasha, both nineteen-year-old interior-design students from Vienna. I instantly connected with the lads and told them tales of my friends Martin and Robert, two of their compatriots from the south Austrian province of Carinthia. While we waited for our special discounted pilgrims' menu of soup followed by grilled fish and fries for €9, I tried to impress them with an Austrian expression Martin and Robert had taught me.

'Lors a ker fleegen!' I said and waited for them both to look at me in amazement. To my surprise and disappointment, I got no reaction.

Sasha scratched his head in confusion and asked me to jot it down.

'L-o-r-s-a-k-e-r-f-l-e-e-g-e-n,' I scribbled into the back page of my journal and pushed it across the table for them to read.

Eyeing my words carefully, he corrected my spelling: 'Loss a kuh fliegn.'

'I sink you write it like siss, but I'm not sure vot it means.' Sasha was trying his best to be polite and sound interested when, really, I think he wanted to change tables.

'It means,' I said, doing a drumroll on the table before letting them have it, 'let the cows fly!'

The macho backslaps I'd hoped for upon demonstrating my knowledge of this crucial Austrian expression that means "party time" weren't forthcoming.

'I sink your friends are maybe a little crazy,' Steffan said, unmoved. 'Ve are from Wienna, not Carinzia, and not saying this!'

Poor Crazy Frank sat with us, not understanding a word of the flying cows debate. Whenever possible, though, I tried to include him in the all-English exchange by asking him if the dinner was good.

'I just can't to get enoughs!' he would reply every time, patting his belly and wailing his own version of the Soft Cell song.

As the restaurant slowly emptied and the staff began resetting the vacated tables, Crazy Frank poked me in the shoulder.

'Nine Three-ty o'clocks,' he said, tapping his watch, warning me of the need to return to the albergue before its fast-approaching 10pm curfew.

When we got back there, the hall was packed with more than a hundred pilgrims sleeping, talking and snoring in barrack-style bunks. On his way to bed after brushing his teeth in the bathroom, Crazy Frank asked me to get him up again in the morning.

'Please. Awake me up before you go go.'

Trying not to disturb those already sleeping with my laughter, I tiptoed off to bed and dropped off with that bloody Wham song torturing my brain.

I thought I'd done everything necessary to ensure a decent night's sleep at last. I'd deployed my earplugs to silence the flaring nostrils of a dribbling Snore-kasaurus just an arm's length away; I'd transformed my bandanna into a blindfold to shield my eyes from the torch wielders; and I'd buried my head into my sleeping bag so the sweaty socks and fetid body odour fouling the air couldn't sting my tormented nostrils a moment longer. Despite all that, in the small hours I was rudely awoken by an Italian *ragazzo* shouting into his mobile phone. Feeling totally helpless, I lay there for a while too tired to move but wishing I had the energy to jump out of bed and shout, 'Shaddapa ya face!' As my frustration was about to boil over and I moved to get out of bed and pull that inconsiderate man's leg hairs, an old lady came to my rescue. With a good old-fashioned finger-wagging and verbal volley, she put him firmly in his place. Not a moment too soon, the selfish swine hung up and walked away to go sit on the naughty chair. I returned to the land of nod, dreaming of secretly putting rocks in his rucksack.

8. THE PROMISE OF NO PROMISES

The woods. Dense. Dark. Daunting. No place for a jumpy Essex boy to be alone at 5.54am. But that's where I was, using my headlamp to guide me along a path overgrown with foliage. Walking through the creepy forest on my own, I soon became anxious and clicked off my headlamp. I wanted my eyes to adjust to the darkness so I'd have better peripheral vision instead of being wrapped in the night with a glaring light one metre ahead. I kept checking behind me to see if anyone was there and agonised over whether I should turn it on again. If I did, a potential murderer would be able to see me coming, but if I kept it off, I wouldn't be able to see him, or her, or maybe even them waiting in the bushes to ambush me. And what about the dogs? If I shone my headlamp into the distance I might catch the reflection of their eyes and have enough time to prepare for a duel. But if I blinded the dog with my light, it might make him mad and give him the upper hand psychologically.

As I reassured myself that this was all just mind games and paranoia, a disturbance in the trees behind me sent my heart racing and I stopped dead in my tracks. Could it be a dog hunting me down or the Camino Cannibal hungry for an English breakfast? Or was it just my overactive imagination?

Apart from the birds in the trees singing their morning melody and the odd car circulating on the road running parallel to the woods, I heard nothing. I stared into the curtains of chlorophyll to my left and right, and behind me into the ominous black void, but saw nothing threatening. My sense of smell failed to detect anything untoward either. All I could pick up was the scent of damp soil and the dew-drenched leaves on the trees. I took great care not to move a muscle just in case any noise drowned out the cunning advances of an attacker.

Proceeding with caution, I thought I was out of the woods until the silence was ruptured by a more recognisable sound – human footsteps, coming my way! My assailant had two legs not four.

The footsteps got louder and close enough for me to hear the boots crunching on the branches beneath them. This is it, I told myself, this is the time to stand up and fight and become a man. All those years watching American wrestling as a kid were about to pay off. From the undergrowth, I grabbed a stick and readied for combat just in case a dropkick wouldn't finish the job. With the stance of a warrior, I trained my eyes on the enemy emerging from between the trees.

Upon identifying the threat, I quickly withdrew the stick I'd been wielding like an Amazonian Indian with a spear and pretended to use it as a back scratcher.

'Hola!' I said sheepishly to the old man with a big white beard and white shoulder-length hair.

I knew this was a Christian pilgrimage but hadn't expected to actually meet Jesus. Upon closer inspection of the Chosen One, I noticed he was a fellow pilgrim and I let my guard down. Very quickly I was back on my way with a casual whistle, using the stick as a walking aid.

Though I'd woken Crazy Frank again as requested, he'd refused to get up and had instead pointed outside, suggesting we meet further on. Knowing full well that the hundred-odd people from the albergue would soon be spilling onto the path, I'd been first out the door. Now I was walking in the darkness by the side of a quiet road with a dimming man in the moon waving me goodbye as he switched off the stars one by one.

As day finally broke, I escaped from the woods and headed into the countryside. Overhead, the sun's rays broke through thick cloud, striking all the hour markings on the sky clock. Cows and sheep were scattered across the rolling green dales, playing hide-and-seek among giant cylindrical haystacks, and the bitter smell of manure occasionally drifted by on the brisk morning breeze. While my eyes feasted on the scenery, the undulating terrain gorged on the little life left in my legs, still tired and stiff from yesterday.

My lassitude was exacerbated further by my failure to find anywhere selling food. Every village I passed was comatose and because I'd left so early, all the shops and cafés were still closed. Growing ever more tired and hungry, I began to lose focus and at one point walked past a yellow arrow painted onto the road, showing me the way. Luckily Jesus had kept pace with me and spotted me walking off into no-man's land. With a short, high-pitched whistle, he caught my attention, and when I looked back over my shoulder he threw both arms to the right like an air steward, putting me back on track.

Another niggling issue causing much irritation was the lengthy process I had to go through every time I wanted to take a photo. I had to drop my rucksack off my shoulders, unzip the side pocket, dig out my camera from underneath my first-aid kit, take the picture, stash the camera away and put my backpack on again. I vowed that when I finished for the day in Larrasoaña, I'd repack my bag more efficiently to save precious time and energy.

Anyone in their right mind would have taken a rest day after such extreme activity the day before. But I was no longer thinking or acting like your average Joe. Take a day off? You had to be joking! We *peregrinos*, as the Spanish called us pilgrims, got up before dawn, with or without sleep, and did it all again. We thrived on the fact that we were in pain; in fact, pain made the journey more satisfying and rewarding. We didn't need soap and water to wake us up! We showered in the promise that a day on the road brought no promises; the possibilities and uncertainties were why we launched from the bed with excitement and anticipation.

After fifteen despairing kilometres without food, and drinking my water sparingly, I met someone who was able to liven me up with some engaging conversation. As the Camino's path through the woods crossed the hazardous N-135 highway, a man walking my way against the traffic waved at me to stop.

'You are on ze Camino?' he asked.

'Yep,' I said, pointing to an information board showing exactly where we were.

'Thanks God! I 'ave been lost on zis stupid road forever!' he said, taking a big gulp of water from his bottle.

Overjoyed to be back on track, Jean Raphael and I walked together and chewed the fat about everything from football to finding yourself. Astonishingly, he had already clocked up eight hundred kilometres on foot from his home in Paris and was covering anything up to fifty kilometres a day. In his mid-thirties and a big supporter of the French football giants Paris Saint-Germain, he was doing the Camino for the second time. Before he did it for the first time, he was a high-flying executive at the dairy giants Danone. Having become disillusioned and dissatisfied in his work, he said he woke one day and asked himself a very serious question:

Do I really want to be in stuck in yoghurt for the rest of my life?

With his career dying a slow and painful death in pots of rhubarb and beetroot, he took action. He quit his job, went walking, found some peace of mind and returned home with renewed purpose. He built his own consulting business, met the love of his life and was soon playing happy families with a daughter now two years old. However, he felt that he had once again lost his way, working all the hours under the sun to support his family. With that familiar sinking-in-a-pot-of-yoghurt feeling, he had returned to the Camino to centre himself while his supportive wife and daughter spent the summer at the in-laws'. On other matters, he suggested I apply Vaseline to my feet every twenty kilometres to prevent blisters. He'd done this all the way since Paris and hadn't had a single one.

When the conversation turned to wild dogs, he suggested a novel way of tackling the problem.

'If you see a dog, give to 'im some sugar.'

'Who told you that?' I mocked.

He explained that an old Frenchman called Jacques had shared this trick of the trade. 'Per'aps you 'ave seen 'im. 'E 'as long white 'air and a big white beard,' he said, tickling an imaginary bush on his cheeks. I quickly figured out he was referring to the Jesus look-a-like who'd given me the fright of my life in the woods earlier.

Jean Raphael described Jacques as an entertaining character who amused him when they walked together by shouting, 'Give me the beast!' to psych himself up. Can you imagine your grandad doing that? No, me neither. Mine would more likely say, 'Give me the TV remote', 'Pass my glasses', or 'Tell your nan to turn down that bloody Elvis Presley'.

I walked with Jean Raphael until we reached Zubiri, where he stopped for a rest and we shook hands and said goodbye.

Just three kilometres down the road, we said hello again in Larrasoaña when he caught up with Jacques and me lunching side by side on a bench. There we were: Jacques, looking every inch cultured and French, book in hand, sipping on red wine from a plastic cup and eating little triangles of cheese; and me, chewing on cheese and ham sandwiches, biscuits and pistachios in the same mouthful, and washing them down with tepid water from my flask. After walking twenty-eight kilometres to Larrasoaña, I'd bought whatever I could consume quickly from the first open shop I'd seen all morning. Though it took the sting out of my hunger, my taste buds were not impressed and threatened to pack their bags and leave if I ever did that to them again. My stomach, equally unimpressed, I could feel was threatening to evict its new occupants any moment.

As I was munching away, Jean Raphael rocked up and gave Jacques a manly bear hug in a moving reunion. Witnessing those two, one of them young, the other old, laughing and joking like best friends, shone sunshine into my heart. It was a perfect example of how the Camino obliterated conventional societal barriers and connected people who ordinarily wouldn't even make eye contact on the street.

When I crossed the elegant medieval stone bridge leading into Larrasoaña, I could not see or hear a soul in the village. Even though it was midday, all the wooden shutters on the white-painted houses were closed and the streets were empty. I wondered where everybody could be. Carrying on, half expecting hundreds of people to come out of nowhere and shout 'Surprise!', I finally spotted signs of life at the albergue. I was greeted by Adrián, a small, portly man wearing a badge with his job title: 'Hospitalero'. The word is so much more welcoming than its English translation, 'Warden', which invokes visions of obese female prison guards covered in tattoos and piercings and jabbing truncheons into my groin for not leaving the floor shiny enough.

Adrián escorted me through the heavy rustic double doors to find two dorms, one upstairs and one downstairs, containing about fifty bunks each. This time I chose mine very carefully and got a bottom bunk, upstairs, in the corner furthest away from the noisy wooden staircase. I prayed Snore-kasaurus wouldn't hunt me down again.

With my bed reserved, I hot-stepped it to the mobile shower block outside, where I got an unexpected eyeful of a sexy señorita. There I was, innocently brushing my teeth at the sink, when an attractive lady came out the shower cubicle smelling of lemons and dropped her towel right in front of me. Completely embarrassed, I looked away as if I hadn't noticed, but while rinsing my mouth out, I had a sneaky peek in the mirror. Her honey-coloured skin and tiny red thong disappearing between two juicy glutes left me totally mesmerised as she dried the glistening hair tumbling down her back. I walked out of there half smirking like a primary-school kid who'd just seen their first sex-education programme.

Later on, at a local café, she sat down at the table next to me while I tended to my blisters and munched on a canoe-sized ham and cheese baguette. Tending to my calluses probably wasn't the sexiest way to seduce her, but I didn't care because

Natalia was the girl I really wanted. I wondered what she was doing to prepare for my arrival. Plucking her eyebrows? Cutting her toenails? Putting all the pieces on the board for a game of strip chess? Whatever she was up to, I hoped I was on her mind as much as she was on mine.

More likely though, she'd be checking the TV listings so she didn't miss one of Spain's biggest annual festivals - San Fermín, the Running of the Bulls. It was the hottest topic of conversation at the albergue. If you've never seen or heard of the Bull Run, I'll quickly fill you in: scores of loonies get chased by six blood-thirsty bulls through Pamplona's narrow streets until they reach the city's bullring (or A&E, with a bullhorn in the butt). Whether we liked it or not, we were going to be in the thick of it because the Camino cuts through the heart of Pamplona and the festivities were due to start there at 8am the following day.

Sasha, Steffan and I were sitting on the steps outside the other albergue in town, debating whether or not to join the party, when we met a Czech named Jan. He hadn't quite caught wind of what was going down.

'I hear they make big street party somewhere?' he said, screwing up his face inquisitively.

'Yes, it's the Bull Run tomorrow in Pamplona. Don't you know already?' Sasha said, incredulous that Jan wasn't 'on the bull'.

Jan didn't come across as the ripest berry in the bunch. Not just because the imminence of San Fermín had flown over his head, but also because of his choice of footwear. I couldn't believe he'd chosen a flimsy pair of sandals to tackle three mountain ranges and 804 kilometres. His poor feet were already plagued with blisters, so I offered a few spare plasters to help him patch himself up. Despite Jan's dizzy nature, I took an instant liking to him. He was a smiley young chap with eighties rock-star hair and got my vote when he told us he'd hitchhiked all the way from Prague to southern France to start his trip. Even though he was in agony with blister problems, he was intent on going ten more kilometres to the next village because he'd heard the albergue there had internet access. He wanted to type up his travels and update his blog. I was full of admiration for his stoic determination to carry on, until, half an hour later, I found a computer inside the building we'd just been sitting outside. Poor Jan! He could have avoided another two hours of anguish if he'd taken two minutes to check inside. I wondered how the hell he was going to get to Santiago in one piece.

Jan's loss was my gain. I chucked €2 into the computer and checked my emails. My decision to go commando had provoked some amusing replies.

>*To: Brad Chermside*

>*From: Ruth S*

>*Subject: Chafing!*

Hello!

How's it going? Can't believe you ditched the tent! And your underwear? Isn't that just gonna chafe? I suppose if it saves your back.

Ruth xxx

Was Ruth trying to tell me it would be better to have sore bollocks than a bad back? It was a dilemma that reminded me of a game called 'Would you rather...?' that I used to annoy my teachers with on long school trips. If they'd been with me then, as fellow pilgrims, I'd have resurrected the game and asked them: would you rather sleep in a hostel full of smelly, snoring pilgrims or spend the night in a pigsty being honked to insomnia? I'd probably have plumped for the pig pen after the horrors of the last few nights.

>*To: Brad Chermside*

>*From: Daniel O*

>*Subject: Swing em!*

Good on ya, mate. So glad to hear that all is going well and that you are getting through it all. You are a better man than I am. As

I told you, after five days, my dad and I drove the rest. I blame him, personally – the fat bastard. Jokes aside, keep on in there and let them balls swing and hang low!

Peace out, bro.

Lots of love, mate,

Daniel

> To: Brad Chermside

> From: Teresa V

> Subject: Minging!

Hello you!

Sounds all very exciting!

Can't believe you're going commando. That's a bit minging!! Surely your undies don't weigh that much. So where are you going to be sleeping if you have no tent?

Well, better get back to work,

T x

Daniel's comments about letting them swing low had me giggling to myself at random moments for days afterwards. Reading Teresa's words, 'Better get back to work', made me feel good about my current plight. While she was sitting at a computer in a cramped office waiting for 5pm, I was roaming Spain with no date set for my return, no appointments in my diary and totally free from the irksome obligations of modern life. At that moment I savoured the precious freedom I'd carved out for myself.

I was genuinely surprised and moved by the interest my friends were showing in my exploits. Even though I was far from home, I could really feel their love when I read their messages of support. As well as the rib-tickling comments about going commando, I had several uplifting messages like the one below.

> To: Brad Chermside

>*From: Maria N*

>*Subject: Hello!*

So great to hear from you. Your journey sounds amazing already, and I hope that overall you experience the best few months of your life. I admire what you are doing and wish to do something as challenging as that one day.

Take care,

Maria x

Words like those from my friends were absolutely priceless and put extra bounce in my boots every time I felt like I was running on empty.

Before my time online expired, I took the opportunity to write to Natalia and let her know of my early progress.

>*To: Natalia*

>*From: Brad Chermside*

>*Subject: Thank You*

Hola Natalia!

I hope you're well. Just wanted to let you know that I've started the Camino. Right now I'm in Navarre so will probably be with you in Melide in around three to four weeks.

It's very nice to be in contact with you and I'm really excited to meet you after finding your email address on €20 in Corfu two years ago.

Thanks again for offering to let me stay at your house. I would like that very much. See you soon!

Brad :)

PS Why did you write your email address on €20 and have you actually ever been to Corfu?

Early evening, I went down to the river that ran by the village with Canadian Catrina and we sat with our aching feet in the soothing cold water. Under a canopy of overhanging trees, we chatted away to the relaxing sound of the gentle current washing armies of helpless bugs and insects downstream. I was sorry to hear she'd be finishing her Camino the next day in Pamplona. She had plans to fly to Amsterdam, meet some friends and finish her travels there because of a job lined up at home with beer giants Michelob.

'Not the greatest job in the world, but I get free beer!' She shrugged, doing her best to look on the bright side.

Pulling our dripping feet from the water, we compared blisters. She had one the size of a Malteser on her right big toe and I had grown a beauty on the inside of my left heel. We took great pleasure in bursting the offending calluses and walked a little easier as we swatted away mosquitoes on our way back up the riverbank.

Dinner that evening wasn't an altogether pleasurable affair thanks to a thunder-faced waitress with a death stare. She rolled her eyes and shamelessly sighed her disapproval if we took more than five seconds to choose what we wanted. Before she could smash her tray over my head for having the audacity to read the menu, I chose a few things at random. Once again, I was sharing a table with Steffan and Sasha and Crazy Frank as well as a family of four from Hamburg. Crazy Frank and I sat quietly, listening to the alien language ping-pong back and forth across the table. My grown-up inner voice was telling me to smile politely, try to understand and join in when I could. My inner child, however, was egging me on to blurt out my Austrian slang about skirts and sausages.

'I think we are lone now,' Crazy Frank whispered to me when we still hadn't found a way into the conversation after two courses. His trademark lyrical summing up of the circumstances and the bargain price of €7.50 were the highlights of a mealtime to forget.

The next course about to be eaten come bedtime was a tall and skinny dreadlocked French femme whose flesh was being seasoned with lust by a strapping Austrian called Franz. She lay back coquettishly on the bunk next to mine while he read her extracts from the Dalai Lama's book, *The Art of Happiness*. Their rampant body language suggested that once the lights went out, the finger Franz was licking to turn the pages might well be used for doing something else.

9. NEVER MIND THE BULLOCKS

I woke up fresh as a daisy after sleeping through the whole night for the first time since leaving England. My trusty earplugs had successfully cancelled out the whispers and moans of Franz and the French girl playing rudies and nudies. Not so much as an '*Oh là là*' got to bang on my eardrums.

In a chipper mood, I bounced down the stairs and stretched my arms outside in the sunshine. The only people around were Stefan and Sasha, unpegging their clothes from a makeshift washing line tied between two tree trunks. Over the moon to see their friendly faces, I shouted good morning at the top of my lungs and got the urge to bombard them with acorns. To my delight, they returned fire. Our blossoming bromance had reached new heights. It was just a matter of time before our parents would be calling each other to arrange our first sleepover.

Though I was the last to leave the albergue, I soon found myself catching up with and passing the early risers. I got a real kick out of wishing everybody '*Buen Camino!*', the pilgrim's equivalent of '*Bon voyage*'. I never knew that saying two words in an alien language to a bunch of strangers in a strange land could make me feel so unreasonably happy. But it really did. And not once along the entire Camino did I tire of it.

I followed stony trails through tunnels of trees alongside the swift and vocal River Arga and the first few hours passed quickly and quietly. Save for the odd bar open to breakfasting pilgrims in the villages scattered along the way, there was little going on. That all changed in Trinidad de Arre, a suburb of graffiti-covered fading white towerblocks on the outskirts of

THE ONLY WAY IS WEST

Pamplona. Cars cruised around, their passengers hanging out of the windows and sunroofs, singing and clapping to deafening Reggaeton music. The streets were buzzing, with locals of all ages coming from around every corner celebrating the public holiday with their tails up and guards down. Without exception, everybody was sporting the San Fermín attire of red neckerchief, white shirt and trousers, and red sash tied around their waist. I felt like a complete outsider: the 'grino gatecrasher wearing the same scruffy, smelly clothes for the third day in a row among a proud parade of traditional red and white.

As I advanced into Pamplona city centre, the harmless fun turned to mindless mayhem. I swerved drunk and disorderly revellers so high on festival fever they were either staggering out of control or had passed out on the sticky pavement. The repugnant stench of sick, stale beer and urine tainted the air and all the shops were boarded up with hurricane-strength defences. The only establishments daring enough to open were dingy bars full of mad-eyed hedonists dancing to deafening music that threatened to blow the speakers. I found it hard to fathom how such chaos could ensue at the time I'd normally be starting work back home.

For a few more streets of shocking dystopia I slalomed vomit, beer cans and shards of broken bottles until I was hit by a wall of hundreds of people squashed into a small plaza outside the albergue. Standing rigid and upright in front of the entrance, the hospitalero barked the rules like a drill sergeant at the queue-jumping mob competing for a bed: the doors would open at midday; only pilgrims already carrying a valid stamped Credencial would be granted entry; doors would be locked and lights turned out at 10pm; the police would be called to arrest anyone breaking the curfew. The more I saw and heard, the less I felt like staying to join the party. The people trying to get in were behaving like animals in a zoo at feeding time.

The Bull Run represented an unwelcome detour from my simple daily goals of finding food, shelter and some insight into my existential dilemmas. All I'd found so far in Pamplona was disorder, debauchery and down-and-outs. I thumbed through the pages of my guidebook to weigh up my options and plan an escape route. Cizur Menor, described as 'a quiet dormitory town of Pamplona' just three kilometres away, suddenly seemed most appealing. I scanned the packed plaza for familiar faces and mingled among the masses to see if I recognised anyone who might come with me. After walking alone for four hours and twenty kilometres, I was craving human contact and conversation to revive me. I bumped into Catrina again, who I knew was going no further, and spoke briefly with a Finnish guy and a Japanese chap, who both had intentions very different to mine.

The Japanese guy was more interested in finding a strip club, a place to cut his hair and a travel agency, having arrived at the airport a day late for his flight home. The order of items on his to-do list seemed to typify the calibre of people attracted to the Bull Run. The Finn's plans were less complicated. He just wanted somewhere to get drunk. He pulled a can from the side pocket of his rucksack and covered me in beer when it gurgled then fizzed open. 'Kit piss!' he shouted, raising the dripping can in the air before chugging it down. I turned away wondering whether that meant 'Cheers' in Finnish or if that was what it tasted of – kitten piss. I later found out from some other Finns on the Camino that it did mean 'Cheers' and that it was actually spelt *'Kippis'*. I've since chosen to believe that it's still a reference to feline urine and have bemused many a Finn by shouting 'Kitten piss!' when clinking glasses.

As more nameless faces squeezed into the plaza, further diminishing the oxygen supply and increasing the sense of claustrophobia, I resigned myself to going it alone. I was searching for a way out through the crowd when I spotted Jan, in a wide-eyed spin from the frenzy of activity around him.

'Hi, Brett. Why so many peoples?' he asked.

'It's the Bull Run, mate. Don't you remember? We told you yesterday!'

I thought I'd leave it until another time to break the news my name was actually Brad. Instead, I got straight to the point and

THE ONLY WAY IS WEST

floated the idea of him coming with me to Cizur Menor. Jan's arm didn't need much twisting, though I was pretty sure if I'd asked him to dress up in a bull suit and chase me through the streets he'd have agreed to that too.

Wriggling out the clutches of the crowd, we headed for the yellow arrows pointing down a quiet backstreet. For a few calmer blocks, the decision seemed like a masterstroke. We moved without challenge down tight, cobbled streets of over-hanging balconies blooming with flowers pots and hanging baskets that curved and stretched out of sight. But as we turned down a narrow avenue of cosy-looking but closed tapas taverns, the decibels rose and we ran into a sea of people crammed into Pamplona's main square.

I ordered Jan to grab onto my backpack as we weaved through the heaving crowds gathered in front of a big stage where technicians were sound-checking. They plucked guitars, bounced sticks off drum skins and tested the microphones by repeating '*Sí, sí*' and tapping on them. It was clear the live music was about to start and would then continue all day and into the early hours. If we didn't make it out before the first notes were played and the crowd erupted, we probably never would.

Impeding our progress were stereotypical tourists from around the globe. Americans with their baseball caps and sou-venir T-shirts randomly yelling 'Yeah!' and 'Woo!' for no ap-parent reason. Japanese tourists en masse, frantically snapping away with their cameras, trying desperately not to miss a mo-ment. Rowdy groups of boisterous Aussies swigging from their beer cans, cracking jokes and laughing loudly in unison. Far out-numbering the foreigners were the natives. They were perched on phone boxes, newspaper kiosks, traffic lights and street signs and were hanging over every single balcony overlooking the sea of red and white. Every so often the earth-shaking boom of fire-crackers brought simultaneous cheers from the hordes and left a smell of smoke and plumes rising over the square.

In the midst of the pandemonium, Jan and I pigeon-stepped through whatever gaps we could find, keeping a close eye on our backpacks in pickpocket heaven.

Cizur Menor, by comparison, was pilgrim heaven – a placid suburb atop a beefy hill overlooking the sunflower and barley fields that had escorted us there. The extra few kilometres were made worthwhile by the warm welcome Jan and I were given by a hospitalero bearing more than a passing resemblance to Harry Potter. In broken English he regrettably informed us that the albergue was *completo* – full – but he'd worked his magic so that the small church next door would take in the overspill. We just had to wait a while and a mattress on the floor in the nave would be ours. I would have accepted a bed full of spiders and scorpions rather than have to go back to the madness we'd just fled.

Feeling destroyed after a taxing day, I slumped against a wall in the shade, kicked off my boots and peeled off my socks. As I was giving my feet and my worsening blisters some much needed TLC, a merry band of international pilgrims came marching in. I threw waves at the French, saluted the South Africans, nodded hellos to the Norwegians and addressed the Americans, all of whom had made it through Pamplona alive.

After waiting patiently and playing the part of British ambassador for a while, I was finally allocated a mattress on the church floor. The peaceful environs of the nave and the comforting smell of the dusty Bibles tucked into the leather pockets in the backs of the pews sent me into a long, energising siesta.

When the muffled voices of people talking outside the church woke me, my eyes strayed to a construction like a passport-photo booth in one of the side aisles. Inspecting it more closely, I clicked that this was in fact the church's confession box. Slipping behind the purple curtain, I took the chance to get a few things off my chest. I dropped the bombshell that, by accident, I once put general waste in the recyclable plastics. I disclosed that when I was a kid, instead of putting chewing gum in the bin, I sometimes launched it down the street like a goalkeeper taking a drop kick (now I always put it in the rubbish - honest!). Lastly, I confessed that when Luke and I used to take the train to college, we would run away from the ticket inspectors even though we had valid tickets. We just liked making them chase us. More often than not, they saw the funny side. Though no answer came from the adjoining box, I felt better for having got my sins out in the open and being a small step closer to the pearly gates.

At sundown, back out in the great wide open, I trudged up a hill to another church, where I was dazzled by breathtaking views stretching to the French border seventy kilometres back. Gazing out at the smooth, arching contours of the Pyrenees aglow in the peachy embers of sunset, at the meadows of sunflowers swaying down below, and at the sprawling conurbation in the centre of the vista, I could beat my chest proudly and say I'd walked the lot.

They say it's better to celebrate how far you've come rather than worry about how far you've still got to go. I celebrated my modest achievement at a bar in the village and treated myself to my 467th cheese and ham baguette in three days. It wasn't until I was on my way back to the albergue, tearing into my takeaway, that I thought to check my change and realised I'd been ripped off. I was highly suspicious that €3.50 back from €20 for a baguette wasn't an honest mistake. This was a dirty, premeditated trick the barman probably played on many unsuspecting travellers and I went to sleep that night planning my ruthless revenge. Like a true gangster, I conspired to storm back in there and take a pee without flushing the chain. To rub salt in his wounds, I would wash my hands, leave the tap running and on my way out stick chewing gum in the ashtray. The bar owner obviously didn't know who he was messing with.

10. UMPTEEN BASTARD HILLS

I was prodded awake in the musty church interior by a strip of dust-laden sunlight shining through a stained-glass window high above the altar. The twenty-odd mattresses squeezed between the pews and the pulpit had all been vacated apart from Jan's. He was still quietly snoring away next to me. For a moment I had the strange but liberating sensation of having lost myself so deeply in the trip that I'd also completely lost track of time. I had to trawl through my memory to work out the day of the week. I knew I'd started walking on a Tuesday and cast my mind back to the first day with Crazy Frank, the second with Jacques and Jean Raphael, and yesterday with Jan. Now it made sense why I'd woken in such a good mood – I had that Friday feeling! It also dawned on me that I hadn't looked in the mirror, brushed my hair or shaved since leaving home. Until people started feeding me raw meat and asking where my owner was, or a van came to take me back to the zoo, I vowed to keep it that way.

Honouring my promise to get Jan up, I gently rocked him awake.

'You sleep well?' I asked as he opened his eyes and slowly came to.

'Yes, I sleep ferry well,' he said, blowing a crusty gale of stale morning breath in my face.

After very nearly keeling over, I retreated to a safe distance and suggested we use the extra life that another great night's sleep had given us and hit the road.

As we shared some muesli bars and a stick of plain baguette

on the go, the first big challenge of the day soon hove into view – a dusty, serpentine, eight-kilometre trail working its way up a range of green hills towards a myriad of wind turbines spinning tirelessly along the ridge. It was extremely heavy going and Jan quickly fell behind when the incline steepened.

When I'd made it to the blustery summit above the clouds at el Alto del Perdón, the Hill of Forgiveness, I asked two French ladies having a break to take a photo of me by a pilgrim monument. Erected in 1996, the steel sculptures set out in a line at the peak depicted the history of the Road to Santiago in the form of a silhouetted pilgrim convoy. At the front of the caravan was a lone figure from the Middle Ages seemingly trying to find his way. Next came two men on horseback, portrayed as enterprising vendors selling their commodities to the ever increasing number of pilgrims. They were followed by another figure with a donkey, supposedly procured from the merchants on horseback. Isolated from all of those figures were then two solitary pilgrims representing the sharp decrease in numbers through the fourteenth to the twentieth century, a result of political, religious and social turbulence. The procession finished in the present day with a male and a female figure walking together, carrying backpacks, showing the pilgrimage's revival. I stood behind the donkey, patted it on the ass, made the ladies chuckle, then said my *merci beaucoups*.

Though I wanted to wait for Jan somewhere on the path, which had disappeared in the mist down below, I had to make a move before the high-altitude wind chills crept into my bones. From up in the heavens it was downhill back through the clouds for thirteen cruciate-ligament-crunching kilometres until the town of Puente la Reina.

Enjoying the full force of the sunshine on my face once again, I stopped to eat outside the albergue and Sasha and Steffan caught up with me. In Pamplona they'd bought a leg of ham as big as a banjo and were aiming to devour it as soon as possible. Not wanting to bear the burden of the extra weight any longer, they were going to cut their losses and throw away whatever was left at the end of the day.

'We sought we would save money but, aaahhh, so heffy!' Sasha moaned.

With their penknives, they tore off piece after piece and kindly offered me a few slices as a little side dish to go with my tuna sandwiches. Over lunch we debated whether to stay in town or carry on another two hours to the next village at Cirauqui.

'There are 338 beds here, but only thirty-four there,' I said, reading aloud from an information sheet. 'Let's do a bit extra and go to Cirauqui so we can find some peace and quiet and break away from the crowds,' I suggested.

With their mouths full of ham, the boys nodded in agreement.

After stopping by a pharmacy for plasters and a supermarket for supplies, we were on our way back into the fields. For most of the exhausting final leg we marched three abreast, matching each other step for step in determined silence. Yet more inclines and declines soon took their toll and my ham-hauling amigos, who were both smokers, had to stop for the occasional breather. Struggling up the umpteenth bastard hill of the day, we were relieved when finally our destination came into sight. The path beckoned us down a dusty descent, snaked through olive groves and vineyards, then shot up into the hilltop village of Cirauqui.

It was prime siesta time when we arrived, trebling the number of people on the empty streets. With our legs still trembling from the dipping and soaring terrain, we fell through the door of the albergue. Surveying the snug surroundings, we instantly knew we'd enjoy our stay. It was homely heaven compared to the hilly hell the Camino had just thrown at us. Underneath a marble staircase, a big comfy sofa and timber shelves stacked with books lured us inside. Cool air crept in through the door and poked a wind-chime into a soporific lullaby. The calming scent of a frankincense stick burning on the bookshelves made the place seem even more inviting.

'I told you it was a good idea, boys,' I boasted whilst admiring the colourful paintings of Camino sunsets and scenery hanging on the yellow walls.

'Yes, zis is great, just great,' Steffan agreed, running a hand over a solid-oak dining table in the centre of the room.

The whole pilgrim army had pulled up the handbrake eight kilometres back and deprived themselves of this little oasis. It was ours and ours alone.

Not long after we'd freshened up with a shower, the dreadlocked French girl I'd first seen flirting with Franz in Larrasoaña arrived too. We'd actually walked a short while together earlier in the day, but she hadn't been chatty or friendly and we soon parted ways. In our brief encounter she hadn't given much away, only that, just like Jean Raphael, she'd started walking from Paris and it was her twenty-ninth day on the road.

Early evening, on the upstairs balcony of the albergue, I also found out one more thing about her – she really liked nuts, particularly pistachio nuts. Sasha, Steffan and I were sitting back with our socks off and feet up when she came and joined us. Trying to extend the hand of friendship, I passed her my bag of pistachios and threw a magnanimous wave in her direction that said, 'Help yourself, mademoiselle.' That's exactly what she did. When I returned to the group after handwashing my walking clothes, she passed me back a bag of crumbs and shells. She'd shamelessly polished off the bloody lot! 'That's the last time she gets her hands on my nuts,' I hissed under my breath as I tossed the bag in the bin.

On a visit to the local grocery store before bedtime, I met someone I would remember more fondly. The shopkeeper enchanted us by handing his wrinkled regulars bags of pre-packed groceries from behind the counter. The plump old man, wearing a black tie and creased grey shirt that revealed large sweat rings every time he reached for the dusty high shelves, knew all his customers' names and what they wanted before they could ask. To his patrons he passed over plastic packets of olives, glass jars of lentils and UHT milk cartons like a genie handing over a lamp. It was a charming throwback to old times and he exemplified the dying art of shopkeeping at its heart-warming best.

When I stepped outside with my own bag containing bread and tins of tuna, I was approached by a dog that looked very similar to a greyhound. Even though he didn't seem dangerous, I was taking no chances. I passed him cautiously while his nose twitched and wiggled its curiosity at the contents of my shopping bag. Staying out of harm's way, I waited for Sasha and Steffan at a safe distance from the dog and took cover behind a big 4x4 jeep parked opposite. I was thinking about crawling under it until I saw a petrified ginger cat had already beaten me to it. It turned out to be a wise decision. When Sasha came out of the shop, the dog barked ferociously and chased him down the street until he escaped by sprinting away with an expression like his hair was on fire.

Once the coast was clear and the dog was out of sight, I caught up with him.

'I sink ze dog wanted to kill me,' he said, doubled over with hands on his knees, trying to get his breath back.

'You must smell of that ham,' I joked as we cautiously made our way back to the albergue, where there had been one more late arrival.

As I pushed the front door open, I saw Crazy Frank trying to get to grips with the hi-tech CD player mounted on the wall in the dining room. With two shiny silver panels and a digital display but no buttons, there didn't appear to be an obvious way of turning the oval-shaped contraption on. I'd be lying if I said I hadn't thought about trying to play some music, but I hadn't wanted to look stupid not being able to switch it on. Crazy Frank had no such inhibitions and was at war with the machine. With a Depeche Mode CD withdrawn from his rucksack and in his hand ready to play, he was trying every which way possible to get it going. Thinking it might be voice activated, he was shouting 'Open! Hello! Good evening!' Despite his best efforts, the machine, which was like something from Star Trek's Starship *Enterprise*, didn't respond. This only served to make him shout louder, with escalating, growling anger.

Watching him through a gap in the front door, Steffan, Sasha and I fell to our knees with laughter as he took to attempting to clap it open. Finally defeated after many unsuccessful attempts, he sat at the dining table leafing through a book he'd grabbed from the shelves. As we came through the door pretending we hadn't seen him, he was muttering what I assumed were swear words in Hungarian. Still angry at the CD player, he didn't even look up from the book to say hello.

When no one was around, just before bedtime, I had a go myself. It took me a good five minutes to find the power button on the underside of the CD player.

With Sasha, Steffan, Crazy Frank and the nut-nabbing French girl the only other people staying in the albergue, the snore risk factor was at its lowest yet. I had high hopes of resting well for the third night in a row after days of sleep deprivation. First to bed was our French friend and we tiptoed around the dorm, taking care not to wake her, while we prepared our rucksacks for the morning. As the Austrian boys and I got into our bunks, the French femme began to snore violently. She sounded like Chewbacca from *Star Wars* having his haemorrhoid cream applied. We didn't know if she was having nightmares or wet dreams about what Franz had done to her back in Larrasoaña, but the three of us fell into yet more fits of giggles. As much as we tried to stop and compose ourselves, every time we looked at each other, we laughed more.

With my cheeks nearly exploding from the suppressed laughter, I closed my eyes on a smile that made my face ache. A cool Basque Country breeze snuck in through the dorm window, stroked my hair and soon put me to sleep. I don't know if I have ever ended a day feeling as happy and intoxicated by life as I did that night. I'd officially fallen for the Camino de Santiago.

11. THE JOY OF BONKING

Dick Beardsley, joint winner of the inaugural London Marathon in 1981, described how it felt to take a good bonking. 'It was like an elephant had jumped onto my shoulders and made me carry it the rest of the way in.' Thankfully, he wasn't confessing to some strange sexual fetish. He was of course talking about the physiological state when the glycogen stores in an athlete's muscles are depleted, causing a major dip in performance. On my fifth day westbound, it was my turn to be bonked. It was the day Camino boy became Camino man.

The morning kicked off in a similar fashion to the day before. Once again I was the last to leave and ate breakfast on the go. For the second day running I passed through dormant towns where the only signs of life were old ladies banging dust out of rugs over their balconies. Yet again, I overtook many fellow 'grinos, with cheerful *'Buen Camino*'s. Everything was going great, until those enthusiastic greetings became few and far between, and my feet started dragging.

After ten kilometres of gruelling uphill battles and downhill duels, I was relieved to make it to Villatuerta. In the middle of a church garden with a tennis-green lawn, I dropped my rucksack off my aching shoulders and collapsed onto a solitary bench. To get better, I told myself, I just needed to refuel, but biting into yet more cheese and ham sandwiches made me nauseous. My stomach couldn't stomach any more of the stale bread, processed meat, tinned tuna and mouldy cheese slices I'd been tossing into it for the last four days. Even more alarming, the acrid smell of chlorine from the water fountains that lingered in my flask meant I could hardly bear to put it to my lips. '*Agua potable*' – drinking water – were the magic words to look for at the taps.

I was now seriously doubting if it were true. It was like drinking poison and eating glass.

When I got back on my feet, an attack of pins and needles caused my left leg to buckle underneath me and I limped pathetically over to a bin and disposed of some rubbish. Shivering and sweating by turns because of a teasing sun playing peek-a-boo among the drifting clouds, I flipped open my guidebook to look for the nearest place to stay. Estella, just half an hour away, would be my salvation.

When I eventually got there, walking like I'd just been dug up, I knew staying over would be the sensible and grown-up thing to do. But there were too many reasons to carry on. Firstly, I'd only walked thirteen and a half kilometres, a measly amount compared to the previous days. Secondly, the albergue slept 125 peregrinos, which meant a potential 250 nose flutes bellowing throughout what could be a torturous night. Lastly and more importantly, Villamayor, where I'd planned to meet Sasha and Steffan, was my goal. Even though I was at my lowest ebb, I was still determined to make it. I reasoned that the extra eight kilometres would be a case of mind over matter and that I'd recuperate and sleep better in an albergue with fewer people.

Waddling wearily out of town, I crossed paths with a local who seemed worried for me. Pointing skywards at the blazing midday sun, he shook his head, warning me not to carry on in temperatures hitting the thirties. I waved away his concerns and foolishly went on my way towards a hell totally self-inflicted.

The road to Villamayor felt more like eighty kilometres instead of eight. My pace slowed considerably and I lost my coordination, clumsily tripping up and down kerbs and occasionally falling over my own feet. The throbbing blisters on my left foot felt like they were on fire and every step I took made the pain worse. I nearly called it a day when I passed a private campsite where the cool, sun-dappled waters of a swimming pool coaxed me over. I would have given anything to leap into the pool and revive my battered body. The best I could do though was stand on the wrong side of the wire fence like a kid with his nose on a sweet-shop window.

My fevered mind was thrown into yet more confusion when I came across la Fuente del Vino – the Red Wine Fountain. You have to see it to believe it. You turn up, turn on the tap and get your laughing gear around an unlimited supply of red wine. I'd heard stories of folk setting up camp there for hours, getting drunk and having a merry old time. In my weak state, I didn't feel that red wine was the elixir to bring me back to life. I lugubriously took a photo to amaze people with back home then stumbled reluctantly on.

Three kilometres under the life-saving cover of a holm-oak forest helped keep a breath of wind in my sails until I reached a seemingly insurmountable escarpment. Any other day I'd have stormed up it, but I needed to psych myself up and mentally prepare for what I thought was the last stretch. As the old saying goes: how do you eat an elephant? One bite at a time. How do you carry one that's bonking you up a beast of a brow? One step at a time. So off I went.

Arriving gingerly at the apex, I got the shot in the veins I needed. Just a cartwheel down the hill away, a church tower rose up between a cluster of houses and Villamayor de Monjardin waited for me with open arms. Mightily relieved to have made it alive, I found a precious circle of shade underneath a tree and took shelter from the soaring temperatures. I wanted to centre myself before entering the village because I painted a sorry picture and was feeling very fragile physically and emotionally.

Regaining my composure, I walked down the hill, through a copse and into the village. A wrinkly gentleman shuffling along the street wearing a big black beret the size of a giant naan bread bade me a laboured 'Buenas tardes'. Three young boys not quite into double figures, babbling away excitedly in high-pitched Spanish, whizzed past me on mini BMX bikes. Time seemed to stand still for a moment while I did a little more reconnaissance of the surroundings. Then my eyes homed in on a roadsign:

'Azqueta'.

Hmm... Azqueta... Azqueta? What did that mean? Then it hit me where it hurt. I realised to my dismay that this was not Villamayor. It was Az-fucking-queta.

My head in my hands, I slumped down on a bench, cried like a baby and accepted defeat. I was distraught. Down and out. My wounds filled with salt when I felt something warm and wet soil my shorts and trickle down my right inner thigh. I looked down and saw that I was bonked to the point of incontinence. To make matters worse, the old man in the beret joined me on the bench, failing to notice the piss trickling down the street from beneath me. Adding to my despair, a Spanish cyclist wheeled up with more good news: Villamayor was a further six kilometres. I felt like dying. There was no way I had that far in me. It was mission impossible. I had no choice but to sleep on the bench.

I stared into space, feeling sorry for myself, regretting having sent my tent home. I worried about how I'd get through my first night under the stars. Would the mosquitoes bite? Did the wild dogs come out at night? Would I be warm enough? Where would I wash my shorts? When would I eat again? Maybe I'd fall asleep and never wake up. But then something dawned on me. There was no way it could be that far to Villamayor. My guidebook had said it was six kilometres from la Fuente del Vino and I'd been walking for an eternity since then.

I checked again. The cyclist had a spoke in his facts. The book reassured me that I was just over a kilometre away. I pulled myself together and with one last push dragged myself up another gruesome gradient and made it down the other side into Villamayor.

Steffan and Sasha were sitting outside the albergue savouring cold beers bought from a bar next door and high-fived me on my dishevelled arrival. Incapable of answering their questions as to what had taken me so long, I went about finding a bed as quickly as possible. Inside the albergue, I met an annoying member of staff who hadn't quite sensed I was in no mood for playing silly buggers.

'Helloooooo, John Waaaaaaayne!' he joked, making fun of my straw hat and the green bandanna tied around my neck.

When all I wanted to do was pass out, he prolonged my anguish by attempting to engage me in a game of Cowboys and Indians, drawing imaginary pistols.

'Peow, peow. Peow, peow!'

My normal playful self would have returned fire, dived for cover and made Red Indian noises. The piss-smelling, bonked version, however, was running on empty and running out of patience. Eventually I prised it out of him that they were yet to open.

'Take a seat outside and relax in the sunshine, Mr Wayne,' he said.

'Thanks for nothing,' I muttered, petulantly under my breath.

Back outside, as I sat underneath a flimsy parasol offering little defence from a satanic sun, I overheard a young English couple talking on a bench across the road. Any other day I would have raced over and introduced myself, but I was praying they wouldn't come and speak to me. I was all out of small talk and pleaded with Steffan to find out how much longer we'd have to wait. He soon returned looking aghast.

'Ve can't stay here. Ze beds are dirty and disgusting, ferry bad,' he warned, before suggesting we try an alternative albergue within hopping distance.

Irked I had to walk some more, I flip-flopped two minutes around the corner, carrying my stinking boots in my hands and sighing like a stroppy adolescent. On a table outside the stone-clad three-storey house, some plastic cups and a jug of water had been placed on a piece of paper flapping in the wind. Though it was yet to open, the message invited us in: '¡Hola peregrinos! We open at 4pm, so please have a drink, find a bed and take a shower.'

I didn't need a second invitation. I went straight inside, clomped up the chunky wooden staircase and launched my rucksack onto a bed, marking my territory. My day became even more calamitous when I fell on the slippery floor in the bathroom after taking a shower. Enough was enough. It was three o'clock in the afternoon. Bedtime.

In the dark dorm of six twin bunks, falling asleep in the mid-afternoon heat wasn't easy. The vinyl mattress clung to my sweating skin and the blanket provided felt like sandpaper. I scratched away at my skin and the bunk's frail metal frame squeaked its annoyance at even the slightest movement. Causing me further discomfort, a splinter of blinding light shone through the ajar shutters. With my nerves fraying, I got up and slammed them closed. Returning to my bed, I zipped up my sleeping bag to protect me from the sticky mattress and itchy blanket. Better to sweat than look like I was suffering with crabs, I concluded. The change of tack worked and I eventually settled and drifted off to the sleepy county of Bonkshire.

Hours later, Steffan woke me with a pill or, as he called it, 'Somezing vor ze fever.' Sasha, recognising my urgent need to refuel with real food, kindly paid €9 and reserved me a spot for dinner and breakfast. I was grateful they were looking out for me and promised to pay him back later.

Though I didn't want to leave my dark room, I knew the first step on the road to recovery was a good, nutritious, cooked meal. Emerging from my cave into the early-evening light, I met three friendly Dutch staff members: Rick and Karen and their daughter Elsa. All were volunteering as part of a programme run by their church in Holland. They got their board and accommodation paid in return for staffing the albergue. Also staying the night was a French woman I'd seen on many occasions on the road. In tow she had a friend and compatriot, a chubby, balding, mid-twenties guy who'd totally ignored me every time I'd said hello. This time though he surprised me and broke the silence.

'Do you like ze Lee-bare-tynes?'

I paused for a few awkward seconds to figure out what he meant.

'The Lee-bare-tynes...? Ah, The Libertines!' I finally cottoned on he was asking my opinion of the London rock band I was none too keen on.

Not wanting to prematurely kill the first conversation I'd had with him, I was diplomatic and said they were a good band but not my cup of tea.

'Ze song "Don't Look Back into ze Sun" is beautiful,' he enthused.

The guy that never spoke turned into the guy that couldn't stop speaking. We took our musical opinions inside to the dinner table and sat opposite each other, ruminating about our favourite artists past and present. Scribbling down some recommendations for each other, on his napkin I wrote the name of English singer-songwriter Ben Howard and on mine he wrote the name of a French artist I'd never heard of and couldn't pronounce. Then our musical musings were cut short by our hosts, who asked us to read John 3:16 from the Bible in our native languages. First we heard it in Dutch, then came the French, followed by the German from Sasha and Steffan, and then, finally, over to me.

'For God so loved the world, that he gave his only begotten son, that whosoever believeth in him should not perish, but have everlasting life.'

Though I'm not a Christian, I read out my lines with all the gusto, passion and belief of a true devotee, and as we cleared the table, I started to perk up. The sumptuous serving of soup and bread followed by pasta, salad and cheesecake had been exactly what the doctor ordered. A long overdue gastro upgrade from the cheese and ham sandwiches and general malnutrition behind my bonking. I'd learned my lesson the hard way – to make it to Santiago I'd need to feast like I'd survived a famine.

Long before the sun melted into the muscly mountains way out west, I went back to bed and slept into the early hours until Steffan snored me awake. Getting up to spend a penny, I gently shook his bunk, trying to jolt him into silence, but got no response. It wasn't until I tripped over in the darkness on my way back from the toilet that I made a breakthrough. Catching my foot on the straps of someone's rucksack, I fell and collided with his bed frame, accidentally shoving it a good few centimetres. The result was magic: he turned over and stopped snoring! I'd found the miracle cure.

A good night's sleep helped a great deal, but I still hadn't fully recovered from my trip to Bonkton. Rick, the big Dutch cheese, suggested I stay another night to fully recover and I thanked him for letting me stay two nights when the maximum was normally just the one.

Over a bountiful continental breakfast, the Austrian boys and I got chatting with Elsa the blonde, blue-eyed chef. From the off she declared she'd come to Spain on God's orders and was in two minds as to whether she should start university or get a job upon returning home. A decision would be made, she said, when a sign from God had been received. Though I admired her devotion, even envied it in some ways, I kept my thoughts to myself that I have never been comfortable with the idea that everything that happens to us in life should be attributed to God. It wasn't that I didn't believe her or was questioning her faith. It was just that I feel such buck-passing relinquishes the power we have in our own two hands to get what we want from life and take personal responsibility for our successes and failures. I simply wished her all the guidance necessary for her crucial decision and thanked her for the delicious breakfast. With the rumbles in the jungle of my stomach silenced by a big brekky, I went back to bed and lay there while Steffan and Sasha packed their bags. I was staying and they were going. This was a reluctant and premature goodbye. Steffan left me with more 'somezing for ze fever' and with that my caring Camino buddies vanished. I was sad to see them go and hoped to catch them up somewhere along the way. My Dutch hosts, like all good Christians on the holiest day, trooped off to church wearing their Sunday best. I politely declined the very thoughtful invitation to join them and chose instead to get some more rest in bed. In principle it was a good idea, but I had failed to take account of the steady stream of passing pilgrims stopping by to use the toilet. They'd come in, raucously stomp their way up the wooden stairs, slam the toilet door closed, grunt noises that I've been trying to erase from my memory ever since, then finally clonk their way back downstairs. Plan A in pieces, I put together a Plan B: throw away everything in my rucksack I couldn't call essential. I was ruthless – a gigantic jar of jam, masking tape, safety pins, shampoo, soap, my Spanish phrasebook and spare pens were all binned. Taking another bonking was not an option. I was so obsessed, I even started ripping out the pages of my guidebook I wouldn't need any more.

By the time the staff returned from church, I'd plotted a calculated yet bold move. Having pretty much eaten and slept my way to recovery, I was ready to dip my toe back in the water by sneaking in a twelve-kilometre walk to Los Arcos. I thanked them for offering me another night's stay and in return they wished me '*Buen Camino*' and went off to have lunch. My backpack notably lighter, I stepped out into the retina-roasting afternoon rays, slipped on my shades and took the baby steps of my Camino rebirth.

12. BUPPLE TROUBLE

Somewhere in between nowhere and goodbye is a daunting place I remember Morgan Freeman speaking of in the movie *Million Dollar Baby*. It's also a place greatly feared by many pilgrims and somewhere I became marooned after losing my way.

Arriving at a two-pronged fork in a barren and remote stretch of trail that was bereft of yellow arrows, I faced an unwanted dilemma: whether to take the inclining path veering right or the other route, which swung left and continued on more level ground. It was so hot and bright, the sunlight stung my eyes when I took off my shades and peered through my binoculars to reconnoitre the terrain. When my vision eventually adjusted, I saw no sign of a yellow arrow. Only a petulant wind, kicking dust clouds into the air and a desolate horizon quaking in the stifling afternoon heat haze. Tossing a mental coin, I made an executive decision and took the path to the right. After walking for five minutes without seeing any yellow arrows or any other footprints in the dirt, I turned back. It had to be the other way.

Back at the fork, I followed the left-hand trail, but after another few minutes without Camino signs or boot marks, I had a rethink. If yesterday had been full of stupid decisions, today had to be full of sensible ones. Only one choice remained: go back to the fork and retrace my steps until a yellow arrow jumped out at me.

Walking east, away from Santiago, was a little unsettling, but it was definitely a case of one step back and two forwards. After a good half hour in reverse, I clocked a knee-high concrete post hidden in an overgrown shrub that I must have missed earlier, putting me back on track.

Prior to my straying from the trail, my Camino reincarnation had begun well enough, the sinuous path snaking its way through vineyards, olive groves and fertile farmland. But with every step the ribbed rack of meaty mountains over yonder had become more defined, the heat more intense and the sparse shade had fallen away. There was little still stirring on the baking, ochre terrain. The only audible stimuli were the insects buzzing, the electricity cables fizzing overhead and planes droning across the heavens. To amuse myself on the humdrum highway, I tennis-served flies with my hands, did the conga with armies of red ants crossing the path and took photos of my shadow in different poses. Waking me from my trance-like state, cheeky grasshoppers would frequently spring in front of me and say, 'Catch me if you can.' As I got closer, ready to pounce, the hopper would leap defiantly into the camouflage and security of the scrub. This was exactly how I'd envisaged the Camino when I was back home – being in the middle of nowhere with nothing and no one in sight.

In the oppressive conditions, I did all I could to stay cool. I tied a bandanna around my neck and used another as a headscarf, with my straw hat keeping both firmly in place. I may have looked like an old lady going to the post office to buy a second-class stamp, but for once I was following the rules.

A full three hours of roving the Spanish outback came to its climax when I took cover in the shade of a log-clad information booth at the entrance to Los Arcos. For my endeavours, I treated myself to a pack of chocolate biscuits and an ice-cold bottle of water from a vending machine. Worn and torn restaurant and bar posters were stuck randomly all over the booth's walls and I scouted some places to eat dinner. There was also a message book filled with the words of soul-searchers from around the world. Most were in Spanish or German, so I thought it was high time for some English.

'I believe life is about learning to build up enough love and power inside yourself, so you have enough love to give to others... *Buen Camino!* Brad – England'

My words in the message book proved how much the Camino

had elevated my thoughts in less than a week. They were typical of the positive mental states I'd been experiencing as I walked. I'd always enjoyed running in my spare time because it gave me time to think and often brought clarity on issues that were playing on my mind. But slow-dancing daily with the elements, walking for hours on end, something I'd never done before, amplified those positive physical and mental effects. It was like a slow-burning, more fulfilling happiness. I'd never smoked anything in my life but imagined walking to be like savouring a long drag of marijuana. Just with a lot more benefits and fewer side effects and not such a strong chance you'd start singing Bob Marley songs. The Greek physician Hippocrates, widely regarded as the father of Western medical science, said over two thousand years ago that walking was life's best medicine. After six days on the road trying out his theory, it was hard to disagree. Like my nan walking out of Romford market with a new £3 plastic ring on her finger, I gambolled gaily on into town.

In Los Arcos, I got reacquainted with many familiar faces, but there was one in particular that I was more pleased to see than all the others. Our eyes met as I passed by the courtyard of the albergue. Jan was chatting with two girls at a stone picnic table. Over the shoulder-high white railings separating us, we screamed joyous hellos and I rushed round to the entrance to join him. Sadly, our reunion was abruptly cut short when the hospitalero told me in a refrigerating tone that they were *completo*. Nevertheless, Jan and I agreed to meet later on, after I'd found somewhere to stay and had grabbed a bite to eat.

Getting turned away was a blessing in disguise. In my quest for a nest, I found success on the very next street, where I had the luxury of a small dorm to myself in a private hostel. Sleeping naked on my back with my legs wide open was how I planned to spend the night.

With my bags dumped in the hostel, I limped around town like a wounded soldier looking for a place to eat. Recognising the distress my blisters were causing me, a pretty señorita stopped to ask if I was okay.

'*Ampollas aquí* – blisters here!' I said, lifting my foot, offering a full frontal of the disaster area.

'Oooooooof,' she grimaced with puckered lips and squinting eyes.

The flames of flirtation were swiftly extinguished by my foot fungi and I hobbled off, vowing to rethink my ways with women. If I didn't want to put my blistered foot in it with Natalia, I'd have to get professional help sooner rather than later and start putting Vaseline on my feet every twenty kilometres like Jean Raphael had recommended.

Gobbling up some spaghetti bolognese on a grubby cafeteria terrace in the main square with the enticing smell of fresh coffee wafting out the door, I watched Los Arcos spring to life after the siesta. In a park in the middle of the tatty plaza, children ran amok around weathered swings, slides and climbing frames. The boys, most of them wearing Barcelona or Real Madrid football shirts, pretended to shoot each other with imaginary guns. '*¡Tomaaaa!*' they bawled in each other's faces before feigning gunshots. At a similarly grating volume, parents and grandparents keeping watch from flaking green benches under oak trees on the perimeter let out shrill cries of '*¡Cuidado!*' At the time I had no idea what they were saying but learned later the kids were yelling 'Take that!' and their guardians 'Be careful!'

People riding mopeds, seemingly intent on the death and destruction of themselves and others, hared down the roads, slaloming around the building traffic. At pedestrian crossings they wore out the pacemakers of the elderly pushing shopping trolleys like Zimmer frames, nearly mowing them down. Outside shops, bars and restaurants around the fringes of the plaza, locals milled around. Women in bakery queues spilling onto the street waved fans in their faces, seeking respite from the heat. Ticket sellers for the national lottery worked café terraces, touting for business. The vast majority of people, though, were engaged in the pastime the Spanish do better than anyone: talking loudly. If it were an Olympic event, they'd take gold, silver and bronze. A group of *chicos* inside the bar of my cafeteria conversed by shouting, gesticulating aggressively and slamming their hands down on the counter. Just as I expected someone to land a punch, there would be a bear hug, a laugh and more raised voices before one of them walked out the door. To survive in the Iberian urban jungle, I really had a lot to learn.

The entertainment over, I sucked up another strand of spaghetti and caught the scent of a fruity female fragrance from the table behind me. Looking over my shoulder, I stole a glimpse of the saucy señorita I'd met earlier, sitting alone, reading the menu. Was she following me? Or was it merely a coincidence that we'd chosen to eat at the same cheap and cheerful establishment? More importantly, had she slipped into something more comfortable just for me? Since I'd last seen her she'd traded her white T-shirt for a yellow crop-top showing off a toned and tantalising midriff. Grey leggings had been exchanged for a green netball-style skirt revealing legs looking smooth as petals and gleaming in the sunlight that was sneaking through a gap in the awning. If ever there was a moment I needed to know Spanish, it was right now. I cursed my secondary school for having made me study French. All I could remember was 'I have a cat', which would have been a random conversation starter, and probably finisher, even if her linguistic skills did cross the Gallic border. I had no choice but to save myself for Natalia and simply savour all the sensory joys this goddess brought to my evening meal.

Wobbling more than walking back through town to meet Jan, I caught the attention of a señora who insisted on helping to heal my blisters. She pushed a palm in my face, ordering me to stop and wait, dashed inside her house and returned at once with a minuscule pill. Holding it in the air, she proceeded to count out loud.

'Uno, dos, tres, cuatro,' she said, counting on her fingers. '¡Cuatro horas!' she continued, raising her voice, which I took to mean I should take one every four hours. Then, with her eyes popping out of her head, she poked her tongue out and pointed underneath it. I nodded non-stop like a parcel-shelf dog to show

I understood – one of those, under the tongue, every four hours. This Spanish stuff wasn't that hard after all.

'*¡Muchas gracias!*' I said appreciatively, bowing my head with my hands clasped together in prayer like a Buddhist monk. Not speaking the language, was making me do strange things to be understood. With that, she pressed a full packet into my hand and vanished into thin air, leaving a cloud of smoke where she had once stood.

Just as I was about to stick one under my tongue, the alarm bells went off. I was about to take a suspect substance; a mysterious medicine; a curious cure; a puzzling pill; a random remedy; a dodgy dose; perhaps a naughty narcotic? Should I be more cautious with this chemical? (Sorry, I thought I was Roald Dahl for a minute.) In normal circumstances I would have put it on my forehead, used it as a bindi and done a Bollywood dance before throwing it away. But I really did need help. Assessing the situation seriously, I noted that the woman had not asked for money, appeared to genuinely care and had probably seen countless pilgrims come and go in a similar state. I decided to trust that the matriarchal figure simply knew how to help. Under the tongue it went.

Hoping I hadn't just swallowed a hallucinogen, I went to meet Jan at his albergue, where we caught up on all things Camino. In the dying evening light he broke some bad news as we sat down to chat in the courtyard.

'I didn't believed Camino was so very hard. I go tomorrow back to Czech Republic,' he said.

'What? You can't walk 160 kilometres then just stop!' I pleaded, desperately trying to make him reconsider.

Remonstrating with him was futile and his mind was made up. His plan was to walk to Logroño tomorrow and then, depending on prices, get a flight, bus or train to Prague. (Jan, as always, was full of surprises and you will read later on about his eventful trip home.)

'Next year, I do Camino again but go to Santiago all kilometres,' he steadfastly declared with a fist in the air.

Earlier in the day Steffan and Sasha had left me and now Jan was going too. I was disappointed to have parted so soon with my three new friends. At least I still had Crazy Frank, if only I could find him.

Bedtime was a tale of two Germans and more drugs. I got back to my cosy dorm to find I no longer had it to myself. Two middle-aged dames of Deutsch descent had just arrived and claimed the remaining pair of single beds.

'Why did you get here so late?' I asked as they bent over to untie their laces with tired groans.

'On ze vay vee ver lost ant hat to make a bus journey to come here. Ze day has been so ferry hart ant long,' replied one of the ladies.

'You haff a problem viz your feet?' the same woman asked, sounding genuinely concerned.

I waved my left foot in the air, which provoked looks of horror on their faces. Her friend, who thus far hadn't said a word, foraged into the depths of her backpack and pulled out a shiny pack of tiny white pills.

'You shall put zem under ze tongue. Zey are homepazick. Ferry good for ze bupples,' she said, closing her eyes and nodding her head in a most reassuring way.

It took me a while to click – 'bupples' meaning bubbles, bubbles meaning blisters. Slipping the packet into my rucksack, I thanked the German ladies for their help and for confirming the pills given to me earlier were not Rohypnol. They were homeopathic. I fell asleep a little easier, knowing I wouldn't wake in the Spanish lady's basement bound and gagged, wearing only scallop shells covering my bits.

13. CRIER'S DIARY

Proper prior planning prevents piss-poor performance. A maxim drummed into me by my boss in my first job after university. They were words I took very seriously as I prepared for potentially the hardest day yet.

For the next thirty kilometres shade would be scarce, water fountains few and far between and the sun turned up to turbo. 'Wear your hat and fill your water bottles,' my guidebook strongly advised. Taking heed of my thus far infallible paperback pal, I did as I was told. While I was there, I stuck another pill 'under ze tongue', slapped Factor 50 all over, used a bandanna to keep the sun off my neck and declared myself fit for the fight.

On the edge of town, where the Camino snuck back into the countryside, I stopped on a bench and scoffed everything edible in my backpack. Four muesli bars, an apple and a banana later, I was back on the road.

On the good-luck charm Chappers had sent, which I still carried with me, he'd signed off with the words: 'I'll be thinking of you roaming and singing your day away.' And that's exactly what I did. Wandering down the paths and dirt tracks, passing clusters of fellow pilgrims recuperating underneath the sparsely scattered trees, I sang loudly and proudly. Some looked at me like I'd been let out for the day, others laughed and a few clapped and cheered me on. After one week with nothing but the bare essentials and a budget of €16 per day, I was happier than I'd ever been in my life. Stronger than I'd ever felt before. No one could say or do anything to take away my sense of indestructibility. When I sang 'Afterglow' by Genesis, I choked back the tears as the words resonated with me more than ever before.

I'd always imagined the song to be about a man finally finding his calling after escaping into the wilderness. Everything his life revolved around before his epiphany was rendered insignificant and worthless. A strange road to be walking. On the Camino I was having a similar realisation. All that I believed before was now being challenged and turned upside down.

It struck me how the 'strange road' I'd walked upon wasn't actually where I was right now. It was my meaningless pre-Camino life and every shallow aspect of my existence: hopelessly dreaming of becoming a rock star, getting drunk every weekend, dating girl after girl but committing to none of them. Compared to this voyage of self-discovery, it was superficial, pointless and immature. Like the life of someone else I pitied and wanted to help.

Once I started crying, I couldn't stop. I tried singing 'In the Cage', another Genesis gem, where Peter Gabriel writes about rocking his baby to sleep with sunshine in his stomach, but I couldn't even finish the first line without having to dry my eyes. In a café the next day, as I wrote up that moment, I drenched the pages blubbering like a wedding day mother imagining how my heart would flood with love rocking my own baby to sleep. What was going on? What had happened to me? I'd sung those words hundreds, possibly a thousand times and never ever cried.

I wondered if it might be the work of a phantom phenomenon I'd read about on various Camino internet forums. There were numerous threads suggesting that the path to Santiago ran directly over some of the earth's energy chakras or ley lines. These are considered to be our planet's meridians, through which its energies and life-force flow, and are allegedly aligned between ancient landmarks and religious sites; the lines are meant to be straight, navigable paths oriented to sunrise and sunset at solstices. In her book, Shirley MacLaine claims that not only are ley lines loaded with the spiritual energy of the earth and the sun, but they are also supercharged by the stars and galaxies. One of these is the Milky Way, believed by pilgrims with paranormal tendencies to unfurl directly over the Camino. Many people on the forum had posted about how the spiritual mines planted along the path had resulted in them having an explosion of emotions and vivid dreams and they reported feeling a strong connection to a supreme, divine energy. One woman even believed that walking the Camino had cured her terminal cancer. Was I too benefiting from this spiritual acupuncture? Could that explain my mood surges, heightened emotional sensitivity and tearful outbursts?

Twenty more kilometres ticked off, I reached the town of Viana, where I straightened myself out with some food before pushing on to Logroño. Three things you hoped for when taking a break were shade, a fountain with drinking water and, if it was your lucky day, grass. In an urban recreation park I hit the jackpot with all three. Sprawling out underneath some trees by a thirst-slaking fountain next to a kids' play area, I planted my burning bare feet on the cool grass. Draining my flask of every last drop, I laid back, closed my eyes and sighed with satisfaction as I breathed in the invigorating smell of the freshly cut green. The drone of distant traffic, the revving of an engine from a nearby mechanic's workshop and the buzz of a hedge trimmer all faded away as I let the grass swallow me up and the ants crawl over me. The richest man, they say, is he who needs the least to be happy. I felt like a billionaire.

With the ants now committing suicide crawling in my pants, I went back to the fountain and cooled off some more by throwing cold water over my head and down my neck. Doubling my pleasure were all the new faces that had come to join me. The first was a very friendly Danish lady. Though I didn't quite catch her unpronounceable name, I did understand when she divulged her dietary objectives for the journey.

'I will not eat ice cream until I arrive to Santiago,' she declared before sinking her teeth into a juicy tomato the size of a cricket ball.

The next arrivals into what was fast becoming the most popular place on the Camino were Paul the Englishman, his

American wife, and their friend Bence the Hungarian. As well as his own rucksack, Paul was also bearing the weight of another, which belonged to a German woman who was further back and struggling with dodgy knees. I told him the Swindon Town football shirt he was wearing ruined such admirable altruism and some harmless banter about our footballing allegiances broke the ice.

Everybody who came to picnic with me on the grass and caught a glimpse of my 'bupples' strongly suggested I seek medical assistance. A young Scottish lass offered some advice to help me survive in the meantime.

'Change your socks half-way through the day. Works wonders,' she promised with a wink and a thumbs-up.

Another pearl came from her English friend.

'Clean your clothes in the shower, saves time and water!' Though nothing to do with my blisters, it was nonetheless a very useful tip.

More helpful hints came from a Kiwi girl. As luck would have it, she was a chiropodist.

'Can I have a squiz at your blisters?'

'I'm not letting you squeeze my blisters,' I barked back.

'Not "squeeze", moron! Squiz, as in "have a look".'

I showed her tentatively, ready to pull my foot away if she did actually try and squeeze them.

'Yeah, nah, you gotta get those seen to, maaaaate,' she warned. 'Until then, change your socks every hour and a half to reduce moisture, and next time you get some boots, make sure they're half a size bigger.'

She had one more piece of advice.

'You need some hiker's wool. You can buy it really cheap online. Soon as you feel a hotspot, you whack some of that on. Straight up, that stuff is mean as. It's like magic and stops them getting any worse.'

As I dug out my journal to jot down the footnotes, I saw a familiar figure coming down the road, dwarfed by the walking stick he was stabbing into the pavement.

'Crazy Fraaaaaaaaank!' I shouted.

Looking tired and bedraggled, he tossed his stick onto the grass and got out his water bottle.

'This day,' he said, chugging his water and panting, 'take my breaths away.'

'Come join us, Top Gun,' I said, clearing space next to me for him to sit down.

While Crazy Frank buried his face in some sandwiches, I re-filled my flask at the fountain where two little girls were having a water fight. My thoughts of 'Oh, aren't they cute and adorable' soon changed to 'Don't you dare or I'll tell your mummy!' One of the girls had grabbed my boots that I'd left there earlier and was threatening to fill them with water. What would it take for them to leave me in peace? Lollipops, a Barbie doll, a puppy, a pony? Normally I was playful and patient with kids, and most of the time I could tire them out with my energy, but now I had to do something scary to save my boots.

I looked back to Crazy Frank, who was wiping mayonnaise from his moustache, and surreptitiously waved my fists at them.

'Relax, no do it,' he sang as the red mist threatened to overcome me.

If Crazy Frank and Frankie Goes to Hollywood hadn't joined forces to stop the blood from rushing to my head, I'd have been going to prison. Taking a deep, calming breath, I waggled a finger of warning, shook my head, snarled a lip and saved my boots from a soaking. Thankfully, my scary face did the trick and the little devils scarpered.

I asked Crazy Frank if he was ready to walk with me.

'I very tired. This night I here. You go. But friend. You are always on mine mind,' he serenaded me and, like he often did, shook my hand with his two.

'Thank you, my friend. I see you later,' I said, pointing ahead.

Most of the last ten kilometres into Logroño I shared with Mikael and Eva, a young Danish couple I'd first seen in St-Jean-Pied-de-Port. Eva was a petite living doll with bobbed, silky blonde hair and pretty eyelashes that fluttered like a butterfly framing blue eyes. Even in her walking apparel she was a beauty, as if she was modelling a line of khaki pilgrim clothing. Mikael was a tall, skinny, nerdy-looking guy with receding spiky fair hair and blue eyes magnified by black rectangular-rimmed spectacles. Though they seemed an unlikely pairing, I found out during our lively conversation that they weren't just boyfriend and girl-friend, they were newlyweds on their honeymoon.

'This was Eva's idea,' Mikael explained. 'She has a pretty face but a wild heart. Everything a man dreams of,' he said, beaming with pride.

'The Camino is like a marriage. Sometimes beautiful, some-times hard, but always growing and learning. It's good training for us,' she said, marching with her chin up like a superhero.

Eva was as tough as she was entrancingly beautiful and walked the walk as well as she talked it. Riddled with blisters, she strode defiantly on, even though a limp was slowing her down. Knowing that places at the albergue in Logroño could well be taken if I stayed with them, I picked up the pace for the final few kilometres and left them behind. It made little differ-ence.

'*Completo,*' said the hospitalera with folded arms and a shake of the head. She did though recommend a convent on the other side of town that hosted pilgrims.

Hot-stepping through the city streets with a Swiss guy who'd also been turned away, we followed directions illustrated on a map and made it just in time. The convent was very nearly but not quite full, and we were delighted to learn that €10 got us a bed in our own private room. When I say our, I don't mean to-gether. I mean private, separate rooms. Sure, I thought the guy was a good fellow, but I didn't feel strongly enough to read him a bedtime story and put water in his hotty-botty.

Logroño was the first big city I got the chance to know and a place I felt at home in as I strolled the streets in the post-si-esta hours. Unlike in Britain, where shops' shutters come down at 6pm and everyone retreats indoors, early evening in Spain is when everyone comes out to play. I perched on a bench in the middle of a busy avenue and watched the world go by as I guzzled cold water.

Steady streams of locals filed in and out of shops. City slickers moved with urgency on their commute home. Café terraces were packed with natives lost in conversation and deploying all manner of hand gestures and exaggerated, cartoon-like facial expressions. Frail elders shuffled slowly down the street, linking arms with their caring younger offspring for support. Elsewhere, roles were reversed and grandparents paraded the latest gurgling additions to their clan in prams they pushed proudly around town. It was a touching demonstration of the united Spanish family unit.

Hot *churro* vans piping out the smell of warm doughnuts teased my chronic pilgrim hunger. The cacophonous crashing of pots, plates and cutlery spilled out of restaurant kitchens preparing for the evening rush of diners. A female busker played a maudlin melody on a violin outside a shop directly opposite. A bohemian rose among conformist thorns, she attracted little attention as the metropolitan masses rushed past like she was a ghost. Each pretty and delicate heart-wrenching note made my lip wobble as her fingers danced gracefully up and down the neck of the violin. I bowed my head so no one could see I'd started crying again and dropped some coins in her violin case. She smiled a grateful smile and carried on playing.

Feeling emotional, I decided to call my mum. I bought a phone card and rang her. It was great to hear her voice again and as usual she had all the answers when I told her of my 'bupple' trouble.

'Go to a chemist's and just show them your foot. They'll give you everything you need,' she ordered me.

Updating me on current affairs back home, she said the weather had been really 'gool-jus', she'd been pottering around in the garden, and her mum, my Nan Smith, had gone dancing down the British Legion the previous weekend in her new Elvis bomber jacket. When we hung up, she said she loved me, and I cried a little bit more. I blamed the ley lines.

On my mother's orders, I hobbled into the next pharmacy I saw and plonked my poor left paw onto the counter like an injured puppy.

'Ah,' the chemist said, raising a confident finger in the air like she'd seen a good deal of this in her time.

From some drawers under the till she started throwing bottles, creams and shiny packets at me. In well-rehearsed but patchy English, I received strict instructions. Until my blisters cleared up I was to dress them in bandages doused in antibiotic cream every day before walking. When finished for the day, I was to apply disinfectant on the blisters to sanitise them. These two simple steps, she promised, should soon clear up my 'bupple trouble' once and for all.

14. THE LESSER-SPOTTED PILGRIM

In the restful setting of my own room in the convent I fell asleep before sundown and woke way before sunrise. At 5am, with still not a crack in the dawn, the city streets were already alive with peregrinos. All the early risers shared the goal of getting to the next stop before midday to avoid the savaging sun.

Spotting the yellow arrows among all the street signs, bill-boards and fly posters in the dark was tricky and I took a wrong turn more than once. Whenever someone saw me looking lost, I'd save face by digging out my camera and taking a picture as if on a planned excursion. Thankfully, with so many pilgrims around, I was able to scan the streets, spot someone going the right way, and chase them surreptitiously.

Due, as always, forever west, I spent those first couple of hours looking over my shoulder determined not to miss the sunrise. As I broke out of the city limits and walked round a huge lake in a picturesque country park, the theatre of first light finally commenced. The spotlights gently brightened and dawn drew its jaundiced spears, charging the retreating darkness to unveil a backdrop of thick forest on surrounding hills. A submerging fish sent ripples pulsing across the lake's previously still waters, breaking the glassy surface and the silence. I was walking close to the water's edge, and the faint but repellent sulphuric scent of rotten eggs coming from the banks killed any grand ideas I had of taking a sunrise skinny-dip. As the light grew ever paler, the birds stirring in the trees around the lake began to chirp and chatter. A fading fingernail of moon dug into the sky, the de-feated night's last act of defiance. How privileged I was to have a private performance and the best seat in the house at nature's theatre.

On my way out the park I met Marcelino, a man with a big heart, a welcoming smile and an unruly white beard on its own pilgrimage to the wild side.

'Peregrino!' he bellowed, with arms wide open.

Set out in front of him on a picnic bench in an area reserved for caravans and campervans was an array of Camino paraphernalia. There were walking staffs, scallop shells, apples, bananas, biscuits, bottles of water and wine. I grabbed an apple and a banana and fished around in my pockets for some coins.

'No!' he said with a stern hand. 'No money. Please, write here,' he insisted, thrusting a notebook at me.

Flipping it open, he displayed page after page of messages written by pilgrims from around the world. Travellers from Slovakia, South Korea, the Philippines, Brazil to name but a few, had written Marcelino words of thanks. I added Basildon to that list of exotic places and impulsively scrawled some lyrics from a song I'd recently written that I thought were fitting for a pilgrimage.

Just a Searcher Like Me

As I walk with a few good men, I wonder how to find more along the way

Do they stare at the stars and feel inner peace?

Do they smile at a stranger and feel released?

It's the searchers I seek

The wisdom that they speak

The lessons that they teach

Just a searcher like me

When I passed his book back, he surprised me again by gifting me a bottle of wine and a walking staff. I tried in vain one more time to offer him money.

'Free, always free. No money. I give only for peregrinos,' he said, before proudly presenting a framed photo of himself in front of the cathedral in Santiago. 'I know,' he said, tapping his finger on his temple. 'I am peregrino many times before and know the life.'

Five minutes after I'd left him behind, Marcelino chuntered past me in a clapped-out car as I skirted a dual carriageway. With his long, dark, grey-streaked hair flailing in the wind and a smile full of teeth desperate to win attention from his lively beard, he stuck his head out the window and blasted on the horn. After circling a roundabout ahead, he came back past me again on the other side of the road. This time he pumped the horn with a football-style 'beep-beep-beep-beep-beep' and added a thumbs-up and that unforgettable smile, just as sincere and warm as when we first met. Marcelino was a guy I knew for five minutes but his willingness to help people experiencing the same triumphs and tribulations he once tasted as a pilgrim meant I'd remember him forever.

Despite spending much of the morning uncomfortably close to busy roads, by 9am I'd made easy work of twenty mostly un-pleasant kilometres. As always, the best way to endure walking against the traffic was a good old singalong. With my memory jogged by Crazy Frank's lyrical remixes, I chuckled to myself, re-membering some of my mother's antics during my childhood. Early morning, she'd be downstairs doing the housework while Matt and I were still in bed. Her favourite radio station would be playing, and she'd join in with any song she vaguely knew, ran-domly changing the words, often to comic effect. Many days, my brother and I would lie giggling in our bunk beds, not wanting to get up and interrupt her while in full flow. 'Don't You Want Me Baby?' would become 'Don't You Want My Bogies?', 'The Wind Beneath My Wings' she'd change to 'The Wind Beneath My Sheets'. Our favourite, though, was her amendment to 'Wake Me Up Before You Go Go': 'Wake Me Up Before You Blow Off'.

I still don't know to this day if she did this because she knew we were listening or because it was a way to amuse herself while cleaning. I do know, though, that it's one of my favourite memories from when I was young. It makes me remember the better times with Dad too. Though he and I were often at odds due to my unfaltering defence of Mum in their slanging matches, we'd forget those differences when we watched West Ham together. Crying on each other's shoulders at the end of the matches was nearly always the outcome. But on one special Sunday afternoon, our beloved Hammers actually won an important game. It was an away fixture against our promotion rivals and a place in the Premier League was at stake. With the Hammers protecting a slender one goal advantage, the home team peppered our goal for the equaliser that would take them up. Having endured wave after wave of attacks, West Ham countered and doubled their lead with five minutes to go, all but ensuring their place in the top division. Yelling 'Yeeeeeeessssssssssss!' at a volume that had our spaniel Hannah cowering behind the sofa, my dad leapt to his feet and threw the roast dinner on his tray all over the carpet. Arms aloft, holding a chicken drumstick in each hand, he came at me for a celebratory hug. It was the one embrace we shared during my childhood. For all our cross words down the years, at least we have that unbeatable chicken-wing hug and West Ham promotion to look back on.

Reminiscing about those happier times, I stopped to re-dress my blisters in the tranquil village of Ventosa. Sitting on some stony steps outside the albergue, demolishing yet more bananas and muesli bars, I was approached by a real-life Mary Poppins. In a soft, high-pitched voice, the woman explained she'd hurt herself and was taking a rest day. Strapped to her ankle with a bandage was a handful of heather.

'Why have you got those on your ankle?' I asked, pointing at the flowers.

'They 'ave 'ealing powers. Just ask them for 'elp and they do eeeet,' she squeaked in a strong Italian accent.

'How do they help? What do they actually do?' I asked, with an inquisitive arching eyebrow.

'I don't know, but I know they do 'elp. Very much-a,' she insisted.

Whispering some indecipherable sweet-talk to a fresh bunch of heather, she sat down next to me and pressed more onto the injured area.

When she first told me about the flowers, I thought her cheese had slid off her crackers. But it was colliding with colourful characters like her and Marcelino that made my adventure so special. She seemed like the kind of person who believed in the unbelievable just because life was more fun like that. And why not?

Shortly after Mary Poppins flew off on an umbrella, a guy wearing headphones the size of breakfast bowls appeared at the bottom of the steps. He looked like a nightclub DJ who'd taken a wrong turn.

'Is zer a café near 'ere?' he shouted in a French accent over the hissing dance music leaking from his cans.

'I think I saw one around the corner,' I yelled back, pointing over his shoulder.

'Zankyou,' he said, returning whence he'd come, throwing his shoulders left and right to the music.

As sanctimonious as it sounds, I couldn't help thinking he was cheating himself out of deeper personal growth by listening to music. While walking, I remained totally disconnected from all technological devices. Switching off my energy-sapping mobile and silencing that annoying little child always begging to be looked at was liberating. Mentally I felt sharper. Clearer. Lighter even. Recent studies have shown that we look at our phones on average 150 times per day and that devices have reduced the human attention span to eight seconds. Less than a goldfish! Keeping my mobile out of mind and sight was a lesson my walk had already taught me. I made a note to incorporate a regular period of digital detox into my post-Camino life to free up some cognitive bandwidth.

And why would I want to listen to music when I could treat my ears to the Camino soundtrack: the insects croaking in the grass and the rustle of lizards scurrying for cover in the bushes. The cowbells ringing in the fields and echoing across the mountain valleys. The birds in rival nests and neighbouring groves competing to out-tweet each other in velocity, volume and prettiness of melody. The leaves on the trees flickering like tickertape fizzing in the wind. The foreign tongues of fellow 'grinos and the church bells chiming in the villages. The advancing and receding buzz of circling bees, wasps and mosquitoes. The lyrics and melodies that came from nowhere and looped over and over to the rhythm of my boots beating the ground. Surely all those audible delights were a more fitting ensemble than 'Smack My Bitch Up', which was bleeding out of his earphones.

The second half of the day was much the same as the first. Long sections of the trail ran alongside noisy main roads, with occasional detours through derelict, graffiti-ridden industrial areas. It was by far the ugliest portion of the Camino so far. On the one occasion when the path did veer off-road, I was held up behind a tractor struggling up a hill in first gear with the engine roaring in my face. To keep my cool, I remembered a valuable lesson from my flirtations with yoga and meditation classes: eat lentils after and not before the session or you'll get thrown out for flatulence. Sorry, not that lesson, another one: where attention goes, energy flows. So I turned my attention towards the heavens; gazing in wonderment at the cloudless baby-blue skies was enough to tickle me pink and let me ignore the tractor perforating my eardrums.

I needed all that power of positive thinking again in Najera, a concrete jungle that brought back unpleasant memories of my years living in Luton. The path was so close to the road, I choked on exhaust fumes and got cracked on the elbow by the wing-mirror of a passing car. Though unhurt, I involuntarily launched a paroxysm of expletives before closing my mouth just in case the driver was a bullfighter with a sword in his car. Adding to my frustration, the waymarks were confusing and inaccurate and I ended up wasting time and energy chasing my tail around town. Getting lost in Luton's Spanish twin-town with the sun at its most inhospitable was far from fun.

Even though the heat was stifling and there was still space at Najera's albergue, I kept going in a bid to break thirty kilometres for the first time. The decision proved to be a good one. The next few hours were a song and dance along a red-earth track as I inhaled the sinus-clearing scent of tall pines throwing glorious shade onto the path. The God-sent countryside extended until it gave way to a single-lane road leading into Azofra, a quaint hamlet of five hundred people kept alive by the modern pilgrim. Its two shops, two restaurants and three albergues, just a puddle-jump away from each other, were its only signs of life.

In a stroke of luck, I chose the albergue with the ribbons and wrapping paper still on. The building was so new, they still hadn't got round to painting the plasterboard walls. Refreshingly, the architects had exercised a little more thought with the design than in others I'd seen thus far. Instead of throwing fifty squeaking double bunks into an echoey, unisex hall, as most albergues tended to, we were paired off into same sex-cubicles containing two single beds, on one of three separate floors. I shared my cubicle with none other than the DJ I'd met earlier in Ventosa. I tried to extend a hand of friendship by making small-talk but he made it very clear he wasn't interested. All attempts at communication were met with one-word conversation killers.

'Where in France are you from?' I asked.

'Montreal.'

Oops, bad start! I tried again. 'Where did you start your Camino?'

'France,' he said flatly, before turning away to carry on unpacking his bag.

I wasn't getting anywhere with him and we ended up just tiptoeing around each other in uncomfortable silence.

Bored of trying to coax conversation out of a social corpse, I ventured downstairs to the dining area, which was full of new faces. A Spanish *chico* sporting tight pink shorts was strutting about topless, flexing his defined muscles at every opportunity. Where I'm from, that would have been more than enough grounds for no end of leg-pulling and a Chinese burn from the local hard-nut. This guy, however, seemed quite at ease camping it up like George Michael at the Club Tropicana.

Those tight shorts would have been much more suitable for the two good-looking brunettes who were boiling pasta in the communal kitchen. If there were an award for the most unlikely pilgrim, those girls would surely have been nominees. They were in their early twenties, gorgeous, sexy, and to my surprise, Australian – I hadn't met any Aussies yet. Like their homeland, they had bright and sunny personalities and both were called Leah. No doubt about it, the Leah Army, as I quickly christened them, were pure retina relish. If an opportunity arose to get intimate with either one of them, I'd need Pope-like powers to resist and save myself for Natalia.

Unsurprisingly, the lesser-spotted Aussie pilgrims soon attracted the attention of the Canadian DJ, who was trying to impress them by cooking up a storm. The girls and I foamed at the mouth as we watched him make a French omelette that put my spaghetti and sauce to shame. If he was throwing me a challenge to win the Leahs' hearts via their stomachs, the wooden spoon was mine. I left the kitchen totally upstaged by that bloody DJ and regretting having wasted my cooking classes at school having butter fights with Tony Butcher. Grabbing a seat at an empty table in the dining area, I was soon joined by another newbie.

'Is it okay to sit here?' a tall, skinny guy with fair hair asked politely in Teutonic tones.

'All yours,' I said, showing him to the seat opposite.

Placing a plastic bag full of goodies on the table, he sat down and did something I'd never seen anyone do: he dipped carrots into a jar of chocolate spread.

'What on earth are you eating?' I asked, absolutely horrified.

'It's good, do you want some?' he said, pushing a carrot smeared in chocolate into my face.

'No, no, I'm fine. You, er, knock yourself out.' I nodded him on.

His quirky cuisine really shouldn't have shocked me. I knew

full well that a famished pilgrim would deem almost anything edible after a hard day's graft.

Having got over the initial choc-horror, I dropped my guard and we got talking. Norbert was twenty-two, from Cologne in Germany, and spoke excellent English. A student of philosophy and theology, he had aspirations of becoming a priest and openly quoted lines from the Bible during our conversation. If the Leah Army were the most unlikely pilgrims, then Norbert was definitely the opposite. When the conversation moved on to blisters, he came up with a novel approach.

'Burst the bubble with a needle, thread through some cotton and tie a knot.'

He went on to elaborate that this technique worked very well because it allowed all the pus to drip out... I'm very sorry if you've just eaten.

I loved how he called them bubbles too, just like his female compatriots back in Los Arcos. That had to be a German thing, I thought, and then chuckled to myself when I remembered that they called gloves 'hand shoes'. What did they call balaclavas – head condoms? Tights – leg jumpers? Socks – feet mittens? Shoes – foot jails?

The more time I spent with Norbert, the more I liked him. When he pulled another surprise later that evening, I knew I'd found one more kindred spirit on the Camino.

'You want some?' he asked, interrupting me while I wrote my journal in the yard.

I was afraid to look up from the page. For God's sake, what fresh horror did he have in store for me this time? Turnips dipped in marmite? Farley's Rusks in mustard? Cucumber sticks in dog food?

'It's called maté, tea from Argentina,' he explained.

'You have maté?' I said, raising my voice like it was too good to be true. 'I'd love some, thanks!'

The tea, made from infusing the leaves and twigs of the yerba plant in hot water, is served in a thermal gourd cup and consumed through a steel straw. Hugely popular in Argentina and Uruguay, the brew is as important to everyday survival as the mobile phone and carried everywhere by the locals. I'd first tried some at university in Florida with two Argentinean amigos who passed the cup around our group of friends like a joint. After a few tentative sips of the concoction, which is said to have antioxidant, anti-inflammatory and cholesterol-lowering properties, I warmed to the sharp taste and in the end couldn't get enough. Sharing a cup with Norbert brought back happy memories of those Florida days and over countless cups of maté we chatted away until bedtime.

After slogging my way through thirty-five kilometres, I collapsed onto my bed and realised how delicate the balance of my journey was. Walking so far in the sizzling conditions had left me with just enough energy to cook something and write in my diary. I didn't go exploring the village as others had done and I wasn't socialising in the albergue as much as everyone else. Although I revelled in the physical challenge, I wasn't doing this to prove my fitness. I was on walkabout to get to know myself better. I reflected in my journal that I needed to do a little less walking and a little more growing.

15. THE DOOR IS ALWAYS OPEN

The day I hit the wall and bonked, twenty-two kilometres had left me bedridden. Now the same distance was nothing more than a warm-up and I really felt I was hitting my stride. Before the morning was out, I'd scored a bed for the night in Grañón, showered and changed and had the rest of the day to play with. Although I had life left in my legs, after thirty-five kilometres twenty-four hours earlier, I didn't want to push myself too far too soon. I also had another reason for staying put in Grañón, the biggest pull: rumours of a banquet style, communal dinner at the parish albergue.

The Hilton it wasn't. The beds were actually thin vinyl mattresses and I counted more than thirty of them slung onto the dusty floor in the attic of the village church. It was, though, undeniably charming and hospitable in the extreme. Not only was dinner served and lodgings offered for a voluntary donation, there also was an open box of cash and coins on a table by the entrance, sitting unattended. Tucked underneath it, a little note welcomed donations of any size but also invited those short of a bob or two to help themselves. I opened it up and slipped €15 into the tin (my donation for dinner and lodgings). Coming from a society where doors are locked, valuables protected and every stranger eyed with suspicion, this was a level of trust I'd never known. Something from a parallel universe I wished was the norm not the exception. I'd not even been in Grañón for an hour but adored the place already.

It seemed at first I was the sole traveller in town as I'd only encountered a few incredibly friendly church volunteers. That was until I saw, stepping down the stairs from the attic into the dining area, those tight pink shorts and long, tanned, shaven legs. Sadly it wasn't the Leah Army but rather George Michael, who'd made it from Azofra before me. Recognising each other, we exchanged a cordial 'Hola' and I wondered if he would scare the church folk with his pink hotpants. I hope they didn't think we were travelling together – brothers, or, even worse, lovers!

Flips-flops on, I hit my hunger with a ham and cheese baguette and sat by a water fountain in the centre of the village as a cast of crazy characters came down the Camino conveyor belt. There was Kevin the Welshman, who was cycling to Santiago and asked me if I too was a 'penguin'.

'Peregrino, you mean?' I replied.

'Pilgrim, penguin, peregrine, all sounds the bloody same to me,' he remarked screwing the cap back onto his bottle.

I met an Irishman who stopped briefly and told me he was walking around the world to raise money for Aids orphans.

'I started about tree months ago and I'm hoping to be done in tree years,' he said, like it was the most normal thing in the world.

He made my exploits walking for a measly month in Spain seem very insignificant.

Before leaving, he gave me his card and invited me to donate to the cause and his journey.

Stephen Malone

Poet, World Walker & Guinness Charity Hero of the Year

Then came another hero. My hero. Crazy Frank.

'How much clock?' he asked me, frantically tapping his finger on his wrist, sweating on whether he'd arrived in time to get a place at the albergue.

'Keep on running.' I wasn't sure if he knew the Spencer Davis Group song, but my thrusting arms got the message across and off he went.

Soon after, I met Tomer, a Jewish film student from Israel. After breaking up with his girlfriend of five years, he went to Tel

Aviv airport and asked to be put on the next flight to anywhere. An hour later he was flying to Barcelona and the next thing he knew, he'd been talked into walking the Camino by some pilgrims he met on the plane.

'I might be the only Jew, but seems we're all searching for something out here,' Tomer said, perfectly summing up the mission of most pilgrims.

After Tomer took off, the Leah Army were the next arrivals, stumbling into town looking the worse for wear.

'My back is killing me,' Little Leah complained, throwing off her rucksack before sticking her steaming head into the cold fountain.

Offering my help, I hoisted up her bulging bag and nearly put my back out too. 'What the hell have you got in there?' I said. 'No wonder your back hurts!'

Later, in the church attic, the girls spread out all their belongings on their vinyl mattresses. It was decision time. They had to work out what they actually needed for the trip, what to send to Santiago to pick up at the post office and what to throw away.

'Throw the conditioner, bin the body butter, burn the magazines,' I dared them.

While the girls sifted through their things, I was really happy to see English Paul step through the door. The first and last time we'd met, he'd been shouldering the burden of an extra rucksack to help out a German dame in distress. This time, he was performing another heroic act, clasping an injured baby bird in his hands.

'Shush, it's an owl,' he whispered.

'I had a dream about an owl the other night,' I said, coming over with a bout of déjà-vu.

'Wow, that's like, so powerful!' said an American lady called Tierra, another recent arrival.

According to her, the owl from my dreams magically manifesting in Paul's hands wasn't merely a coincidence. It was the work of a divine power pulling the strings of synchronicity from a higher spiritual plane.

'It's the amazing collective energy we're subconsciously creating on this incredible journey together,' Tierra hypothesised.

I loved her trademark American enthusiasm. Almost as much as I wanted to be more like Paul. I wanted to come to the rescue of injured pilgrims, save the lives of baby birds and feed them dead flies (which Paul was right then catching and killing). Later that evening he even entertained a small audience by playing Spanish guitar and holding conversations in three different languages. Was there anything this guy couldn't do? Could he reproduce my party trick and balance a full bottle of beer on his forehead while doing the 'YMCA'? Could he lick the end of his nose with his tongue like I could? I bet you just tried that, didn't you?

Word of the banquet style dinner had obviously spread. In the cosy dining room of wooden floorboards, tawdry ornaments and rickety furniture, there were more than fifty of us squeezed around three long tables covered with white paper tablecloths. People perched on plastic chairs, wooden seats and metal stools with plastic plates and cutlery at the ready. We had to be patient before we could eat though. Norbert announced he was going to bring in a retired priest still living in the church grounds for a special saying of grace.

The spilt second the frail old man hobbled into the room underneath the attic clutching Norbert's hand for support, conversations halted and everybody fell silent. It was like he'd cast a wordless spell over all of us. Speaking Spanish in a deep, gravelly voice, he took long pauses between sentences, which were met with a serene, captivating silence each time. Most of us present didn't understand what he was saying but we listened and nodded like we did. He finished his short speech by doing the sign of the cross and the Christians around the tables followed suit. Norbert translated for us.

'He says he is 102 years old. He was born in this church and he will die in this church. He says that, regardless of where you're from or in what or whom you believe, the door is always open for all of you. Enjoy your meal, *buen Camino* and *bon appetite!*'

With that, everybody stood up to applaud and his crinkled centenarian's face lit up like a birthday cake.

Over dinner, strangers quickly became friends, filling each other's cups and piling up each other's plates before their own. It was the happy family meal scene I'd never experienced but wanted to make happen every day for my future wife and kids. Questions pinballed around the tables. The most common lines of enquiry were:

What's your reason for doing the Camino?

Irish Peter was another person doing the Camino to mend a broken heart after a messy relationship break-up.

Have you got any blisters?

French Bernard, who, remarkably, was walking the whole route barefoot, hadn't had a single blister to nurse.

Where did you start your Camino and are you going all the way to Santiago?

Like a medieval pilgrim, German Gerald had started walking from his front door in Munich and was indeed going all the way.

Next to me at the table was Crazy Frank and opposite were the Leah Army. Crazy Frank hardly ate a bean as he stared across the table at Big Leah's ample cleavage, gazing like a fortune teller at a crystal ball.

Under the table, I poked him in the ribs, warning him to pack it in.

'Sorry,' he said, leaning in, 'I got a booby kind of love.'

Doing my best to divert attention away from Crazy Frank's leering, I asked the girls about their lives. Their answers proved they were as lovely as they were pretty. Little Leah talked about how much she missed her boyfriend, a childhood sweetheart with whom she planned to marry and have children. Big Leah spoke fondly of her family, the presents she wanted to buy them and how she hoped to reunite with an old friend in London after the trip. They were real girl-next-door material, a catch for any bachelor.

When the girls got up to go help with the pots and pans, Crazy Frank pointed at Big Leah. 'She hot. Like batteries,' he said with eyes as big as bowling balls.

Since I knew he wouldn't understand a telling-off, I had no choice but to laugh.

With all hands on deck to help with the dishes, the washing-up was completed in no time, after which we were escorted into a small side chapel for a service. Directing proceedings was a lively and energetic man with a greying beard and wearing a scruffy, slightly faded black vest, shorts and sandals. His casual clothing and unruly facial hair suggested he wasn't a man of the clergy but his faith was clear for all to see. He led by example, reading out psalms with passion and singing hymns like a patriot screaming a national anthem. Although most of the foreigners understood very little, we respectfully joined in whenever possible, even if an occasional echo of 'Amen' was the best we could muster.

At the end of the brief service we were asked by two Spanish ladies to introduce ourselves and divulge our nationalities. The church's congregation, we were told, would read our names out and pray for us in their Sunday service. These people were so nice, I wanted to make them global governors. The baton passed quickly around the room.

'I am Simone, from the Ned-erlands.'

'I am Wim, the father of Simone.'

'My name is Barbara ant I am from Charmany.'

'Hi, I'm Tina from Denmark.'

'My name is Tierra, I'm from the USA and I'd like to say I'm so happy to be here with you all.'

My turn.

'Brad, Inglaterra,' I said, trying to sound Spanish with a trill of the tongue on the 'terra'.

The lady writing down everybody's names looked at me blankly. I tried again.

'My – name – is – Brad, from Eng – land. Eng – lish,' I said v-e-r-y s-l-o-w-l-y this time. My Spanish accent obviously still needed a lot of work.

More blank looks were followed by a quick consultation with

the woman beside her.

'Can you say your name again, please?' the other lady asked apologetically.

'My name is Brad. Like Brad Pitt.'

Hallelujah! Finally they got it and my mention of Brad Pitt gave everyone a little chuckle. The lady jotting down the names gave me a big smile and a shrug of the shoulders as if to apologise for the unnecessary fuss.

If that moment was a little awkward, it was nothing compared to when the guy leading the service taunted a poor Austrian lady with yodels.

'A-oooooo-stria, A-oooooo-stria!' he shouted, pointing at her and laughing maniacally while looking round the room for someone to join him in mocking her.

'Door-door-deeeeeeeee-door-de-door-de-door.' He carried on teasing the bemused lady. Even as the introductions went on past her, he continued with his wildly out of tune, inaccurate, yet entertaining Spanish interpretation of a yodel. I never actually found out whether this guy was the village priest or the village idiot. He could quite easily have been both.

If every church service I'd ever attended had been as entertaining as this one, I might well have converted instead of remaining on the spiritual fence. My first brush with religion came in my teens when I voluntarily picked up my brother's Bible for the first time. Though we hadn't had a religious upbringing in any way, Matt was curious and I saw him reading it regularly. Wanting to be like my big brother and knowing that kids at our local church got chocolate bourbon biscuits after services, I thought I'd give it a read. After several attempts to get into it, I closed the covers, thinking it was more like reading Chinese and a lot of hassle for a biscuit. The complex language used in the Bible just didn't connect with or speak to my teenage mind.

During my travels as a spiritual tourist, sampling Buddhism, yoga and chanting with Hare Krishnas, I had desperately hoped something would reach out and grab me. I enjoyed Buddhism's practices of loving kindness, yoga's tenets of non-violence and the tingles of relaxation Hare Krishna chants gave me, but I still hadn't found my spiritual home or a divine doctrine I could fervently follow. Experimenting with Christianity again when I was a youth worker for my local church, I attended Mass on Sundays, hoping to be convinced and ultimately converted. My favourite part was when we had to turn and hug the person next to us and say, 'Peace be with you.' I loved that! Aside from hugging random grannies and getting a whiff of their potpourri perfume, though, nothing gave me the urge to go up to the altar and receive Communion. I just sat in my pew while the rest of the congregation went up to kneel at the priest's feet.

In the end, attending Mass became for me like being on a fifth date with someone really nice who you want to fall for but just can't. Like listening to an album everyone else loves but you can't get into it. Like considering the manifesto of a politician you really like personally but remain unconvinced about voting for.

In more recent times, I've enjoyed visiting churches and sitting alone for a while when there's no services. It's there, I've found that same higher vibration, purer consciousness and connection with a divine energy as I find in the middle of a forest, standing on a mountain top or sitting on my surfboard in the ocean looking out at the waves.

Part of me was hoping that, on the Camino, I'd finally see the light. Perhaps in one of the churches that adorned every single village, town and city. Or possibly I'd be convinced by some of the peregrinos who were doing the Camino in the same month as me, 39 per cent of whom, according to the pilgrim office in Santiago, were walking for religious reasons. I was open, ready and willing to be drawn to Christianity, but, up until then, had found no teaching that inspired me to tattoo it across my heart.

At sunset after the service, Norbert and I carefully felt our way up the dark spiral staircase leading to the top of the church belltower. We took in the extensive views across the provincial border of La Rioja to the thirsty and very sparsely populated countryside belonging to the region of Castilla y León. I'd be spending most of the next week out there, all alone in Spain's desiccated backcountry.

Directly beneath us, in the church's immaculately kept gardens, Tierra was meditating in the lotus position under a tree, and nearby on the plush grass a few people were sprawled on their stomachs writing their diaries. On the cratered streets bereft of road markings, greying locals sat on their doorsteps chatting to family, neighbours and passers-by while yapping dogs soiled rusty street signs. Most people had their front doors and ground-floor windows open so anyone could pop their head in and say hello. It was an expression of the sort of trust that had seemingly disappeared forever from modern society but that perhaps constituted the most valuable asset of that poor rural community.

According to United Nations figures, in 2016 Spain had 17,000 centenarians. Which meant that out of every 100,000 Spaniards, 37.5 of them had made it to a hundred or beyond. Spain played third fiddle globally to Portugal, with 38.9, and Japan, in first place with 48 centenarians per 100,000 of population, but was streets ahead of the UK, at 21.5. The sense of community I witnessed in Grañón and all along the Camino was obviously putting years on people's lives.

Also enjoying the clear, temperate evening with the town's elders were flocks of chirruping swifts speeding inexhaustible circuits over the orange and brown tiles of the dilapidated rooftops.

After our bout of bird watching and marvelling at the views, Norbert and I got down to business and discussed the real reason we'd climbed the church tower. We'd met to hatch a plan for camping out. He was the man with all the camping equipment and I'd persuaded him to rough it outside in Tosantos the following night. When I broached the idea of taking the Leah Army with us, his response disappointed and surprised me. I'd grown to like Norbert a lot but thought he was being judgemental and self-righteous in his attitude towards them. According to him, they didn't understand the Christian ethos of the trip and therefore weren't worthy pilgrims. Without even talking to them, he'd made the assumption that they'd just come for a suntan and some exercise.

Norbert wasn't the first person to question the Leah Army's pilgrim status. In Pamplona, where they'd started – or Papalonia, as the cyclist Welsh Kevin had called it earlier on – they were initially refused a Credencial because they looked too pretty and the staff suspected they were just after cheap accommodation.

Ignoring Norbert's high-and-mighty stance, I went ahead anyway and invited the Leah Army to join us and they accepted. I felt a little guilty about having gone against Norbert's wishes, but I thought he should get to know them better before passing judgement. The deal was sealed. We'd all meet tomorrow night in Tosantos and sleep under the stars. If Norbert doesn't kill me first.

The Door Is Always Open

The door is always open... come and go as you please

Put down your bag, put up your feet, come and drink some tea

The door is always open... make yourself at home

I know you need a friend cos it's lonely on the road

The door is always open... no, it will never close,

Take a shower, freshen up, give me your dirty clothes

The door is always open... even when I'm not in

So help yourself to a drink or two, there's whisky, wine and gin

The door is always open... sit down and take a seat

Go lay on the couch and get outta the heat

16. VERY NIGHT!

By 9am on a normal working day back home, I wouldn't have got much done. At best I might have choked on burnt toast, turned my flat upside down looking for clean boxers and put on odd football socks for the ten-mile drive to work that would take me a painful ninety minutes.

By the same time on the morning I left Grañón, I'd travelled further on foot than my daily commute in the car. Seventeen kilometres already to the good, I was just an hour from Tosantos, where I'd planned to meet Norbert and the Leah Army. My legs felt strong, able and ready to do a thousand more kilometres, but on my mind were the words I'd recently written in my journal: 'I need to do a little less walking and a little more growing.'

In light of which, I decided I would write down all the lyrics, melodies and lofty meditations of the road that were rattling around in my brain. A rest area just before my target destination described as 'a picnic spot by a stream' sounded like the ideal place. But, for the first time, my guidebook let me down. Thick weeds and litter covered the cracks in the bone-dry earth where once a stream may have flowed. The picnic benches had seen better days too, ravaged by woodworm, eaten away by the elements and full of splinters. I had no other option but to reluctantly put the lid back on my pen, slip my journal back in my bag and push on.

Tosantos was as much of a let-down as the supposed picnic area. Though I scoured the streets of distressed houses, clapped-out cars and oinking and manure-secreting farmyards for somewhere to write and camp, my search was unsuccessful. I was left with an unwanted dilemma: keep moving and cover my biggest distance yet or keep my word to Norbert and the girls but have to endure the whole day twiddling my thumbs and choking on the smell of manure.

As much as I had the urge to carry on, I couldn't go back on my promise to meet them. So the hunt continued in earnest. However, further reconnaissance of the lifeless village in ruins proved futile. Frustrated, I ripped a page from my journal and stuck a message for Norbert and the Leah Army to a Camino signpost with some surgical tape from my first-aid kit.

Dear Norbert and the Leah Army!

I got here very early and hung around for a long while to wait for you guys but got restless so I'm going to Villafranca. It's only another eight kilometres, so try and make it there. If you can't, I hope to see you all another day.

Buen Camino!

Brad:)

As I crossed the village square with a renewed sense of purpose, a white van came speeding down the road, manically blasting its horn. The previously comatose plaza quickly filled up with old women coming from around every corner. Purses in hands, they raced each other towards the vehicle, now parked up and with its back doors swung open. I half expected Tom Jones to appear and get their knobbly knees trembling, such was the look of excitement on their craggy faces. Emerging through the doors though wasn't the Welsh crooner; it was a man selling bread, milk, biscuits and cakes. The old ladies peered around each other to get a peek inside the van and counted their coins as they waited in the queue. I joined them and bought a baguette and a jar of chocolate spread. Finally I had a good reason to remember my lost hour in Tosantos – the Bread Man and his granny groupies. I imagined the old dears having posters of him bare-chested with his white overalls popped open on their walls next to their framed photos of the Pope.

Sitting at a bus stop, I plumped my jowls with bread smeared in chocolate spread and took the opportunity to have some fun.

Roaming the streets were a few chickens, so I broke off some pieces of baguette and launched them at the stupid cluckers. They fought each other for one small piece of bread while several other bits remained untouched next to them. Two cheeky little dogs, seizing their chance, ran from the front garden of a house opposite and craftily lapped up the remaining pieces, leaving most of the chickens empty-clawed. The fun you can have with some chickens, dogs and a piece of bread, eh?

I knew next to nothing about Villafranca de Montes de Oca, the place I intended to spend the night. 'French Town of the Goose Mountains', its English translation, gave me some idea as to what I could expect. A much more appropriate name would have been 'motorway service station'. The scab of the Camino consisted of nothing more than a bar with dozens of lorries parked outside gunning their engines as they prepared to re-join the busy road carving through the village. Not a goose, mountain or French person to speak of.

San Juan de Ortega, my next hope for a bed, was thirteen kilometres further and I knew it would be folly to proceed in the skin-frying afternoon heat. With no choice but to stay put, I kicked myself for having left Tosantos, where, at the very least, I would have had good company.

I wasn't surprised to find there were only five people checked into the albergue. Hanging out my clothes to dry in the communal garden, I met one of them, a Spaniard who, like me, wasn't impressed with what he'd seen of the town. Coming over from his chair under the trees, he revealed a cunning getaway plan: sleep away the hot afternoon, then get moving again when it cooled down in the evening. I told him he was a genius and thanked him for the great idea. Despite my best efforts to resist his generosity, he insisted I help myself to his leftover macaroni cheese. As I very gratefully did so, I decided I would do the same - walk on into the sunset when the afternoon passed.

After a siesta with the soothing voice of Jack Johnson, I set off for San Juan de Ortega, thirteen kilometres away. The path began with a long climb into the heart of a shaded oak wood before the sandy track levelled and took me back out into the blinding sunshine. The trail was a pilgrim's playground, decorated with fallen logs and boulders I jumped on and off for kicks, and surrounded by dense forest where I hugged the bulky tree trunks and stroked the smooth leaves. The next challenge was a dizzy descent to a wooden footbridge across a bubbling brook, followed by another hulk of a hike up a hill. Before I could call it a night, one last big test for the thighs came from a steep, rock-strewn slope, easier to run down than walk.

Walking in the evening was very different. In the morning you felt the sun climb in the east and take aim at the back of your neck as you headed west. The setting sun, however, forever losing altitude, slid painfully slowly down the western sky, bathing the path before you in a harsh, disorienting light. Even with a tilt of the hat to shield your eyes, you could still only see just a few feet in front of you. At dusk your only friends were the butterflies bouncing around gracefully like leaves in the wind. They were far outnumbered by your enemies – the insects dive-bombing your face and buzzing in and around your defenceless ears.

Tumbling from an isolated pine-forest trail in the lilac twilight, I stood staring bug-eyed at the impressive setting of the albergue in San Juan de Ortega. Beside the Camino path a stately nine-hundred-year-old monastery soared over a sixteenth-century cobblestoned courtyard where groups of pilgrims had congregated outside an adjoining bar. Of its 108 beds, 107 were already spoken for and I was lucky to snare the last squeaky wooden bunk, even if the springs in its mattress made it feel like a bed of nails.

Entering the dated but welcoming watering hole next door was like strolling into my local pub on a Friday night. Smiles, waves and hellos came from everywhere. Mikael and Eva, the Danish couple, high-fived me on my way to the bar. The Finnish guy I'd spoken to in Pamplona gave me the thumbs-up as he fed a coin into the flashing fruit machine. The four Italians who'd taken a photo of me at the French border on the first day screamed a cheerful *'Ciao!'* and waved in unison as they hacked their forks into a wedge of tortilla. Tierra, Barefoot Bernard and Irish Peter shouted from their table outside for me to come join them. I signalled that I'd get a beer and be there in a minute. Sidling up to me at the bar, Crazy Frank offered me an olive from his tapas dish.

'Welcome to the house of the funs,' he said, skanking into a little Madness-style ska dance.

'Egészségedre!' I said, raising my beer in the air.

Toasting my perfect pronunciation of 'Cheers!' in Hungarian, he applauded me before reciprocating by raising his own glass.

Outside in the courtyard, I joined the somewhat glazed-looking inseparable trio of Tierra, Barefoot Bernard and Peter, who told me they'd consumed more alcohol than water traipsing the forty-five kilometres from Grañón.

'Sounds more like the longest pub crawl in the world,' I said.

'Cheers to that!' said Irish Peter before downing a large beer.

When the fantastic three went off to bed, Crazy Frank jumped in their grave and in the campfire atmosphere opened his heart and shared the story of how the Crazy came out of the Frank. Since he could only express himself using song titles and the odd word, he illustrated the inconceivable chain of events on several napkins pieced together like a comic strip. So the story went: he'd just done time behind bars for pulping the living daylights out of someone who had inappropriately touched his girlfriend in the club where he worked not as a glass collector, bingo caller or tribute to his dead-ringer Barry Chuckle but as a strip-club bouncer. I know – I couldn't believe it either. From his wallet he withdrew a small photo of a beautiful, slender redhead and cradled it to his heart. It was his girlfriend Szilvi who he lived with in Budapest and who worked in the same club as a stripper.

From the man who resembled a fun-sized Freddie Mercury, this was almost too much to take in. I'd imagined him as a steam-train driver, a whistling postman or a cheerful milkman. But a little bouncer in a strip club packing a big punch to protect his stripper girlfriend? I never would have guessed.

Crazy Frank looked me squarely in the eyes, awaiting my response. Somewhat taken by surprise by his story and lost for words, I replied in the only way I knew he'd understand.

'The only way is up,' I encouraged him, pointing up to the sky.

'After Santiago,' he said, 'stop Crazy Frank.' And he scribbled onto another napkin a messy drawing of him driving a forklift truck and a woman I figured was Szilvi studying to be a nurse. 'New works. Ch-ch-changes!'

Glancing up at the inky, star-spangled firmament and then around the dark, empty courtyard, he checked his watch. 'Very night,' he observed.

That Crazy Frank was walking to Santiago in penance for his crimes, like many medieval pilgrims had done before him, was the most unlikely bedtime story I'd ever heard.

17. THE COSMIC WARRIOR

The next evening, I was blessed to be enjoying once again the sharp, witty and quirky company of the fantastic three: Barefoot Bernard, Irish Peter and Tierra. We'd swapped the sixteenth-century courtyard of the night before for the oasis of an albergue hidden away in a leafy park in the city of Burgos. As we sat round a wooden picnic table sinking more coldies, we were joined by a couple of Austrian girls just starting their journeys to Santiago. The tall, creaking trees leaning over the log cabins of the albergue shimmied in the brisk evening breeze. Mopeds, buses, and police cars sounding their sirens circled the park, an unwelcome reminder that we were hiding out inside the lungs of a city and not in a forested wilderness as the army of trees fooled us into believing. A big group of locals who had assembled on a patch of grass beyond the trees chatted away interminably in raised voices. From time to time the wind carried the mouthwatering aroma of their seafood paella to our noses. With night falling, they were doing what most do on a Saturday – throwing a party.

We were doing something I'd never done on a Saturday night, or any other for that matter – discussing Mayan astrology. Barefoot Bernard, our resident expert on the subject, had our undivided attention. The Austrian girls leaned in, captivated. Peter lit a cigarette. Tierra nodded and gave me a look with big eyes that said, 'Hold onto your seat, you're about to be blown away.'

Pulling out a tatty-looking book in which he'd made some notes in scruffy handwriting, Bernard told me some things no one had ever said to me before and never will again.

'Your Mayan sign is ze Cosmic Warrior. Ze presence of intelligence. You transcend fearlessness and endure in order to question. Your destiny is to question free will wizout fear.' He read aloud, pausing after each sentence and making strong eye contact like he was laying down a challenge.

I'd been called many names in my life, including Spermside and Germside; an eleven-year-old boy once called me Mr Circumcised in a PE lesson I was teaching, much to my amusement. But Cosmic Warrior was definitely a first.

My nose would have outgrown Pinocchio's if I'd pretended I knew what he was talking about, but the idea quickly grew on me. I visualised myself as a supernatural superhero, planet-hopping on a solar-powered horse, planting my seed of intelligence and championing free will and fearlessness for all. This would definitely be something to impress Natalia with! She could be my Lois Lane. My Miss Moneypenny. Being a superhero, I'd probably need to invest in a golden cape, shiny belt and headband and advertise for an assistant too. A job for Crazy Frank perhaps?

Irish Peter's sign was the Planetary Magician: the manifestation of timelessness, guided by the wind. 'Pretty fucking cool,' he said, taking a drag on his cigarette.

Grabbing my journal, Bernard kindly drew some symbols to further explain my sign, imparting more mystical mishmash that flew straight over my head. I understood the most important part though: the Cosmic Warrior was the Mayan calendar's equivalent to my Sagittarius star sign.

Bernard was a fascinating person who lavished everyone he met, male and female, with his time and attention. The bottomless well of unconditional love he harboured naturally drew people to him. Dressing like the Dalai Lama, with an orange shawl draped over his shoulders and prayer beads round his neck, and walking barefoot, he was quite clearly a man guided by deep-seated spiritual beliefs. Tierra, another person fascinated by all things esoteric, seemed totally besotted with him and hung on his every word. It was surely only a matter of time before their spiritual encounters turned sexual.

Before donning my warrior cape, I'd had an eventful passage to Burgos, the half-way mark to Santiago. My long day had begun well before the previous night ended. Even the birds were pecking each other awake to check out the crazy people leaving at the ungodly hour of 4.45am. Well aware that the first ten kilometres would take me up and over dark, spooky moorland, there was no way I was going it alone. If I'd known I was a Cosmic Warrior at that point, I would have got changed in a phone box and flown over the moors on my winged horse. But, still unaware of my nascent cosmic superpowers, I dragged my tired body screaming for more sleep out of bed to join a convoy of French and Italians for safety in numbers.

Hardly any of us knew each other, but we stuck together in the mist and darkness like Scooby Doo and the Gang hunting down a baddie. The leader of the pack was an obese, bearded gentleman who had stained the night with his maniacal snoring. He probably felt guilty for having kept the whole town awake and took it upon himself to right that noisy wrong by lighting the way. Shining his torch into the dark to locate those crucial yellow arrows and stop us from walking to our deaths off hidden hill ledges was his route to forgiveness.

When daylight broke, I picked up the pace to wake up my body and went solo even though thick hill fog was still severely limiting visibility on the path ahead. Every muscle in my legs ached and I fought crippling cramp in my hamstrings as I hauled them up to the morning's windy and shivery peak. Stopping briefly to quieten my stomach tremors with two muffins from my backpack, I heard some voices in an unfamiliar foreign tongue coming up the hill.

Materialising out the thick fog were two pretty fairies, one a redhead and the other a brunette.

'You are Brad?' asked the redhead.

'Yeah?' I said, coughing on my muffin, completely taken aback that they knew my name.

'We have something for you,' she said in an emotionless Eastern European tone.

Whatever could it be? I was so hungry, I was hoping they had magically turned some mist into candyfloss.

After rummaging in her rucksack, she handed me a small square of paper. I unfolded it.

To my delight and astonishment, it was a message from Czech Jan with his email address. I looked again at the fog fairies, and then it all made sense. They were the Slovak girls I'd seen him chatting with in Los Arcos nearly a week ago.

Jan and I had made vague plans to say our final goodbyes in Logroño but sadly missed each other. I thought he had come and gone from my life, but thanks to the ladies we'd be able to stay in touch.

Walking with the fairies in the fog for a short while, I found out they were in their early twenties, had just spent six months studying in Madrid and were heading back home to Bratislava from Santiago. Some on the Camino like to tell their life stories within minutes of you meeting them. Others don't give away very much at all. The ladies were in the latter category, and penetrating their cold, hard, Eastern European shells was harder work than the walk itself. Feeling like I could do no more to keep the conversation going, I said thanks again for Jan's email, then sped up and left them behind.

Scrambling down a hazardous path of loose damp soil, slippery shale and stones as sharp as dinosaur teeth, I finally escaped the disorientating cocoon of hill mist and reached level ground. The rewards were the day's first light and some much needed warmth after a cold, unpleasant start to the day.

Crossing a wide-open plateau of barley fields, I kept my pedal to the metal until Orbaneja, where I stopped by a bakery. Unable to resist the smell of fresh, hot bread, I popped in and tore into a chocolate croissant. In a few rapacious bites, I kept hunger at bay for a little while longer and powered on into the outskirts of Burgos.

As the traffic became busier, the people got less polite and the city walls closed in, I began hearing noisy explosions at ever more frequent intervals. I carried on with trepidation into the suburbs lined with multi-coloured bunting until I met a rowdy group of youths banging on doors and windows, knocking up the neighbourhood. One of the crazy gang then pulled a flare gun from his bag and fired it into the sky.

BOOOOOOOOOOOOOOOOOOOOOOOOOOOOOOOM!

He did it again!

BOOOOOOOOOOOOOOOOOOOOOOOOOOOOOOOM!

Then the flare firer saw me.

'Peregriiiiiinoooooo!' he shouted, running at me for a hug.

Clocking my presence, the whole bunch, maybe ten to fifteen of them, congaed over and forced me to drink some happy juice from their hip flasks. I reluctantly accepted, thinking it would be red wine, but the mystery concoction tasted more like cheap cider.

'Gracias,' I said, doing my best not to spit it back out.

The mystery of the explosions uncovered, I bade the party animals farewell, reached for my water bottle to wash my mouth out and walked on, shaking my head in disbelief. It was quarter to nine on a Saturday morning! If I were to hammer on people's doors so early back home, I'd be chased down the street by tea-towel-wielding, apron-wearing housewives. I discovered later that night that they were celebrating the final day of the city's annual two-week fiesta season.

The final stretch into Burgos wasn't much fun, battling a cold headwind in the shadows of high-rise developments, with city traffic roaring past in both directions. I choked on exhaust fumes, tripped over uneven paving and swore at drivers speeding over pedestrian crossings and leaving me shaken. Ignorant bastards! If I'd known at the time I was a Cosmic Warrior, I'd have made my flying horse crap on their windscreens.

Many people spoke of taking a bus to skip this unpleasant chunk, but I strongly disagreed with that. After all, the saying wasn't 'When the going gets tough, the tough get a bus!' The tough pilgrims puffed their chests out defiantly through the grottier parts of the Camino and went on to appreciate the days in the mountains and the wilderness even more. To my mind, those who took a bus when they had the time to to walk, were selling themselves short.

Stopping at some traffic lights in the heart of the city, I bumped into some South African girls I'd met back in Cizur Menor. This time I got all their names: Lauren, Tracey, Nicola and Sarah. With them was Jono, a likeable, laidback, strapping Aussie who nearly crushed the bones in my hand when he introduced himself. As the green man started flashing and a forty-five-second countdown to cross the road began, the girls talked about a guy who'd robbed them of sleep the last two nights with his snoring.

'Yeah, he's the Corner Snorer,' said Tracey, the curly-haired redhead. 'He always takes a corner bunk and snores the hell out the place.'

'There he is now!' Nicola said, pointing at the man buying some cigarettes at a kiosk by the traffic lights on the other side of the road.

It was none other than the bearded pig snorer, last night's protagonist. The guy's nasal dredging was like no other I'd heard before. If you woke up in the middle of the night, you'd think Darth Vader was somewhere in the room violating a pig.

Further story sharing about the Camino's many snorers ensued as dual carriageway became avenue, avenue became side street, side street became tree-lined park path and tree-lined park path became log-cabin albergue. I'd broken the back of a gruelling twenty-seven kilometres without taking a break, powered by two muffins and a croissant. Add to that the forty-five kilometres I'd crossed off the day before – that was seventy-two kilometres in less than forty-eight hours. I was absolutely destroyed and wanted to eat everything in sight. A squirrel, sensing my desire to make a Snickers out of him, scrambled up a tree.

Most peregrinos were talking of going sightseeing but I didn't have the energy. I only wanted to write my diary, rest my legs and get some food. I made a quick sortie into town with Jono, Nicola and Tracey and brought some snacks back to the albergue, where we waited for opening time. A bargain €5 bought me a bed, and after a cold shower and another siesta with Jack Johnson, I woke up to some fantastic news: a giant-sized pan of paella had been generously donated by the locals partying in the park. I'd heard many accounts of people walking the Camino penniless, living off the land and relying on the kindness of others. I could now see how they survived. This was the third day in a row I'd been blessed with food from strangers without looking for it.

Just before nightfall, I popped out to get supplies for the next day and returned to find that a team of medical professionals had set up a tent to give a long queue of pilgrims some pedi-pandering. I got in the line and showed the multi-cultural gathering waiting to be seen just how good the English are at queueing. Those trying to cut the line were politely directed to the back. When my turn came around, the woman who cleaned up my foot didn't speak much English, but communicating with her wasn't a problem. She began my treatment by ripping off the Compeed on my blisters and giving me a telling-off.

'Compeed – no!' she said, then doused my blisters in cream and dressed them in gauzes.

Though it didn't hurt, I pretended it did, just to flirt a little. I quite liked my Spanish foot nurse.

'Oooooowww!' I moaned.

She apologised profusely and her face quickly turned scarlet with a mixture of worry and embarrassment. When she saw I was joking, she gestured to stick a needle in my arse.

'Por favor,' I said with a wink.

'Crazy man!' she said and patted my foot for me to get out of the way for the next person.

After flirting with my pretty foot nurse, I checked my emails on a computer in the albergue before bed. I was very excited to see that both Chappers and Natalia had written to me.

> To: Brad Chermside

>*From: Paul Chapman*
>*Subject: Sunrise, ooh Sunrise*
Brad

Hey there fella!

Sorry I haven't replied before, but I literally just got to the library to read your emails. I am sorry to hear that you were ill and glad that you have recovered.

I am also a little glad that you were ill and it was a chance to enhance the trip even more for your own personal growth. Brad, I don't want to say I've done it all before, but I know what you are going through.

I know that beautiful rising sun. I know that heat and that sun hitting you. I know that isolation, where you go for days without communicating. I went weeks and came off of it a little insular. Like you, I know the power and the single-minded determination it takes to keep plodding and keep pushing yourself. I know the pain and the feeling of getting up and doing it all again, and yep, I know those photos. Those random photos. Photos of your shadow, of which I too have a few. I'm interested to know if you feel like your boots are your wife yet? I am also keen to know what you threw away and what happened that night that led to the tent being dumped.

And all too well, I know you know now the spirit of the human when someone is not in the best form.

It's priceless, bloody priceless. Your words are doing that funny tingling thing to my body. I am inspired also and willing you on. Not that I need to, because I see that you don't need any more willing. You have entered that trip zone that will not let anything or anyone sway you from your goal. Your determination and focus and zest are as strong as ever. Fear is good, solitude is good, loneliness is good, realising you have never done too much for people is even better. What goes around does come around. Sunrise, ooh sunrise.

You will never be the same when you come home. You are going

*to have this new resilience that will stand you in such good
stead. Brad, your spirit will never be broken because no one or
nothing can break it but you deciding to let that happen. No one
can break you but you, Bradders.*

Carry on forward, I am a proud man.

It was the first I'd heard from Chappers since he sent me the
good-luck charm. His moving words put a lump in my throat,
a tear in my eye and a million more miles in my boots. He was
the one person who wouldn't be bored by my stories when I returned home because he'd been there, done it and got the mal-
aria from these kinds of trips before. He would nod, listen and
ask questions while the rest of the world would look to change
the subject as soon as possible. He was going to be a close ally
against the post-trip comedown he'd warned would be coming
for me.

I typed Chappers a reply, saying what I'd been thinking to
myself every day since the trip had begun: that walking the
Camino, I was simultaneously having the hardest and best time
of my life. I went on to explain how the simple daily pursuits
of finding food, water and shelter had given me a sense of fulfil-
ment and satisfaction I hadn't felt before. How depriving myself
of First World indulgences had transformed simple things like
a hot shower, bottled water and a stick of plain baguette into
five-star fantasies. How my comfort zone had shrunk to nothing more than a warm sleeping bag and a rucksack packed with
sufficient supplies to last until the next town. How I'd learned
that luxuries and distractions outside of that comfort zone
were my nemesis. Partners in crime with sloth and procrastin-
ation. The arch enemy of proaction, progress and motivation.
How having the clearly defined goal of Santiago brought out of
me degrees of discipline, willpower and focus I didn't know I
had. How surpassing self-imposed physical and mental limits
had convinced me I could now achieve anything I put my mind
to. How the generosity I'd been blessed with on the Camino

made me believe more than ever in the kindness of the human spirit.

I could have gone on and on with all the insights the Camino had given me, but my time online was running out. I pressed send, typed a message to all my contacts to let everyone know I was still going strong, then hurriedly clicked on the message from Natalia.

> *>To: Brad*
>
> *>From: Natalia*
>
> *>Subject: Re: Thank You*
>
> *Hola Brad!!!!!!*
>
> *You must not to thank me for staying on my house. Is my pleasure and you must always to have some rest on el Camino.*
>
> *Never I go to Corfu so is amazing you find this money in this place! As you say is crazy we meet this way but this is the life.*
>
> *You want that I say why I write my email on this money? I say you this when you are here.*
>
> *Write me please when you are close to here.*
>
> *¡Besos!*
>
> *Natalia*

Just like in the first email, when she included a photo of her face covered by her hair, she'd left me in suspense again. I'd have to wait until we met in Melide to find out why she wrote her email address on the €20.

Before I could reply, my internet time ran out and I walked outside thinking the day couldn't possibly hold any more surprises. I was wrong. Coming through the trees and out the darkness were the Leah Army, looking scruffy and like they were about to drop as they opened the white, waist-high gates to the albergue. When they saw me they screamed my name and we ran for each other, embracing in a jubilant group hug. Quarter to eleven at night and they'd just arrived, having traipsed forty kilometres in sixteen hours.

The grumpy hospitalera, already gathering her belongings to finish her shift, wasn't as pleased to see them as me. '*Completo,*' she sneered, with her arms folded on her desk, as if she took pleasure in saying that single word that every pilgrim feared.

'Ah, whatever, we'll sleep in the park and have a ball,' vowed Little Leah in determined tones.

I was so impressed with how they managed to laugh it off. These girls were tough and resilient. You certainly wouldn't catch them taking a bus.

Knowing they'd be cold sleeping in the park, I offered the ladies my bed and told them I'd be happy to rough it outside. The hospitalera, though, had other ideas. She caught me trying to smuggle the girls inside and ordered them away from the log cabins. I tried explaining they'd be sharing my bed and I'd sleep outside, but the heartless jobsworth was having none of it. The girls had to leave.

Knowing neither of them had a sleeping bag, I gave them mine and they went to sleep in the park. Even though I put on all the clothes I had and curled into a foetal position to keep warm, I still woke up trembling several times as my body lost precious heat while I slept. The drop in body temperature and the cold bite of night were not the only things making me shiver. I was also shivering with terror at the thought of everything that could go wrong on the inhumane terrain that awaited me tomorrow.

TORTUGA.COM
COSMIC WARRIOR
PRESENCE OF INTELLIGENCE

DESTINY KIN : TO QUESTION
THE FREE WILL
WITHOUT FEAR

GUIDE KIN : SUN
TO ENLIGHTEN
THE UNIVERSAL FIRE

ANTIPODA KIN :
WORLDBRIDGER
TO EQUALISE
THE DEATH

ANALOG KIN
NIGHT
TO DREAM
TE ABUNDANCE

OCCULT KIN
TO SURVIVE
THE VITAL FORCE

I endure in order to question, transcending
the fearlessness, I seal the output of intelligence
with the cosmic tone of presence.
I am guided by the power of universal fire.

18. SHEPHERDS, PUNKS AND HIPPIES

Between the cities of Burgos and León, a vast, arid plateau of wheat and barley more fit for camels than humans stretched out for almost two hundred kilometres. With the mercury threatening to hit the forties, limited water sources and scarce shade, this merciless no-man's land known as the Meseta seemed a dreadful prospect to most pilgrims. The treasonous 'bus' word was muttered in hushed tones by those without the appetite for attempting such testing terrain at the height of summer. Though I had my own fears about crossing the Meseta, a big part of me was also anticipating with relish the physical challenge, solitude and tranquillity the next seven days would bring. I pitied those who planned to take a bus to beat the heat.

I took my virgin steps on the Meseta at daybreak. Lances of light pierced the charcoal sky, picking out the silhouette of a lone figure on the path ahead, awash in aurora gold. Blocking my passage was an abundance of livestock being nosed back into the herd by a dog barking ferociously. Coming closer to the bend in the path, I realised the man grunting and whistling at the animals wasn't a pilgrim. He was, in fact, a shepherd. The first one I'd ever seen who wasn't a toddler in a Nativity play. I checked around to see if his proud, crying mum was nearby. She wasn't. This was definitely a real one, with real livestock, not just a cuddly sheep tucked under his arm. As I skirted the bleating animals, holding my breath so I didn't pass out from the stench of their dung deposits, the pot-bellied old man wished me '*Buen Camino*' in a gruff voice. It was a poignant moment, sharing a sunrise with someone doing a job thousands of years old who knew this intimidating land better than most. Just knowing he was out with me in that desolate, secluded world made me feel safer.

The traffic, pollution and impoliteness of the hustle-bustle in Burgos made me cherish the serenity of the wilderness more than ever. Exhaust fumes gave way to the agreeable scent of barley and oat crops waltzing to the whispering light winds. Constant Spanish blabbering faded into immaculate silence. Endless kilometres of flat and featureless golden fields chasing infinite horizons meant my only companions were the passengers in the planes scratching vapour trails into the boundless blue sky. Those who were on buses being dribbled on by the smelly stranger next to them were missing out.

Before venturing onto the Meseta, in the 'very morning', as Crazy Frank would have put it, my precious sleep had been rudely interrupted by a pair of clown-sized shoes kicking against my bedpost. I reached gingerly for my mp3 player to check the time – 3.47am.

'Clumsy, selfish, f*****g bastard!' I muttered angrily to myself.

Kept awake by the sound of carrier-bag rustling, the intermittent ripping of Velcro and the continuous mumbling of those already getting ready to leave, I weighed up my options. I could stay in bed, trying in vain to mute the hubbub by sticking my earplugs so far into my brain I'd need a fireman to get them out; do some time behind bars for stamping on the toes of the person who had kicked my bed; or I could reluctantly join the unbeatable arseholes who were making so much noise. Later on, I'd be grateful they woke me to get a head start on the heat. In the dead of night though, when my dream about doing naked pottery with Natalia like Demi Moore and Patrick Swayze in the movie *Ghost* was cruelly cut short, I was livid.

After carefully cleaning and dressing my blisters, in the darkness I searched among the trees in the park for the Leah Army, to fetch my sleeping bag. Eventually I found them back at the albergue, where they'd come looking for me to make sure I got it back. As the girls waved sleepy goodbyes, we exchanged email addresses and promised to keep in touch.

Ready to do some hard yards, I went to get my boots from the designated area where Crazy Frank was shooing away a stray cat.

'Sorry,' he said. Heaving a pensive sigh, his eyes receded into his head as he looked for words from his rations of English that might just make sense. 'Cat very fuck. Here. Peeesh. Peeesh,' he informed me, drawing my attention to the assortment of boots, running shoes and sandals laid out.

I was becoming more astute at deciphering Crazy Frank's English: the cat was horny and he'd caught the fearless feline soiling someone's boots. Thankfully our furry foe 'Piss in Boots' hadn't deemed mine worthy of a golden shower.

As usual, getting out of the city in the dark proved difficult. Small groups of bewildered pilgrims gathered spontaneously under dim streetlights, running fingers over maps like school kids on a scavenger hunt, sniffing out clues. Only by trial and error did the majority break through the city walls and wander into the fields of gold beyond.

The biggest challenge on the lonely desert road was not actually the sun, heat or lack of water. It was the countless stones and rocks strewn along the path. I'd be casually strolling, studying armies of ants or watching lizards big as baby alligators skittering for cover, when I'd be abruptly launched forwards. Gazing towards the ground, more often than not I'd find the culprit was a rock the size of Gibraltar. Time and time again I told myself to be more careful, look where I was going and lift my feet a little higher. Just when I thought my toes had been stubbed for the last time, I'd trip over another. After eating dirt and grazing my hands yet again, I'd swear to the sky with my nostrils flared and fists clenched. Stumbling over those bastard rocks and stones infuriated me so much and drained me of precious energy.

With the hours merging and the murderous heat from the ground burning through my boots, I plodded on, taking little sips of water to rinse my dry mouth as the sun flexed its muscles to melt me into the path. After a morning spent scanning the horizon, I finally spied a green oasis of plush lawns and birches brushing the Meseta sky, bringing some life and colour to the barren landscape. It seemed I'd finally found the place I'd been keeping an eye out for to write down all the lyrics, melodies and songs flooding my brain. I excitedly picked up the pace and, getting closer, saw just off the path a ruined bomb-shelter-type structure hidden among the trees. Curious, I trod round the back of the building, into the trees, and discovered the edifice was actually an albergue with a small, shallow swimming pool. After a hundred kilometres and only eight hours of sleep in two days, this was just what I needed.

Lounging around the edge of the pool, immersing their poor feet in the water, were a smattering of pilgrims chatting away. Close by, on a grassy clearing, some tents were pitched in the shade cast by the birches. I heard raised voices coming from the albergue and, stepping inside, encountered a grotty room furnished with ten or so bunk beds. A balding, chubby guy was lying back in a top bunk, resting his head in his hands with his belly in the air.

'Don't talk to me with that thing on your back!' he said in a Dutch accent. 'Make yourself at home.'

'Thank you very much,' I said, dropping my rucksack on a bed opposite and plonking down on it.

Catching me unawares, he jumped off the bed and stood over me, hands on hips. 'The boss of this place is starting a punk-rock revolution,' he said, raising his eyebrows in a way that suggested I should be impressed.

'R-e-a-l-l-y?' I replied, trying to sound convinced.

'Yeah, man!'

Proving he was a man of action, he climbed back into his bunk for another lie-down.

Hoping the 'revolution' wouldn't start for another few hours so I could get some writing done first, I carried on my surveil-lance. Stepping out through a side door, I hopped over ripped rubbish sacks, empty beer bottles and cigarette ends thought-lessly tossed onto the ground. The place was an all-you-can-crawl-over buffet of grime for cockroaches. Then, out of no-where, the Dutch punk rocker came running naked through the door and executed a suicidal back flip into the foot-deep pool, splashing those bathing their feet in the water. It was like some-thing from an 18-to-30s holiday, not the oasis in the desert I thought I'd discovered. The sooner I took leave of the place the better.

I went back inside to use the toilet, and a pushy German girl with tired, bloodshot eyes insisted I drink their coffee. Just put-ting the cup to my lips made my stomach turn and after one swig of the rank, dirty-dish-coloured brew, I ditched the cup and made my excuses for leaving.

'Where are you going, man? I've been here ten days. It's para-dise!' protested the back-flipping, punk-rocking Dutchman.

'You should stay wiz us! It's ze best place. Ve make parties every night,' pleaded the German girl.

In the last act of madness, blocking my exit was the man who'd taunted the Austrian lady with yodels at the church in Grañón. Smoking a cigarette in the doorway, he was making fun of those staying there.

''Ippies,' he said in mocking tones with two fingers for peace in the air, blowing smoke rings. Dropping the 'h' from hippies the way Spaniards do, he continued to mock them. ''Ippies, 'ip-pies, 'ippies.'

I humoured him with a pat on the arm, stepped past and marched up the pebbly path through the trees that led back to the Camino.

I was not at all tempted to accept their party invitation and I was glad to see the back of the place. I was already having my own party every day, exploring a mysterious foreign land, meeting inspiring people, young and old, from all over the world. A party meant drinking. Drinking meant a hangover. A hangover meant I wouldn't be able to walk, talk, smile or enjoy the treats each exciting new day was bringing. I was in love with life as it was and didn't need alcohol to enhance my experience or a hangover to break my rhythm. I was focused on getting to

Santiago sober and adopting a different lifestyle to the one that had failed to fulfil me back home.

It was by now the hour of mad dogs, Englishmen and, quite surprisingly, Danish ladies and Hungarian men. I caught up with Tina from Copenhagen and Crazy Frank in a field with not so much as a scarecrow, haystack or ploughing tractor to speak of.

'Good afternoon!' I said cheerfully, approaching them from behind.

'You are walking very fast,' Tina replied, in typically blunt Scandinavian manner.

Happy to have some companions after having gone solo most of the day, I dropped down a gear and traversed the plain with them. It quickly struck me how tall Tina was alongside Crazy Frank. After some small-talk about the heat, Tina explained she'd soon be turning thirty and would celebrate by striding into Santiago on the big day.

'She. Three-ty. Birthday,' Crazy Frank said, nodding and pointing to Tina, unaware we'd just run that sketch.

'Well, I might not see you, so, um, happy thirtieth,' I congratulated her prematurely.

'Thank you so much,' she said with a grateful hand on heart.

In Hontanas, a village poked into a rare fold in the table-top terrain, Crazy Frank and Tina left me behind when I stopped to refill my water at a fountain. As they disappeared down the street and the sound of Crazy Frank's stick thwacking the ground faded away, I parked my bum on a wall and rehydrated in satisfied silence.

I wasn't expecting anything special from Hontanas. It was reminiscent of most rural settlements on the Camino: rusty, broken-down farm vehicles with missing wheels left to rot in random locations; a steepled church tower standing sentinel over crumbling homes; more fowl than folk on pot-holed streets lined with adobe houses, many of them with shattered windows. On my way out of town, though, was a treasure I would uncover nowhere else on nearly nine hundred kilometres of Camino.

Behind a head-high wire fence, the sunlight sprinkled a million sparkling diamonds across the cool blue waters of a public swimming pool. There were white plastic sunbeds, light blue parasols and vending machines selling cold drinks, ice creams and snacks. Spanish pop music wheezed out of tinny speakers mounted around the fence and the tang of chlorine invoked memories of Thursday morning swimming lessons in primary school. Not a soul was using it. Not even any of the chickens roaming around, which reminded me of another useless fact our bass player James Nash once told me: 'Chickens can't actually swim.' I could though. And that's just what I did.

Spinning on my heels, I went to the albergue I'd just passed and, like a rock star making a quick-costume change backstage, got ready for a dip.

I'd just traipsed thirty kilometres in the Spanish Sahara, but the stiffness and tenderness in my sizzling, beaten body melted away the instant I lowered myself into the cold water. Looking out over the hinterland, resting my arms on the poolside with the sun kissing my face and water recharging my body was pilgrim porn. There couldn't have been a better way to unwind before the next day, when I would break fifty kilometres on the brutal Meseta.

19. GOOD NEWS, BAD NEWS

> To: All Contacts
> From: Brad Chermside
> Subject: Good News, Bad News, Good News

Well! I've been an absolute lean, mean, Camino walking machine since I last wrote from Burgos. The last four days have been a rollercoaster, with lots of good news and bad news. Allow me to enlighten you all.

Good News

I'm trotting past a church in the middle of nowhere and this guy comes out shouting, 'Hey, peregrino! Where are you going? You want some coffee or tea?!'
'Hey! Why not?' I say.

Bad News

I realise when I stop for coffee that I've dropped my camera somewhere between the church and the last town fifteen kilometres back – bugger and balls!

Good News

Even though I stuff my face with bread and biscuits to wash down the coffee, the man won't accept any money from me. He just wants my signature, country of birth and a message of thanks in his guestbook. He won't even accept one of my peanut M&M's.

Bad News

Armies of unrecognisable insects carrying weapons ambush me on many occasions. I'm sure I see one armed with an AK-47 and another with a penknife. When I fail to swat them away, they fly off in a victory roll, laugh in my face and come for me again just when I think they've gone. I hate them.

Good News

After leaving the church, I get chatting to a Spanish guy on the road. He takes my phone number and says he'll call me if he speaks to anyone who finds a camera.

Bad News

While eating lunch on a village bench, a guy with the hairiest back on earth comes and sits next to me, which puts me off my baguette and pâté. He could have made a poodle out of all that curly hair!

Good News

Even though I've lost my camera, I'm feeling very good and hoping to break fifty kilometres in one day. If I'm gonna do it any day, it's gonna be today as, for the first time in forever, the sun is on holiday behind the clouds.

Bad News

For a long period the trail is sandwiched between a noisy motorway and fields irrigated with chemicals that constantly sting my throat and make me cough. The horizon is neverending and I've nothing but traffic, toxic fields and vicious swarms of insects for company.

Good News

Straight ahead, springing up from the prairie like a toddler's foldout book, there's a church spire on the horizon – Carrión de los Condes, just six kilometres away.

Bad News

I have nappy rash on my inner buttocks and have to walk on my tiptoes to ease the chafing.

Good News

For the first time I break fifty kilometres in a day and walk a gibungus fifty-eight kilometres – bloody hell! Needless to say, I was whacked out and needed a friendly face!

Bad News

No room at the inn, and I can't find another place to stay in Carrión de los Condes.

Good News

I hear someone shout something from across the street. 'Loss a kuh fliegn!' they cry! This means: Let the cows fly and let's party!

It's Steffan and Sasha, my two Austrian buddies who left me behind when I took a rest day because I fell ill. So I get my friendly faces and also they show me another place to get a room.

Even More Good News

For the first time on my trip I turn on my phone, hoping for some news of my camera. Unbelievably, the Spanish chico I met earlier in the day has texted to say someone found it and he has it with him. He promises to give it to a cyclist who will drop it in Terradillos, twenty-seven kilometres ahead, for me to pick up tomorrow. Praise the Lord! It's a miracle!

Bad News

In the bunk next to me, the loudest snorer on earth is trying to break his own record. It sounds like he's having his prostate examined by Edward Scissorhands.

Good News

I listen to Ben Howard's 'I Forget Where We Were', to forget the snoring and put me peacefully to sleep. I love that album. It's like a musical hug.

Bad News

I really want to walk a shorter distance today but, annoyingly, the next town with a shop is forty kilometres away.

Good News

I pick up my camera in Terradillos. Am I the luckiest man on earth or what!

Bad News

I'm hungry, tired and really ratty that I have to walk forty kilometres just to find a shop. Did I mention I'm hungry?! I am sooooo bloody hungry! Do I really need ten fingers? Maybe I could cover one in chocolate and tell myself it's a Cadbury's Finger.

Good News

At seventeen kilometres, a village with a shop!

Bad News

¡CERRADO! – CLOSED! – says the sign on the door.

Good News

As I roll into Monomentos at about 1pm, a white van man punching his horn like crazy skids into the village square. It's better than a shop – it's the Bread Man! He flings open the back door of his van and grannies queue up to buy loaves, rolls, cakes and soft drinks. I join the line and buy a whole baguette, dip it in some mayonnaise and lick the jar clean. Hmmmmmmmmmmm-mmmmmmmmmm!

Bad News

Sahagún, my goal, is still eleven kilometres away. It's horribly hot and I hate having to take each step. It's the hardest day so far. Even harder than the fifty-eight kilometres because the sun is unleashing its fury and I really didn't want to walk this far.

Good News

I get to Sahagún about 4pm, drool over a chilled fizzy water from a vending machine and stock up on supplies in the first shop I've seen all day.

Bad News

My guidebook reminds me of tomorrow's terrifying terrain – a soulless twenty-one kilometres with little shade and water sources that are few and hard to spot. 'Only the weeds and wild-flowers have changed in the two millennia since the ancient Roman path was laid,' the author warns.

Good News

It's half six the next morning and I've already gobbled up four-teen kilometres.

Bad News

It's time to take on the twenty-one kilometres of barren, companionless, sun-baked land I read of last night.

Good News

Just over half-way through this Martian territory, my guidebook promises refuge in a shady picnic area of poplar groves and streams to soothe aching feet. I fantasise about cooling off in the stream with a mermaid who'll feed me fish and stroke my hair with her fins.

Bad News

My mermaid fantasies are crushed when I discover the stream has all but dried up at the height of summer. I trudge on, sulking like an infant.

Good News

I survive the hot, sweaty and empty twenty-one kilometres and arrive alive in the town of Reliegos. Outside a large, gated house there is an eight-litre water tank with a message inviting us to take a cup and fill up for free! I sink countless cups of water and thank the heavens.

Bad News

At the albergue, I recognise nobody, feel lonely and long for friends after so many days without meaningful human contact. I miss Crazy Frank's comedy English, the bubbly personalities of the Leah Army, the cosmic ruminations of Peter, Bernard and Tierra. I long for a chat with Norbert, Steffan and Sasha, three guys that are best-mate material. I consider slowing down to let them catch me up.

Good News

I stop feeling sorry for myself and think more clearly. I contemplate that just like life, the Camino is about being thankful for all you have and learning something from the great people you meet along the way. It's about remaining positive, looking forward to what lies ahead and believing your best days are yet to come. It's about wearing on your sleeve the Camino motto: 'Ultreya – Move forward with courage'.

Brad:)

Love and Peace (or else!)

20. THE MOONWALK

After so much time alone in the back of beyond, with my friendship senses sharpened, I thought I'd be happy to re-join civilisation in the humming metropolis of León, but I wasn't. The overload of stimuli on the manic streets were a shock to the system and threw me off-centre. People barged past, tutted their disgust and murdered me with irate eyes as they slalomed round my rucksack. The ground shook from the shrill drilling of roadworks, and the acid rain of condensation from air-conditioning units in the high-rise flats dripped onto my head. Worst of all, nobody returned my smiles.

Being back in the smoke wasn't just muck and nettles and did have something of a silver lining. At a pedestrian crossing, I was hypnotised by the intoxicating scent of a señorita's perfume and instinctively pursued her across to the other side. Realising I'd strayed from the Camino path and that my impulsive reaction could be misconstrued as sexual harassment, I put my tongue back in my mouth and crossed back over the road. After weeks of smelling little else but general 'grino grime, my appreciation for sensual treats such as a female fragrance was greater than ever. That didn't excuse my behaviour though and my case for the defence wouldn't have gone far in court.

'But, Your Honour, I just wanted to sniff her. Nothing else – honest!'

'Guilty!' the judge would cry!

'Make this strange creature listen to Justin Bieber for the rest of the way. Not only that – from now on you must hop to Santiago wearing ankle weights.'

At the albergue in León I encountered a man who'd ended up doing just that – hopping the Camino when the pain of his blisters became too much. We met in the kitchen of the albergue when I was so keen to find a friend that I approached the bespec-tacled, pale, ginger-haired gent.

'You want some mayo for your sandwich?' I offered, as he spooned the contents of a big tin of tuna into a baguette the size of a rounders bat.

'That's really kind of you, thank you,' he said, spreading the mayo over his French bread before cutting it in two and offering me the other half. Dangling free food in front of a pilgrim was like offering a pint of virgin's blood to a vampire. How could I say no?

We slid behind a table in the kitchen and as we chomped away on our French bread, Tore from Denmark told me all about himself. He spoke briefly about his studies to become a civil engineer and at length about two subjects: his burning blisters and an Austrian girl he'd met a few days back. On his phone he showed me photos of his feet, black and blue with bruises, rid-dled with blisters, and his toenails a mixture of sickly, gangren-ous colours. Unable to fit his feet into his boots any longer, like a Nordic warrior he was hopping, skipping and limping on in sandals and socks. His heart was aching just as much as his feet, pining for a girl called Kathi from Austria. He'd fallen in love when they'd spent a long evening having a deep and meaningful conversation and staring at the stars on a magical Meseta night.

'Such a pretty face, sympathetic eyes and happy smile,' he said wistfully, gazing into space. 'I can't stop thinking about her.'

Our bellies full of baguette, I made us a cup of green tea from supplies left behind by past pilgrims and told him something I couldn't stop thinking about. Placing the cups on the table, I sat down and put to him a serious proposition.

'Would you like to walk at night with me?' I asked, taking a sip of my tea.

'Actually,' he said, pressing a spoon onto his green teabag to speed up the infusion, 'the moon will be full tonight and the next twenty kilometres are by the roadside. If you're going to walk in the dark, tonight is the perfect time. So, yes, great idea, I'll do it,' he agreed. 'But I need to sleep first,' he said. 'I'll wake up at 3am and we'll leave then and walk four hours in the dark.'

We shook on it.

Before the León cathedral chimed eight, I was in bed wearing my walking clothes ready to stride out the door at 3am. Tucked away in a bottom bunk in the corner of the forty-five-person dorm, I quickly dropped off and snoozed until Tore woke me. All the lights were still on and people were still getting ready for bed. This was quite clearly not the previously agreed 3am wake-up call. I stared at Tore for a moment in bewilderment. His mouth was moving but I couldn't hear a word so pulled out my earplugs.

'Brad, can you hear me now?' he asked.

I nodded with all the energy I could muster.

'Did you know the albergue is a monastery?' he asked me in a panic.

I shook my head, still squinting from the surgical lighting.

'Well, I just found out they lock the doors at 9.30 tonight and don't open them again until six in the morning. It's part of the noble night silence.'

'Eh? Noble night science?'

'No! Noble – night – silence. It means we can't leave at 3am. We'll be locked in. We can't walk tonight!'

The bad news jolted me awake.

'Okay, so let's go now. We can leave before they lock the doors,' I said, quickly sitting up, determined to follow through with our plans.

'No. No way. Sorry, Brad. I need my sleep,' he insisted.

That was it. Our moonwalking plans were quite literally put to bed. Walking off into the Spanish night alone wasn't a sensible thing to do and I knew my overactive imagination would make me a nervous wreck. I reluctantly accepted it just wasn't to be.

Disappointed, I rolled out of bed and took the much less dangerous option of attending a blessing with the resident monks.

There were dozens of pilgrims crammed into an adjoining side chapel with limited seating. I offered my seat to an elderly Spanish lady and leant against a wall for the duration of the proceedings, for which there was no English translation. Totally confused by the Spanish jibber-jabber, I quickly lost interest, with fatigue feeding my restlessness that I had to stand for the service.

Becoming ever more disengaged, a bright idea popped into my head. What if I got out before they locked me in and went without Tore? Surely I was brave enough to go it alone and annihilate my fears? Santiago didn't become a saint and a martyr by being scared of the dark. Clark Kent didn't become Superman by being frightened of things that went bump in the night. Nobody would have called the Ghostbusters if they'd been too afraid to go out after the sun had gone down. Best of all, this would be another tale of swashbuckling bravery with which to sweep Natalia off her feet. The right time was now!

Taking the night hostage, I shuffled furtively towards the door, sneaked out the side chapel and ran to my bunk. Stuffing my sleeping bag hastily into my backpack, I bolted through the monastery doors at 9.27pm. I'd escaped the prison of the noble night silence with three minutes to spare and headed straight for the city centre with my pulse racing.

Being downtown while my pilgrim pals slept felt mischievous. Like a kid allowed to stay up past bedtime and discover a whole new world. In a brightly lit central plaza presided over by an ornate and majestic cathedral I sat at a café watching the locals on fashion parade. Throngs of well-dressed couples, young and old, strutted the streets like they were coming down the catwalk. Most of the men had dark, slicked-back hair, pressed trousers, shiny shoes and tailor-made shirts with the sleeves rolled up; the women were mainly brunettes, with their long hair floating, high heels clicking and glamorous dresses swirling in the evening breeze. Playing out late, squadrons of kids chased the same single football like bees around honey, while others raced each other on scooters and skates. The children who couldn't get a kick of the ball took to clambering over a Hollywood-style sign spelling out the letters of the city.

Though it was a Thursday, the whole place had a real Saturday night vibe. Numerous bars around the edge of the plaza were bleeding dance music onto the streets and beginning to fill up. If this had been my home town, that was probably where I'd have been too. More than likely drunk, spending way too much money and in a sticky situation with a couple of women I'd been dating but wouldn't commit to. I much preferred being a detached observer from afar and in some way pitied the people in the bars because I knew only too well what awaited them. The greasy food on the way home. The one-night stand. The awkward goodbye the next morning. The next day completely wasted, fighting a hangover. That was once my life. Not any more.

The tricky part was figuring out what changes to make to my life. A big part of me still wanted to carry on singing in the band. But returning to that same shallow lifestyle and running the business I'd built around band life was another matter. It appealed about as much as entering the sleazy nightclub opposite, whose outside walls a *chico* was currently spraying with jets of urine. When I got home, would it be time to turn my songwriting into a hobby instead of a reason for living? Would it be the right moment to research a new career path with the aim of getting paid for something I actually enjoyed? A line my brother Matt once said to me had stuck in my mind ever since: 'Love your job, never work a day.' If those words were true, I definitely needed to call time on my days as a football coach. What I might do instead, though, I really had no clue, and the way forward was still so unclear. I was certain of only two things. I wanted to like my job and I wanted this walk to go on forever.

As the clock edged towards midnight, I strolled the pokey side streets, having second thoughts about walking off into the night. Fear was eating me up and I entertained the idea of sleeping somewhere in the city. Locals stared, wondering what the hell a pilgrim was doing downtown so late, as I eyed up potential safe places to rest. I found a cosy spot underneath an iron staircase within the grounds of the cathedral and seriously contemplated staying there. But remembering the words of Jack Kerouac in his classic book *On the Road* made the final decision for me: 'Beyond the glittering streets was darkness and beyond the darkness, the west. I had to go.'

Procrastinating no longer, I sat on the cathedral steps, swapped flip-flops for boots and snacked on a hot sandwich from a fast-food joint opposite. At 1am, repeating to myself the Camino motto – 'Move forward with courage' – I started following the yellow arrows out of the city towards the westbound highway. Pretty soon, though, I was lost. Thanks to a combination of my bad map-reading, a lack of waymarks and poor streetlighting, I'd gone way off course. Try as I might, I just couldn't find my way back. The Camino seemed to be hidden in the haystack of dark streets, avenues and buildings.

Standing under a streetlamp with my guidebook open, trying to figure out where I'd gone wrong, I heard two old ladies nattering away in English across the road. Both appeared to have had one too many and were staggering a little. So when they crossed the street towards me, I let them pass, then followed behind at a distance. I was too sober and anxious to entertain a drunken conversation.

Without warning, one of the greying ladies spun round and looked me up and down. Oh God, here we go, I thought.

'You lost?' she asked.

'Um. Yeah, I am. I can't find my way back to the Camino,' I replied.

'It's your lucky day, pilgrim!' she said, slurring her words. 'My house is actually on the Camino. Follow me to the bridge over the railway ahead and from there you'll be on the right track.' She pointed forwards, nearly falling over in the process.

'Thank you so much! You've saved my life,' I said, gushing with gratitude and relief.

Turned out the lovely, slightly inebriated lady who'd saved my bacon wasn't a tourist at all. Before marrying a local and moving to León twenty years ago, she'd been a fellow citizen of Essex and lived just ten miles from where I was born and raised. How lucky was I to be found when lost in the Spanish night by a friendly face from home?

I accompanied the ladies to the bridge and said another big thank you before setting off purposefully through the suburbs. I traversed a couple more spooky railway bridges and passed a plethora of nightclubbers walking in the opposite direction. I was expecting some drunken abuse but surprisingly none of them paid me any attention.

Finally free of the city limits, the Camino presented me with two possible routes. I could tiptoe ten kilometres through the forest full of creepy crawlies and swaddled in darkness or take the route hugging the highway. There was no way I was going into that forest on my own. Taking the highway by the pearly light of the moon and the tungsten glow of the streetlights was the safest option.

Reassuring myself that I had nothing to fear was easier said than done and my paranoia returned with a vengeance as I walked into the blinding lights of the traffic. I'd somehow convinced myself that every truck driver was Natalia's ex-boyfriend hunting me down in cold revenge and that he'd erased all the yellow arrows. Along the highway, I didn't see one for miles and was worried sick I'd gone off course again. The most frightening moment came when I walked underneath the highway via an underpass with no lighting whatsoever. I clicked on my headlamp and sprinted into that dark tunnel with my heart pounding. My paranoia was telling me I was being chased from behind by Natalia's ex and that his accomplice was waiting for me with a Taser gun at the end of the tunnel. The store of madness in my mind was straining my logic and driving me crazy.

After a few hours of motorway moonwalking, I'd proved my point. I'd done what I'd said I wanted to do and smashed my fears in the face. Though I was proud of myself, I was no longer enjoying the experience. My anxiety had worn me out. I was tired of thinking everyone wanted to kill me and tired of being tired.

Just when I needed it, a footbridge leading to a church bell-tower on the other side of the dual carriageway provided a safe haven. I crossed the bridge hoping to find a cosy doorway, comfy bench or patch of grass in the church grounds where I could sleep a while. At the foot of the tower I tried the door handle, more in curiosity than in the hope it would be unlocked. To my surprise it creaked open. I mounted the stairs to the top and discovered the bells were actually defunct, meaning I wouldn't get woken up every fifteen minutes if I stayed up there. Shining my headlamp on the ground expecting to see it spattered in pigeon poo brought more good news. It was spotless. I unrolled my sleeping bag, strapped my body belt packed with my passport and wallet under my clothes and dropped my head onto my backpack. Despite the four lanes of cacophonous traffic roaring past, I was gone.

21. SCHOOL FOR ADULTS

Judging by the height and brightness of the sun, I guessed the day was still in its pyjamas when I woke to the disturbance of a truck driver blasting someone on his horn. Having slept in my sleeping bag with my clothes on, I was lathered in sweat, and lying on the rock-hard concrete had given me terrible backache. I was not a pretty sight as I moaned and groaned my way back down the steps to the bottom of the church tower. Feeling groggy and dehydrated, as if I had a hangover, I swished the precious last drops of my water around my cottonmouth and prioritised finding more.

Returning to where I'd left off in the early hours, I began chipping away at the remaining twenty kilometres of trail sandwiched between the motorway on my right and irrigated farmland to my left. The vacant and lifeless horizon seldom changed. Only rarely were there bends in the road, and I prayed something around the corner would break the monotony. A village with food, water and shade were always top of the wish list. Walking in what was essentially a ditch littered with traffic debris, I trudged on defiantly for hours, repeating the mantra 'stronger and faster' every time a vehicle sped past spewing fumes into my face.

It wasn't until mid-morning that the Camino finally veered off the motorway and into a village. I seized the chance to refill my water supply at a fountain. As I sat emptying my flask on a bench under two oaks across the road, a rotund old man came and positioned himself next to me. Even though I told him my Spanish was bad, the old fella, dressed in a pink shirt, white tie and brown trousers, nattered away like he'd known me all his life. Every so often he raised his cigar in the air to press points he felt passionately about. When he finished his smoke, he delved into the right-hand pocket of his brown trousers and scattered small pieces of bread on the ground. It wasn't long before a handful of pigeons flew in to join us while he carried on talking at me. As the flying rats pecked away, all I could glean was that he was originally from Barcelona and he'd lived in the village for twenty-four years. I stayed for way longer than I'd planned, listening politely and nodding my head as if I knew what he was talking about. When he took a rare pause to clean his thick, round-framed spectacles, I stood up to leave and said '*Adios*' with a firm handshake. He hit me back with a '*Buen Camino*', a pat on the back, a chesty laugh-cum-cough and a few more unintelligible words. The loveable, pigeon-whispering pensioner was the highlight of a morning on the motorway to forget.

In Hospital de Órbigo, nearly ten kilometres further up the highway, the cockles of my heart were warmed by another great man. I chose a private albergue above the municipal and parish alternatives and was immediately made to feel at home by Filippo, the Italian hospitalero. I needed some degree of comfort to catch up on sleep and cleanse myself, having roughed it the night before. Filippo's place was clean, bright and spacious and well worth the €12. The walls were alive in sunburst orange and perfectly complemented by ocean-blue window and door-frames. The pebble flooring kept the place cool and there was a blank canvas and paints charmingly provided for anyone who might like to have a go with a brush themselves. Those who'd already done so had their works hung up in the communal area of long walnut tables and chairs, on either side of a tick-tock-ing antique grandfather clock. Among the dozens of colourful paintings adorning the lustrous interior were silhouetted pilgrims heading for distant mountains, a pair of battered old boots, and pilgrims on horseback.

In the modern kitchen, freshly mopped and smelling of bleach, Filippo was busy rustling up something special. He treated me like a VIP. As soon as I perched on one of the beech dining chairs at the big white marble table, he stuck a beer in front of me and raised his bottle to mine.

'*¡Salud!* – cheers!' we both said in unison.

While he busied himself stirring and seasoning the food simmering in the pans on the gas stoves, we spoke about all things Camino. Since he didn't speak English and I didn't speak Italian, we agreed to communicate in fragmented French. Though I couldn't say much, I was still able to understand a lot, having studied the language for seven years at school and college. With my brain in overdrive trying to comprehend as much as possible, I grasped that he'd walked the Camino three years ago and had enjoyed the experience so much that he dreamt of opening his own albergue. Now he'd turned that dream into a job and his mission was to reciprocate with the same generosity he'd enjoyed on his own journey to Santiago. True to his word, when he finished cooking, he switched off the gas rings, turned to me and asked if I'd like some of the meal he'd prepared.

'*Sí, por favor,*' I said, forgetting I was supposed to be talking French.

Setting a plate down in front of me, he piled on the entire contents of the pans. All for me, none for him! I was at a loss for words. Especially French ones. All I could do was stand up and shake his hand in gratitude. Completely gobsmacked by his kindness, I tried to insist that we at least share the food, but he waved off my suggestion. Drying his hands with a tea towel before hanging it on a hook on the wall to dry, all he asked was that I wash up.

It was a small price to pay for the best meal I'd eaten on Spanish soil. Surrounded by seven empty seats, all alone, I chewed away on the chicken, vegetables and pasta drowning in a tangy tomato sauce, feeling somewhat embarrassed. I'd done nothing to deserve such a selfless gesture from someone I'd known for not even an hour. Had I been too hasty in accepting? Should I have refused and insisted he ate it? I made a point to try and return the favour in some way.

After being blessed with yet another free meal, I caught up on some much needed sleep, then walked into town and called

Mum from a phone box. Still feeling a little lonely after the isolation of the Meseta, I was eager to hear her voice.

'Be bloody careful,' she said when I told her about my moon-walking mission. Abruptly changing the subject, her voice slipped into a cadence suggesting she might have a pleasant surprise in store. 'I've got someone here you've not seen in a while that wants to say hello.'

Who could it be? My dog Hannah? She must have heard my voice. I looked around the street to make sure no one was about to see me woof down the phone.

The receiver changed hands.

'Brad, I know why you like travelling.' Unless my dog had learned to speak in a cute, high-pitched voice with a Yorkshire accent, I was sure I was talking to my seven-year-old cousin Callum. 'Because you don't go to school anymore, it's like school for adults.'

I told him he was a little clever clogs and he told me he was going to do what I was doing when he grew up.

'Not until you're a big boy!' his Dad, my Uncle Paul, shouted in the background.

After I hung up, the significance of the words I'd just said to Mum struck me: 'I'll call you next week from Santiago.'

That was it. Barely seven days and this would all be over. My daily 'Buen Camino's. The random acts of kindness from strangers. The deliberations on Mayan astrology, healing flowers and talk of walking with the man on the moon would be things of the past. How would I find characters like Marcelino, Filippo and Crazy Frank amid the daily grind upon my reluctant return to Blighty? I couldn't bear the fact that this adventure was coming to an end and I was having too good a time to think about how to change my life for the better when I got home.

As the day slid into early evening, I met Elizabeth, a garrulous Austrian girl, in the common room at Filippo's place. We shared a watermelon the size of a basketball with an entertaining group from the Basque Country who'd arrived late. All of the Basque brigade were cycling the Camino. One guy in the party made sure I could not forget he was a true Basque.

'In the Basque Country, we do not espeak Espaneesh. We espeak Basque,' he said with his chin in the air, beating his chest with pride every time he said 'Basque'. 'In the Basque Country [cue beat on the chest], I am a policeman and we have many *terroristas*. In the Basque Country we must wear protective clothing from the guns and carry arms.'

In my head I rehearsed similar sentences singing the praises of my homeland: 'In Essex we do not speak English, we speak Cockney rhyming slang. In Essex we wear hoodies to scare grandmas and protect ourselves against the rain and cold outside McDonald's. In Essex we try to look well 'ard by walking like we have a stone in our shoe and by tattooing our names on our forearms so we don't forget them.' That didn't sound anywhere near as impressive, so I stayed quiet while nodding as if in silent wonder.

As I was getting the Basque Country lowdown, a tall, stunning, blue-eyed blonde walked through the common room to the yard outside and began hanging up her washing. The conversation carried on without me as I watched in awe through the window while she pegged her socks onto the clothesline. Coming back inside, she introduced herself as Inke from Holland, then quickly disappeared up the black iron staircase to the dorms. I was hoping she'd come back and rescue me from the Basque Country bobby yapping on about his noble quest to protect his citizens that spoke Basque and not Spanish. Sadly, she didn't return. Though I'd promised to save myself for Natalia, I couldn't stop thinking of Inke. I would have to find her tomorrow.

22. THE INKE TRAIL

Hot on Inke's trail, I'd plotted a fifteen-kilometre amble to the city of Astorga. Its attractions included markets, a cathedral and Gaudí architecture, and I was sure the beautiful blonde I'd seen the previous evening would stop there for the night.

Around midday, as the sun climbed to its zenith, my heart was exploding out my chest. I'd just bounded up and down two separate summits, both nearly a thousand metres high, and within five kilometres of each other. At Alto Santo Toribio I paused for a moment to catch my breath and absorb the sweeping panorama. Six kilometres ahead, past an expansive, fecund valley, the gaunt, spherical, twin towers of Astorga's famous Episcopal Palace graced the hazy blue sky. Beyond, the colossal, intimidating shadows of the Mountains of León commanded the horizon. Lurking somewhere among the broad, curving peaks, smoothed off like the surface of dancing seas, was Foncebadón, the 'abandoned village of wild dogs'. The sober realisation that I was only a day away from the place where Shirley MacLaine had feared for her life refuelled my four-legged fears. I made a point to keep a lookout for somewhere to buy some Love Hearts.

But in Astorga I was on the lookout for Inke. If she had stopped over, I figured the best place to find her would be the central plaza. Most people in the city were sure to pass by there at some point. So, late afternoon, I stationed myself at a café and staked out the lively main square whilst updating my journal. With a cold water on the table and a pen in my hand, I hadn't even filled a page when I was interrupted.

'Is it okay to sit with you?' asked a female voice politely.

I put down my pen and couldn't believe my eyes. It was her –

Inke!

I couldn't pull out a chair quick enough.

'Of course.'

She ordered a coffee and I hurriedly closed my journal, making sure she couldn't see I'd just been writing about how I was looking for her.

'Would you like to come to the Chocolate Museum with me? It's just down one of these little side streets,' she proposed, stirring her coffee.

'Chocolate Museum? Um. Yeah, why not. Let's go!'

Like a gentleman, I insisted on paying the bill, and when she'd finished her coffee, off we went – together! I couldn't believe my luck.

The most fascinating thing about the museum was watching Inke gawp, point and shriek in amazement at the exhibits – chocolate-making equipment; traditional hot chocolate mugs and jugs; even chocolate bars that cost a whopping €200. Inke suggested we buy a bar at the more economical price of €3 and wash it down with another coffee back in the central plaza.

'Great idea!' I agreed.

Back at the café in the square, chewing on our chocolate, I did some detective work. Inke was a heavy-metal-loving, fresh-air junkie who made a living as a professional psychic. If she were able to read my mind, she'd have seen visions of me watching her eat a Cadbury's Flake seductively while doing a striptease to the sounds of Metallica. I did my best to think of fluffy bouncing rabbits just in case she was trying to hack into my consciousness. For the first time in a long while, I had the pleasure of spending a sustained period of time in female company. Eventually she left me to go for an afternoon nap; I wished she'd stayed even longer.

For once, I didn't need a siesta. I had treated myself to a lie-in and a slap-up continental breakfast at the albergue in Hospital de Órbigo that morning. Being the last to wake, I'd eaten alone and felt like the lord of the manor at the head of the big marble kitchen table. Bowls of fruit, croissants, toast and cereals, jugs of orange juice and pots of tea and coffee, all with my name on – I didn't know where to start. Spoilt for choice, I went at the toast with a knife, smothering the bread in melting butter and jam. As I did so, I saw the Basque Country crew wheeling their bicycles past the kitchen door. Wanting to wish them well, I stuck my head round the door and shouted '*Buen Camino*', waving a jammy knife at them. As one, they all shouted '*Gracias*', clipped their helmets safely on, hopped onto their saddles and pedalled out onto the road.

When I could eat no more, I got ready to leave too, but first I wanted to say a proper farewell to Filippo. I found him back upstairs in the dorms, sweeping up, and thanked him from the bottom of my heart for his hospitality. He handed me a bunch of flyers for his albergue and asked me to spread the word. I promised I'd tell the world about the Albergue San Miguel and the best hospitalero on the Camino. I only knew Filippo for a day, but, just like with Marcelino, his kindness will always inspire me to go the extra mile for others.

Half-way down the final two-kilometre descent into Astorga, I thought I spotted an old man taking small, deliberate steps with the aid of two sticks. As I walked down the hill towards him, I got a pleasant surprise.

'Oi! Denmark!' I shouted, accelerating my pace to catch up with Tore. I gave him a manly, probably over-enthusiastic, slap on the back. He responded with a faint yelp of pain.

'Oops, sorry! Blisters still hurting?' I asked.

'Really bad,' he said, screwing up his eyes, taking another agonising step.

For someone to be suffering with such bad blisters so far into the journey was far from the norm. After nearly three weeks of daily poundings, the skin around my calluses had finally toughened up to the task and I walked in pain-free bliss. Sadly, Tore couldn't say the same and I admired him for his sheer bloody-mindedness to power through such discomfort.

It wasn't long before we got on to talking about my moon-walk. I told him all about how the city came alive as the clock closed in on midnight. About getting lost then saved by an old lady from home and about sleeping at the top of the church bell-tower. He sighed in disappointment at having missed out.

'I'm glad I did it, but I wouldn't do it again. I'm still tired from not having slept properly that night,' I reflected, trying to make him feel better about his decision not to go with me.

Walking at a snail's pace with Tore became a little frustrating after a while and, sensing my restlessness, he insisted I go on ahead.

'Drinks are on me in Astorga,' I promised, feeling guilty about leaving him to wobble all alone down the steep drop, hurtling towards a road full of traffic running in and out of town.

Arriving in the city, I was lured into staying at a small, private albergue by a young English-speaking lady touting for business on the street. I coughed up five bucks for a bunk and was pleased to see that most of my room's thirty beds were occupied by young Spanish females. This meant not having to spend the night in a room full of snoring old men – something that made me very happy. Nearly as happy as when I saw Inke again outside Gaudí's impressive Episcopal Palace that evening.

The opulent neo-Gothic edifice of pearl-grey granite and svelte turrets stood resplendent against the azure sky, ablaze in the tangerine light of the falling sun. We stopped briefly to chat on the street by the front gates and I tried to impress her by saying something that might sound clever about Antoni Gaudí's work.

'Those thin spherical towers and spired roofs are very different to Gaudí's Parc Güell in Barcelona,' I said, looking up at the building like I was surveying it. With that one sentence I'd exhausted all my architectural vocabulary, but I'd obviously impressed her. This time she gave me not one but three kisses on the cheek when she said goodbye and went to queue up to enter the palace. I stood there with my hands on both cheeks, vowing never to wash my face again. If things didn't work out with Natalia, now only a week or so away, I really hoped they might with Inke.

Heading back to the albergue, rubbing my cheeks where Inke's velvet lips had kissed me goodbye, I saw Tore limping through the streets. Easily recognisable from a distance with his sandals and shin-high white socks, I caught him up and we made for a bar in the city square. From there we watched swarms of locals in fancy dress wreak havoc. People wearing a variety of eye-catching costumes appeared from around every corner. A guy in a dark brown bull suit chased a crowd of *chicos* around the plaza in a hilarious re-enactment of the Running of the Bulls. They were followed in hot pursuit by a large group of young se-ñoritas dressed as football referees, blowing whistles and wear-ing figure-hugging gold jerseys and black hot-pants with socks up to their knees.

We relaxed, slowly savouring our beers and picking at the complimentary olive tapas while watching as events got louder and wilder. I explained to Tore how such shenanigans in Eng-land would be sure to end in a sorry scene involving drunken fights, police vans, ambulances and women simultaneously vomiting and urinating with their knickers around their ankles. The Spanish, on the contrary, I'd noticed, knew how to party in a good-natured manner without the aid of binge drinking. We both agreed we preferred the Spanish way and raised a glass to having our own fun when we got to Santiago.

Come bedtime, my growing love for the Spanish way of life was put to the test back at the albergue. The raised voices of a rowdy gang of youngsters shouting across the kitchen table were permeating the dorm walls, disturbing those trying to sleep.

Arthur, an eighteen-year-old from Germany I'd met earlier, shot up in his bunk when I entered the dorm.

'These people are so rude to eat when we are sleeping,' he complained. 'Zey are speaking so lout!'

'Because of the hot weather, the Spanish wake up later, work later and eat later. It's a culture thing,' I countered, trying to calm him down and convincing myself not to get annoyed too.

Arthur lay back down in bed with a frustrated grunt.

I'd been warned already that the closer I got to Santiago, the more likely I was to encounter large, noisy groups in party mood. Plastic pilgrims as I christened them.

By no means am I referring to *all* those walking the minimum required to pick up their Compostela. My admiration extends to anyone being intrepid enough to take a break from everyday life and do something they've always longed to. That is to be celebrated and congratulated whether hiking some, or all of the trail.

When mentioning plastic pilgrims, I'm referring to a small, yet loud and noticeable minority. A new crew in town breaking curfews, waking people still sleeping in the mornings by packing their bags and being inconsiderate like the mob in the kitchen.

Sadly, they'd become more prevalent around the last hundred kilometre mark due to the rule in place stating that a pilgrim need only walk that far to get the Certificate of Completion.

Spying some surplus beds through a gap in the folding partition wall, I grabbed my things and snuck around into the adjoining, empty dorm. The cunning move proved a masterstroke and the extra barrier perfectly muted the racket coming from the kitchen. I wriggled into my sleeping bag in the room full of empty bunks, praying I wouldn't have nightmares about crossing Foncebadón, the abandoned village of wild dogs, tomorrow.

23. GRIZZLY IN THE MIST

I woke with one thing on my mind: raucous revenge. I battled a mad urge to run around the dorms clanging pots and pans to wake the inconsiderate bastards from last night. Even though the devil on my shoulder was daring me to do it, my conscience won me over. Two wrongs didn't make a right; an eye for an eye made the world blind; what went around came around. With moral one-liners like that spoiling the fun, I left it in the capable hands of the karma police. Instead, I did my good deed for the day and offered a large bar of chocolate I had to three Spaniards I'd seen numerous times but had never got to meet. They gratefully accepted, full of smiles, and just like that I made three new friends.

As I prepared to leave, the devil inside was still whispering fiendish ideas; hide their backpacks; take the laces out their boots; find their cameras and take lots of photos of myself in their spare underwear. I left in a hurry before I got myself into trouble.

The streetlights were still on when I left the albergue and mingled with a plenitude of nightclubbers staggering home from their Saturday night out. What totally different worlds we were living in. While they drunk themselves to a stupor, I slept. While they stumbled into bed, I was taking the first steps of a forty-kilometre mountain hike. A few months ago I would have been doing the same as them on a Sunday morning. My thoughts were much the same as they had been a few nights earlier – I preferred what I was doing now.

Leaving Astorga behind, I paced myself on the first gentle climb into the Mountains of León, well aware that thirty monstrous, uphill kilometres loomed. On meadowland between two tough climbs, seven kilometres to the good, I was crept up on by five pilgrims on horseback. '*Buen Camino,*' they said one by one as they galloped past. My hairs stood on end as they raced off across the plain and dissolved into the fissured mountainsides ahead, lit by the crimson clouds of morning that were docked on the peaks.

As the altitude increased, so too did the levels of poverty in the dilapidated settlements. El Ganso, at over a thousand metres high, had somehow managed to endure, despite having no running water and buildings so derelict they looked like they'd been shaken by an earthquake. Surreally, a cowboy-themed bar complete with saloon-style swing-doors and American beer stood among the ramshackle homes. It was still way too early in the day to be drinking alcohol, so I jumped onto a wall outside and breakfasted on a plain piece of baguette and muesli bars.

The second place I took a break, some twelve kilometres further up, near Foncebadón, was on a damp and grassy knoll under dirty skies looking over valleys and gorges steeped in mist. To protect myself from the dew on the ground, I unravelled my roll mat and lay on my back, using my rucksack as a pillow. Chewing on the last of my muesli bars, I prayed for safe passage through the village. There was no bailing out now. No taxi I could call, no helicopters I could hire, and nowhere to buy Love Hearts. I stood up and grabbed a big stick ready to fend off any four-legged fiend.

Continuing up a steep, boulder-ridden track through a wall of fog, I passed a spooky wooden cross on my left at the entrance to the village. Fearing that this must be where they buried the bones of those who lost their lives, I nervously sped past it. Sibilant radio music and some banging and clanging coming from a couple of houses under construction were the first signs of life. So far, though, not a barmy bow-wow anywhere. Not so much as a squeaky toy, saliva-drenched tennis ball or recently laid lozenge. The atmosphere was calm, but I had a sickening feeling this was the calm before a pack of wild dogs stormed me.

Quaking in my boots, expecting to be set upon any moment, I was relieved to find the unexpected safe haven of a recently opened albergue. As I stood on the wooden decking of its porch, a middle-aged *chico* came out to greet me and offered to refill my water supply. I seized the opportunity.

Remaining there on the porch, I surveyed the boulder-strewn path and peered into the mist for potential peril. The coast seemed clear. Now was my chance to get through the last stretch of the village.

Stepping anxiously back outside, I trundled up the rocky path, flanked on both sides by beds of grass, and saw my fears come to life. Impeding any further progress was a big, brown-coated beast eerily enveloped in hill fog. He was so huge, I was convinced the dog had a grizzly bear somewhere in his family tree. Sensing my slow and cautious approach, his ears stiffened to attention and his head whiplashed off the ground. His nose began to twitch inquisitively and I worried he'd picked up the scent of my fear and was already seasoning my flesh. My heart raced, my palms began to sweat and I got ready to use my stick. Doing my best not to make any sudden moves, I left as wide a berth as possible around him.

When he laid his head back down and returned to dreaming of biscuits and chasing cats, I accelerated up the foggy track, wiping the sweat off my brow. I'd done it! I was through Shirley MacLaine's supposedly abandoned village of wild dogs without having been barked at or having my face licked or my crown jewels sniffed.

With the weight of Foncebadón finally off my shoulders, I continued climbing until Cruz de Ferro, the official highest point on the Camino at 1,505 metres. A tall weather-beaten oak pole with an iron cross atop and a huge mound of rocks around the bottom marked the momentous spot. It's custom-ary to place a gift of gratitude (or symbol that you're leaving behind a past burden) on the rock pile at the foot of the pole and all manner of pilgrim paraphernalia had been left behind: boots, sandals, photos, caps, scallop shells, rocks with messages written on them in many different languages. Down to the bare essentials of my kit list, there was nothing in my bag I could do without and leave behind. To remember the moment, though, I asked a Swedish guy I'd met earlier to take a photo of me by the pole.

While I was pulling my smiles and thumbs-up to the camera, a surly old man stumbling up the mound of rocks towards me caught my attention. With his eyes detonating with rage, he began launching many of the gifts left behind off the rocks and shouting incessantly in angry Spanish. Shocked groups of tourists recently arrived at the landmark in coaches quickly dispersed to avoid being hit by the objects raining down. With no security or police around, the man was left alone to continue shooting his mouth off and throwing things around. I quickly got out of harm's way and walked on, thinking he was simply a bitter and twisted old fool.

Having hit the highest summit, I was feeling good and bounced my way down from the peak. I shouted into the fog-filled valleys just to hear my echo and stopped on several occasions to moo at grazing cows. 'And they say we're mad?' I'm sure I heard one of them saying to another while rolling its eyes.

The long route down into yet thicker mist was dotted with tiny settlements. Knowing I could stay at any one of them allowed me to be picky. Manjarín, a place made famous among pilgrims by a man named Tomás, a modern-day upholder of the Knights Templar tradition, was one option.

In the Middle Ages, the Knights Templar were a highly trained elite Christian army fighting religious wars on behalf of the Latin Church. They were instrumental in the capturing of Jerusalem from the Muslims in 1099, a conquest that then inspired thousands of Christians to make pilgrimages to the Holy City. Though the city was liberated, the route to Jerusalem was plagued with bandits, and hundreds of pilgrims were slaughtered en route. In response, the Knights Templar began providing safe passage for all Christian pilgrims, including those walking the road to Santiago. They built accommodation, hospitals and places of worship for the half a million devotees believed to have trodden the Camino in the twelfth and thirteenth centuries. They became a powerful organisation, were subject to no authority but the Pope's, owned vast amounts of money, land and businesses, and were even said at one time to own the entire island of Cyprus.

Tomás had taken it upon himself to continue the original mission of the Templars, guiding and helping pilgrims on their way to Santiago de Compostela. Though it wasn't quite Cyprus, he'd bought an abandoned stone house and converted it into an albergue. Thanks to him, pilgrims now had shelter where once they had to beg for mercy from the elements in one of the Camino's most isolated locations. His stock continued to grow thanks to the free food and drink on offer and the daily pilgrim-blessing ritual.

When I got there, I had an important daily ritual of my own to complete. I burst into the albergue and asked a group of people sitting round a table for the toilets. A bearded man at the head of the table, whom I assumed was Tomás, thrust some kitchen roll at me and pointed to the cold and windy mountainside out back. Crisis averted, I returned to the stone shack and handed back the remaining kitchen roll. Everyone at the table knew what I'd just done, so I thought it wasn't the best time to start shaking hands with people. I said a bashful thank you and got out of there quick smart.

The longer I carried on, the more my muscles ached, and the sorer the chafing in my nether regions became. Just like the altitude, my energy levels were plummeting. Not a moment too soon, the black-tiled rooftops of El Acebo, glistening with mountain dew in the misty valley below, saved the day. Dragging my feet around the village in the hunt for a highly recommended tavern proved frustrating and fruitless. When at long last I found the house pictured in my guidebook, I rapped on the door and got no answer. I assumed they were either *completo*, closed or hiding behind the sofa giggling at me, trying not to be seen or heard. Shattered, irritated and hungry, I continued my search for digs.

Scouting the village of beige stone-walled houses and over-hanging wooden balconies, I realised I'd lost my camera. In a panic, I retraced my steps around the village and hurried back to the bar where I'd bought a drink when I first arrived.

A waitress, as unfriendly as she was obese, made my heart sink when I asked if a camera had been handed in.

'No,' she said curtly, looking right through me.

I was distraught. All the photographic memories of a journey I would cherish for the rest of my life were gone. The realisation was sickening, but I hoped that just like when I'd dropped it on the Meseta, someone would magically return it to me again tomorrow.

24. MEN ONLY!

I was turfed out the wrong side of the bed by two Spanish men talking loudly at 5am, hesitantly stuffing various objects into different compartments of their rucksacks, unsure of where to store them. Considerate pilgrims like myself did this before bed so we wouldn't disturb people still sleeping in the morning. Plastic pilgrims like these and the uproarious young bloods at the albergue in Astorga would continue to be a source of much vexation for the remainder of the way.

Not only did I lose my camera yesterday and my rag with these guys for having woken me up early, I also lost my travel towel. In a sleep-deprived and petulant tantrum, I stormed out the albergue and forgot to unpeg it from the line where I'd hung it out to dry. Now I would have to use one of the two T-shirts I had with me to dry myself. I'd definitely had better starts to a day.

Resuming my descent of the mountain in thick woods, I trod carefully over hazardous, slippery boulders where yellow arrows were hard to see in the murky dawn. I fretted that I'd lost my way until a sign for the village of Riego de Ambrós confirmed I was still on course.

The settlement comprised a single street of big, renovated mountain getaway homes owned by wealthy people from nearby cities and led into a covering of giant sweet-chest-nut trees. Three kilometres further down the valley, first light grazed the world as I walked out from the trees and onto bitu-men. A clear view of a stunning Roman bridge and its myriad arches over the River Meruelo leading into the handsome town of Molinaseca called me over. I couldn't get there quick enough.

Crossing the bridge, I could have been in an elegant oil painting. Reflected in the still water were the pines on the sloping grassy riverbanks, the pointed belfry tower of the twelfth-century church and the perfect circles of the mirrored bridge arches. I tossed a big piece of baguette into the river and a thousand fish came to the surface and nipped away, making it disappear in seconds. The way they fought for the bread reminded me of the old ladies rushing to the Bread Man in the remote villages.

Molinaseca was one of the prettiest places on the Camino. Lanterns mounted on black iron arms overhung streets that were no more than three people wide and gave it a Victorian flavour. Quaint supermarkets, shoe shops and cafes with goods displayed on wooden shelves through boutique style windows added a touch of class. Wine-barrel bar stools drilled into the ground outside taverns tempted you to peer through the window at the local cheese and wines on offer. Disappointingly, though, everything was still closed. I made a promise to myself that if one day I returned to the Camino, a stay in Molinaseca would be a must.

Carrying on down the mountain through vineyards and cherry orchards and then over another, larger, Roman bridge with just three even bigger arches brought me into Ponferrada. Behind me on the surprisingly tranquil city streets was possibly the biggest, meanest-looking pilgrim I'd ever seen. Marek from Poland was a house on legs. On first impression, his gigantic appearance was a little intimidating: he had biceps the size of my thighs, legs as thick as tree trunks and ears as big as my feet. But once you'd seen that he was limping, you'd probably be brave enough to call him a *Sitzpinkler* ('one who sits down to wee' in German) and run off, confident that he couldn't catch you.

Marek told me he could only manage to walk for an hour each day and he moved with the aid of two fat poles. By that I don't mean two porky Polish people holding his hands. I'm referring to the big sticks he was slamming into the ground like skis. I felt really bad for him and just couldn't walk off without offering to help in some way. Considering his enormous frame, a piggyback was out of the question, as was a fireman's carry, but I did offer to take the weight of his rucksack for a while. Polite in his refusal, he said there was no need as he was planning to stop in the city.

We quickly found out after arriving at the albergue that it didn't open for another four hours and that the whole city had its shutters down for a bank holiday. I had one eye on staying over to visit a twelfth-century castle built by the Knights Templar, but since that was closed too, I called Marek a big Polish fairy and ran off. Not really. I told him to get well soon and wished him 'Buen Camino'.

Beyond Ponferrada was twenty kilometres of flat terrain through numerous villages, vineyards and shady woodland – very easy going after the extremities of the previous twenty-four hours. For most of the way I trailed a hip-looking dude wearing a green bandanna, a New York Knicks basketball vest and shorts, white shin-high socks and Converse baseball boots. I really wanted to talk to him but sadly couldn't match his relentless pace.

I was sad to see he didn't stop in Cacabelos, where I ended my day and amused a terrace full of diners on my arrival. The sound of cutlery on plates and cross-table chatter halted abruptly as, directly across the road from them, I fell onto my back on the pavement, using my rucksack to cushion the impact. Supine, motionless and with arms wide open, I sighed with satisfaction and stared at the sky, too tired to move an inch or care what the diners thought. Another thirty-three kilometres put to the sword, another new town and another new albergue were all that mattered.

Apart from Filippo's place, the albergue in Cacabelos was probably the best I'd seen. Seventy single beds were paired up in thirty-five spacious wooden sheds stuck together like beach huts forming a circle around a sandy communal area with picnic benches in the middle. I was fortunate to have a dorm to myself and sprawled out naked, enjoying some rare privacy and fresh air on certain body parts beginning to pickle themselves.

In the communal area, I lunched with Elizabeth, the sweet

Austrian girl I'd first met in Hospital de Órbigo. Very kindly she offered to share some beef chunks in sauce and bread she'd taken away from a restaurant. Though it looked more like a dog-food sandwich, I stuck my face into it like a castaway into a carcass. Elizabeth was an extremely clever thing in a small package. Being fluent in five European languages – German, Italian, English, French and Spanish, just in case you were wondering – and with 'molecular geneticist' as her job title, she sounded as well as looked like a *Big Bang Theory* protagonist. Though we didn't have a lot in common, I found her world of glow-in-the-dark cats, Hepatitis-B-inoculated bananas, and pigs with human organs spellbinding. Anything was possible in her line of work.

Retiring to our dorms to sleep off the hot and irritable afternoon hours, I overheard a conversation through the thin walls, a few doors down.

'Eef you had to rate 'im one to ten, what would you g-e-e-v?' asked a male in an Italian accent.

'I don't want to say,' Elizabeth said. 'I like him, that's all I can say.'

'Ah! Ah!' the Italian teased. 'So you like the Ingleesh man!'

Even though I looked like I'd been sleeping in rubbish bins for the last few weeks, it appeared I was the subject of their conversation. Flattered and amused, I popped in my earplugs, dropped into a siesta and promised my tired body I wouldn't move it for the next few hours.

Come last light, I went hunting for food. While I was out and about, a guy sped by me with rush-hour urgency puffing his cheeks.

'*Buen Camino,*' I said as he shot past, checking his watch.

'I'm sorry?' he replied with a puzzled look.

'*Buen Camino,*' I repeated. 'It's like "Bon Voyage" for the Camino.'

'Oh yeah? Well thanks!' he said. 'We just flew into Madrid last night from Texas, caught a train this morning to Ponferrada and hit the ground running.'

'We?'

THE ONLY WAY IS WEST

'Oh yeah, sorry – my wife. She's a few kilometres back there somewhere. She's gotta keep hustling because we got a plane home in a week.'

I couldn't believe he'd marched off and left his spouse wandering around Spain, playing catch-up. He didn't care a dime though.

'I told her, walking up those hills and mountains, she's gotta lean forwards to take the weight off her back and pressure off her knees.'

While I shook my head in disbelief, sympathising with his poor wife, he carried on.

'Yeah, I've done the pilgrimage to Jerusalem as well, and before that to Mount Athos in Greece. Anyways, nice talking to ya,' he said, before bursting back into a power walk.

Just when I thought I'd seen the last of him, he spun back around.

'Hey, by the way, if I had to recommend either Jerusalem or Mount Athos, I'd say Mount Athos every time. You gotta get written permission. And...' he said, pausing to press the point, 'you got an excuse to leave the wife at home. It's men only, brother!'

I bet his poor missus was wishing the Camino was men only too. I feared for her with what lay ahead. Tomorrow she'd spend most of the day leaning forwards to save her back and knees. Awaiting us, just over the regional frontier in Galicia, was the steepest climb on the Camino, up to the soaring summit of O Cebreiro at 1,300 metres.

To fortify myself for the next day's twenty-seven-kilometre stairway to heaven, I ate at a café close to the albergue. Sitting beneath a green canopy emblazoned with 'Café Bar Santiago' in yellow lettering, at one of the three wicker tables outside the sun-faded, lemon-yellow property, I slavered as I read the menu. After agonising over whether to have a sirloin steak or chicken escalopes, I plumped instead for a fourteen-inch pepperoni pizza for a bargain €5. The motherly owner who served me in broken but endearing English took my order and requested I sign her guestbook while she prepared my pizza. The pages were full of appetite-whetting messages about how good the food was:

Excellent! Great! Amazing! Tasty! Super duper! Mega good! Most importantly, full of love!

Thank you!

Marcis and Marta, Latvia

I was told the Camino provides miracles. I believe your kindness and goodwill is one of those miracles. The food was fantastic and after a thirty-seven-kilometre day, I feel ready to go again!

All the best to you,

Darren, Atlanta, Georgia, USA

Licking my lips, with my pizza destroyed, I concurred with every word. My hospitable host, with her dark gypsy eyes and wispy jet-black hair, had provided unbeatable five-star food and service at zero-star prices. She couldn't do enough for me either. She carefully centred the vase of plastic flowers on my table like the final brushstroke of an artist, refilled my complimentary glass of mineral water countless times and even troubled herself to lift my duffel bag off the ground and onto the chair beside me.

'*Hormigas,*' she said, pointing to the ants playing Ring-a-Roses around the bag in which I kept my valuables so I didn't have to cart my rucksack around at night. She really didn't have to do that and I must have said *gracias* thirty times to show my appreciation for her humbling hospitality.

After clearing my table, she asked to take a picture to stick on the wall inside along with hundreds of photos of other happy customers. With my hands on my belly to show I was full of food and happy beans, I smiled as the camera flashed in my face. She then offered me a takeaway sandwich for the morning for €2.50, but knowing I had my rucksack already loaded with snacks, I politely refused. Unperturbed, she disappeared inside and a few minutes later came back outside with a carrier bag containing apples and bananas. She insisted I take them for free and then, just like Dad had started to do whenever I visited him, she waved me off until I was out of sight.

That delightful lady's warmth, kindness and humanity typified the spirit of many of the people I met along the way. It was because of that same spirit that so many pilgrims returned to walk the trail time and again and the reason I'd become addicted to the Camino.

25. THE RUNNING MAN

Coming back to earth after a long, uninterrupted sleep in the sweet solitude of a private room was nothing short of life changing. A much better way to start the day than firing insults under my breath at the first faces I saw, as I'd done yesterday.

In a perky mood, I left the albergue and within minutes began the long, tiresome climb up to O Cebreiro. It was still dark, and my headlamp guided me through more chestnut woods, vineyards and a clutter of villages. As usual, I saw no one but the odd pilgrim and heard nothing apart from dogs playing bark tennis across the silent dawn. It was like listening to Monica Seles serve with a high-pitched squeal and having it returned by Serena Williams's deeper, guttural grunt.

The sun surfaced at the perfect moment, taking the covers off Villafranca del Bierzo, a pretty village with a French influence, famous for red wine. Cobbled streets, gated mansions and palaces, and the River Búrbia passing under the arches of another majestic Roman bridge were enough to make me consider staying put. I stopped to weigh up my options while I ripped open a pack of muesli bars and took in the ostentatious surroundings. Had it been a little later, I may well have stayed to explore, but with the whole town asleep and only a stray cat for company, I decided it was time to move on. Still feeling fresh after a revitalising sleep, I knew there was no better time to attack O Cebreiro.

With the Galician border just a hike away and the altitude increasing with every step, the landscape began to change in character. Everything was greener. The soil underfoot was looser and sometimes muddy. Tall pines outnumbered and towered over chestnut trees. The air was cooler and the occasional gusts of wind scented with vanilla from the sap dripping off the pines had more bite. Encounters with animals became more frequent. I passed wild donkeys and ponies roaming, and chickens and peacocks that ran for their lives when they saw me coming, diving into hedges as if they were being shot at. At one point I had a stand-off with a cow bearing huge horns blocking my way. I remembered reading about how cows were officially the most deadly large animal in Britain. Seventy-four people, mostly farmers and walkers, butted, trampled or crushed to death in the previous fifteen years. Would I be number seventy-five? I did my best to stay calm as I realised it was probably a bull and stopped to check if I was wearing anything red that could make him charge. So far he seemed okay, no smoke blowing from his nose or ears and no pawing the dirt with his forefeet. The space between him and the overgrown hedges on both sides was minimal. I could just make it past. I approached cautiously. He stood still, swinging his tail and I squeezed past him with my heart in my mouth. And to think I'd been worried about the dogs!

Having survived a potentially life-or-death situation, I continued my ascent. From a high vantage point, I peered through a clearing between the trees and caught a view of those walking the shorter route along the motorway that hooked round the mountain. From my platform in the sky, they looked like an army of ants in procession as they followed each other along the road. I was so happy to be up in the silent heavens instead of taking the easier but less rewarding route by the roadside. I grabbed a big stick from the pine forest to gain some extra rhythm and went on my way, counting to four each time between pounding it into the dirt.

Several strenuous but fulfilling hours later, the path briefly dived down again to Trabadelo before continuing upwards for another eighteen hellish kilometres to O Cebreiro. I bought some food in a supermarket and sat against a wall outside where I tore off pieces of baguette like a dog with a toy in its mouth. It soon became apparent this was where the roadside route united with the mountain path and the shop began to fill with a slew of people buying supplies. I quickly got off my numb arse and made tracks to stay ahead of the crowds.

I was soon passing through a smattering of tiny mountain villages on my way into the pewter sky. I said a quick hello and goodbye to Portela. Felt sorry for the inhabitants of Vega de Valcarce because of a noisy flyover marring an otherwise idyllic setting in a verdant valley. When I got to Herrerías, with seven kilometres and the steepest part of the climb still to go, I took a welcome break. In a grassy picnic area with a cool mountain stream rushing by, I dipped my feet into the soothing water and was soon joined by a small group of Germans. None of them were very talkative and silence prevailed until an American girl, Evelyn, arrived. Speaking German to the Germans and English with me, she was a ball of bubbly, positive energy and her jolly presence perked everyone up.

Further up, in La Faba, I met her again. Her invigorating company was just what I needed when I was zigzagging with tiredness and running on empty for the final push. She was at a stall on a hairpin bend in the road talking to a dreadlocked Argentine guy selling handmade jewellery, painted rocks and other cheap but charming items. I stopped to see if anything caught my eye. What he was selling didn't. What he was drinking did. He had a flask of maté, the tea I'd drunk with Norbert in Azofra and with my Argentine friends in Florida. The vendor was so impressed an Englishman knew his national brew, he kindly offered to share it with me. As I sipped maté with this hip and happy guy, Evelyn said she needed to get going to keep her muscles warm. Not wanting to miss an opportunity to walk with her, I thanked the generous gent and we left together.

Deepening my acquaintance with Evelyn, I found out she was a student of Medieval Renaissance history, originally from Oregon but now living in New York City. Always full of surprises, when I oinked at some pigs in a field, she responded with the best horse impression I'd ever heard.

'You speak pig?' she asked, as if it were a serious question. 'I don't speak pig but I'm fluent in horse.' Then she let off a horsey squeal, confirming she really did speak horse.

Evelyn was a little loopy but her eccentric character was a perfect fit for the Camino. Her wacky company kept me going for the last few kilometres and we walked together across the Galician border and into O Cebreiro. A concrete marker warned us of how close we were to the end of our adventure: 152 kilometres to Santiago. I was fast running out of pilgrimage and still wasn't ready for this epic adventure to end. Would anyone speak horse to me in England? I doubted it very much.

In O Cebreiro we were on the roof of Galicia, looking across endless rows of gigantic green mountains outgrowing each other like Matryoshka dolls under a galaxy of smoky clouds. The view, like gazing through an airplane window, was staggering. Almost inconceivable.

Checking into the albergue, I noted the back-breaking beds in the sleeping quarters and opted instead for a space on the floor in the overspill hall. In the kitchen I was overjoyed to see Crazy Frank again for the first time since the middle of the Meseta. He was addressing five slightly confused-looking ladies who were sitting around him at the table.

'Everybody touch the pussy,' he said with a finger on his wrist.

I balked. Someone had to stop him before he was put behind bars again. I was sure he was trying to say 'pulse' but pronouncing it 'pulsie', or rather 'pussy'. I quickly stepped in.

'Pulse! He means "pulse"!' I said, my voice quivering in panic as I tapped my finger frantically on my wrist.

Thankfully, none of the assembled ladies were native English speakers and so were unaware of the colloquial significance. I could only assume the reason he was telling the ladies to touch their 'pulsies' was to prove how such extreme altitude accelerated the heart rate. Crazy Frank's comedy English was turning into lewd, incarcerating English. As I led him out the kitchen, away from danger, he very nearly landed himself in trouble again.

'Pussy, pussy,' he said, blowing kisses at the ladies.

I grabbed him by the collar of his anorak and dragged him away to the outside terrace.

'No "pussy", Frank. Never!' I chided. '"Pussy",' I said, pointing south, 'is this for the ladies, for the girls.'

'Ahhhhhh.' He finally got it.

'My country. Hungary. For pussy. Kisses.'

His country was hungry for pussy kisses? I had no idea what he was talking about but pressed the point again with a stern finger. '"Pussy" in English – never. Very bad. No!'

It was only later on, when his compatriot Bence made an appearance, that all the dots connected. The word *puszi* in Hungarian, he told me, pronounced softly, like in 'pussycat', actually meant 'kisses'. I might well have just saved Crazy Frank's Camino from the *puszi* of death and another stint behind bars.

Far more deserving of that sort of fate were the two coach loads of French plastic pilgrims who came from their lodgings to use our showers. Any chance of getting a hot shower on a cold mountain peak went down the drain when they raided our albergue. This was a prime example of what irritated me about the glory-hunters. The hardcore, grafting 'grino braved the wind, rain and sun to reach the top of the mountain but missed out on hot water because of people who had their fat arses chauffeured up there.

Being invited out for dinner with Evelyn and a group of Spaniards made up for the sense of injustice I felt at having been cheated out of a hot shower. In the restaurant next door we grabbed a table for six and Evelyn introduced me to her Spanish friends. There were two guys, José and Santiago, and three girls, Núria, Leyra and Montse. All were fantastic company and made me feel so comfortable and welcome in their group.

Santiago, a train driver, was a towering, stocky guy with a grizzly auburn beard. I told him he didn't need a backpack and could store all his belongings in the bush on his chin. He laughed and gave me a pat on the back that nearly knocked me off my chair. He was a real gentle giant, and every time we saw each other on the road after that initial meeting he gave me a thumbs-up and a wink. I could see in his eyes a timidness that undermined his macho appearance. His friend José, a PE teacher, looked more like a typical Spaniard. Short, dark, slicked-back hair, olive skin and big brown happy Spanish eyes. The girls with them were full of questions. Where was I from? What was my job? Did I have a girlfriend? Why was I there on the Camino? They were the first Spaniards I'd met that spoke very good English and this was the first time I'd connected with the natives.

Throughout dinner, Evelyn conversed with them in fluent Spanish and I sat back in quiet admiration. What a show-off she was. German with the Germans, horse with the horses and now Spanish with the Spaniards. I let the locals take the lead in ordering some Galician specialities. For an incredibly economical €9, we were served little noodles swimming in chicken soup, fresh fish and potato-skin chips. I was told to pull the flakes of fish from the bones, douse them in lemon juice and wolf them down coated in their crispy golden skin. The chips were possibly the tastiest I'd ever had, still with their skins on and dipped in a garlic-flavoured sauce. We remained at the table long after we'd finished eating and I felt so incredibly blessed to have been invited out with such a great bunch.

Later that evening I met more fantastic people, once again thanks to my new friendship with Evelyn, who knew everybody. In a cobbled cul-de-sac of thatched cottages, souvenir shops and cheap hostels presided over by a ninth-century stone church, pilgrims had congregated outside a bar. I got talking to an American I'd seen numerous times on the road doing something insane: running the Camino. He wore a white baseball cap backwards, a quick-drying nylon T-shirt and running shorts and shoes. Without fail he always carried a walking staff and had run past me with it several times like a Neanderthal hunter with a spear. Finally I could put a name to the face: Brad was an early-forties lecturer in law at Colombia University in New York City. He spoke fluent Spanish too and was good friends with another pilgrim.

'Meet Luís, my long-lost brother,' Brad said, bidding me to shake hands with none other than the yodelling maniac from Grañón.

'Hol-a-a-a-a-a-a-a-a-a-a-a!' Luís said, grabbing my one hand with his two before launching into a laugh. Luís laughed after everything he said. And even though I couldn't understand most of what he said, I laughed too, and so did everybody else. He was such a funny character, with a captivating presence and personality. You couldn't help but love him. It was hard to believe this guy was fifty-three years old when he was acting his shoe size. Every move he made had an air of childish mischief about it and he seemed to take nothing seriously. As he sank beer after beer, he described the forthcoming terrain to Brad, Evelyn and me.

'Bing bong, bing bong, bing bong,' he said, making hand signals to show the going would be all ups and downs. As usual he let out wild infectious laughter after he spoke and we couldn't help but follow, even though we didn't know what was so funny.

I asked Brad to explain to him that I'd thought he was the priest in Grañón because he'd taken the pilgrim service. In response, he slapped the table in amusement, threw his head back and guffawed at my incorrect assumptions. What a personality he was! I want to be like Luís when I grow up, I thought.

While the laughter rang out, another of Evelyn's many acquaintances, Piotr, a real Polish priest, joined us at the table. 'I was hoping to be able to take some services in some of the towns but I haven't been allowed,' he said with palpable disappointment.

'Oh that's so gay!' Brad blurted out in an unnecessarily brusque manner.

After that, Piotr fell quiet and didn't add much to the conversation. I actually thought he was quite cool and all of us were a little flabbergasted by Brad's, off-key reaction. A typical straight-talking New Yorker. Evelyn, feeling a little uncomfortable, and adroit at putting everyone around her at ease, quickly changed the subject. Luís sat there in ignorant bliss, in his own happy world, smoking a cigarette, drinking his beer and looking around for something or someone to laugh at.

Just before bed I spoke briefly with an Italian I recognised from the albergue in Hospital de Órbigo. Since then I'd been carrying an extra sleeping mat that someone had left behind and that I thought might be missed. I showed him the mat but he insisted it wasn't his. The conversation didn't go much further due to the language barrier. He made a humorous and unnecessary apology for his lack of English.

'In my 'ead, eez English, eez Francia, eez Germain, eez Spanyolo, eez Italiano. Eez di land of confusion – *Mama mia!*' he cried, with his head in his hands.

Yomping thirty-seven kilometres up a mountain had been punishing for my body, but the pay-off for my spirit had been huge, thanks to the glittering personalities that had lit up the day. On the cold, hard, laminated flooring of the hall in the albergue, I got cocooned in my sleeping bag and let the first Galician night swallow me up. I fell asleep with one beautiful thought – isn't it wonderful to be alive!

26. SPACE INVADERS

The next day to Samos was a hard road to hoe. It began with the wind and rain attacking me from all angles; my backpack got drenched and, ill-prepared for inclement weather, I got soaked to the bone. Now I understood why Galicia was often spoken of in the same breath as Ireland – the land was lush and green, and the weather dismal, grey and wet.

With my quads still burning from scaling O Cebreiro, coming down the mountain was notably harder than going up it. As well as feeling stiff from yesterday, I had a sharp, pinching pain at the bottom of my right shin. Running Man Brad later diagnosed the symptoms as shin splints, a common overuse injury causing inflammation of the muscles, tendons and bone tissue around the tibia. It had more than likely been brought on by the harsh mountainous terrain and was a sure sign I should take my foot off the gas.

Adding insult to injury, the coach loads of hot-water-robbing French plastic pilgrims had been let loose on the trail. Large groups of them impeded my progress down the helter-skelter path. When I eventually got around them by weaving my way in and out of their retinue, not one of them could return my numerous '*Buen Camino*'s. Why were they incapable of learning the two words that created such an air of goodwill among pilgrims of all nationalities? I'd heard Slovakians and South Africans, Australians and Austrians, Danish and the Dutch deliver the magic words with passion, sincerity and alacrity. But our French friends were sticking to '*Bonjour*' with a snooty nose in the air. The group were rude, ignorant and selfish and I really wanted to get ahead and never have to deal with them again. Which was why, even with suspected shin splints nipping away at my energy, I kept on gunning for Samos instead of Triacastela, where I suspected they'd stop.

Each hamlet I passed through – Liñares, Hospital de la Condesa, Padornelo, Fonfria, Biduedo – had similar features. Big dogs lying in the road, too lazy to do anything but wiggle their noses as I tiptoed around them with trepidation. The sharp, nauseating stench of cowpats on the farms and horse dung dumped on the roads. Sheep, goats, pigs and cows fenced in on private farmland and chickens clucking away in backyards. Houses, cottages and half-built apartment blocks in a decrepit state as if they'd just suffered a wave of airstrikes. There were other peculiar, rectangular shed-like constructions too, unlike any I'd ever seen – roughly the length of an estate car, raised on concrete pillars and with triangular thatched roofs. The crosses mounted on the points of the roofs made me think that local families perhaps buried the bodies of their loved ones inside – or was it somewhere to leave the corpses of plastic pilgrims who riled you? Reading up on them later, I discovered they were *hórreos* – two-thousand-year-old structures unique to Galicia, raised off the ground to keep corncobs and other crops safe from rodents before they were threshed.

There were also frequent sightings of tiny, circular, stone-walled dwellings with conical roofs thatched with rye. Undercover work on those buildings revealed them to be *pallozas* with a history that dated back to the Celtic era, when they were used to house cattle during harsh winters. They were so small and odd-looking, I thought Bilbo Baggins from *The Hobbit* had started building little holiday homes for himself along the Camino. Bilbo would probably be a lot friendlier than the Galicians too. The majority were cold, expressionless, didn't bat an eyelid when they saw me and seldom said hello. I assumed it was the effect of all those plastic pilgrims, so common in Galicia that they were probably more a nuisance than a novelty to the locals.

As I descended out of the clouds and into brighter, warmer and drier weather, a welcome tranche of level terrain escorted me into Triacastela. Knowing that most people would be staying there and that the albergues would be overrun by plastic pilgrims, I pushed on.

Traversing pleasant woodland and chasing the tittering River Ouribio for most of the next ten kilometres helped put the pain of my shin splints to the back of my mind. Before the afternoon was out, I spied the distinctive architecture of a Benedictine monastery albergue and the town of Samos, framed by an opening in the conifers.

After crossing a bridge with scallop shells cast into the black iron railings, I followed the course of the river through some bushes and up to the road. In the albergue, which, refreshingly, was not even half full, I was reunited with many pilgrims from the previous night. Santiago, José and the three girls had all got there from O Cebreiro, along with Brad. I was sad to see Evelyn hadn't come this far but the ebullient presence of Luís made up for that.

That night, I had dinner with him, Brad and another American, a young girl called Abbie. Without doubt, it was the best meal I ate all summer. Even though it blew my daily budget apart, the exquisite cuisine was worth every cent. Our Spanish speakers Brad and Luís ordered the dishes and we were served five courses of heaven for the hungry: little fried green peppers covered in sea salt and octopus salad, fried squid doused in lemon juice, and black rice with cuttlefish. Dessert was a Catalan flan with a crispy caramel topping. The six-pack I'd been hoping to sculpt for Natalia on the Camino was now more like Lurpak.

At the dinner table Luís made me chortle time and again even though I had no idea what he was saying. When he spoke to the waitresses he seemed loud, brash and rude, but they laughed with him. He was a hurricane of happy energy that couldn't sit still. Earlier in the day, he'd run past me with his backpack bouncing up and down and a cigarette in his hand, shouting, 'Brad Pitt! Brad Pitt!' Pretty amazing for a man seventy-three years young.

On our way back to the monastery, with rain slapping the pavement like a pressure washer, Luís, full of mischief as usual, ran ahead of me. He waited by a tree and as I passed underneath, he kicked the trunk so all the raindrops fell off the leaves and soaked me further. He skipped away laughing and I chased him into a shop doorway where I got him in a headlock and asked Brad to take a photo with the disposable camera I'd purchased. Luís was officially the Spanish Crazy Frank.

With my belly believing Christmas had come early and my taste buds feeling like royalty, I just about squeezed into my sleeping bag. I was one of the last to turn in, so all the lights were out and the prom of nostrils was already playing. As I was nodding off, Abbie knelt down by my bunk and thanked me for inviting her out to eat. She was such a smiley girl but had a sadness in her eyes because of a troubled life. Over dinner she'd told us the short version of a long story about why she'd come to Spain. Made to feel like a family outcast because of drug and alcohol problems, she'd found a shoulder to cry on in a Spanish guy she met online. Dreaming of a happier life, she flew over to meet the man she'd been messaging every day for the last six months. She explained how she loved the Camino because she felt free of judgement and welcome among a friendly, loving and accepting tribe. As a pilgrim, she was no longer an outcast. She was simply searching for answers like the rest of us. I wished her all the luck in the world for her big date and that her dreams came true.

Sarria, where Abbie planned to meet her mystery man, was an important milestone on the Road to Santiago. With little over a hundred kilometres left, this was where the majority of plastic pilgrims invaded the path. They were everywhere. We were far outnumbered. Why had there been no sign of them on that twenty-one-kilometre stretch bereft of shade, water and shelter? Where were they on those hot Meseta days when the horizon had seemed to get further away not closer? Why couldn't they have been there on that first dramatic climb over the Pyrenees? And yet now, with Santiago so close, they were everywhere. At times, irritation got the better of me, but I was determined not to let others sour the greatest journey of my life.

With the pain of my shin splints slowing me down, I watched people race by while the River Ouribio held my hand in the woods again for the first few hours. They checked their watches and studied maps and information boards to assess their chances of winning the grand prize at the end of the day: a bed at the next albergue. With such a sharp increase in the number of pilgrims and only limited places, the guarantee of a roof over my head was gone. I wasn't fazed in the slightest about not knowing where I'd sleep the night and this demonstrated very clearly how vagabonding across Spain had changed me. In the past I'd been a serial worrier. I'd panic about anything and everything that could go wrong and be fraught with anxiety if things weren't going as I wanted or planned. I remember once crying my eyes out as a young boy when Mum was still inside a shop after closing time. I thought she was never going to come out and was trapped in there. Perhaps such anxiety stemmed from going to sleep at night as a kid listening to my parents arguing. I often lay in bed wondering if one of them might be gone when I woke up, how we'd pay the bills and who I'd actually choose to live with if it happened. Chappers, who knew me like a brother, was well aware of my anxious personality, which was why he'd written on his good-luck charm: 'Remember, don't stress. Everything will be fine in the end!'

Please understand that this is far from a plea for sympathy. I wouldn't change anything about my life because, as clichéd as it sounds, without the pains of the past, I probably wouldn't have escaped overseas and had so many unforgettable, life-moulding experiences. I'm mentioning these memories as a way of measuring how far I'd come. The pre-Camino Brad would have stressed about not being guaranteed a place to stay. But life on the road had taught me to roll with the punches, keep on swinging and trust everything would fall into its predestined place. After all, the Camino had always provided and had never left me in need. When I bonked in Villamayor, the Dutch family and the

Austrian boys Sasha and Steffan came to my rescue. When I got lost in León, my Essex angel saved the day. When I'd been hungry, some kind soul had often magically arrived with food. If I didn't get a bed, I'd crash somewhere under the stars. I'd done so once and was more than happy and prepared to do so again.

For the duration of the overcast day, the path undulated gently through blooming oak woods, along quiet country lanes, and through tilled fields and numerous forgettable villages. Aside from some extremely spartan albergues even squatters would have turned their backs on, the local communities had little provisions for the tired pilgrim. Ferreiros, nearly ten kilometres from where I would be staying in Portomarín, was the only place on the thirty-kilometre stretch from Samos that had a bar open.

Having bitten off another forty kilometres, I arrived very late into Portomarín and jumped on the last bed in a filthy public-school building converted into pilgrim digs. Though there was space for 160, I didn't recognise a soul. I was surrounded. Noisy plastic pilgrims had taken over. They shouted into mobiles. They played games on their phones and watched videos with the volume turned up. They trashed the bathrooms with toiletry bottles, plasters and soggy toilet roll and left the sinks peppered with post-shave hair. Turning a blind eye and looking on the bright side was the only option – at least the albergue was free of charge. On my way to the shower I popped €5 into a donation box hoping they'd give it to the overworked morning cleaners.

After raiding the shops for some tinned tuna and bread, I returned to the albergue and found a vacant table in the open-air dining area. As I loaded my baguette with tuna, I was approached by the guy I'd tried catching up near Cacabelos forty-eight hours earlier. Pulling up a chair, the young, cool-looking dude with the green bandanna introduced himself as Reece in an endearing Irish lilt. Having just turned eighteen, he'd decided to embark on a pilgrimage after his local Catholic priest encouraged him to get his walking boots on.

'The Camino is a crash course of life lessons in a month. It teaches you how to deal with anything life can trow at you,' Reece said the pastor had told him.

Though he'd initially travelled with two friends from his congregation, he hadn't seen them since they'd pulled a disappearing act with some girls they met. I gave him a high-five for having the discipline to keep walking and the resilience to carry on alone. On the subject of ladies, I gave Reece the lowdown on Natalia and how nervous I felt now she was only a day away.

'Go on. Call her now, will ye. It'll be grand!' he dared me. 'Ye cairn't just be, loyke, hey, I'm de crazy fecker who emailed you from Greece two years ago. I'm round the corner, fancy a point? She'll still have toyme ta pap ta Victoria's Secret!' he said, toying with me.

I knew Reece was right. Not about Victoria's Secret. The bit about her needing some notice that the madman that had followed her from Corfu to her home town was coming knocking. I was petrified of making the call though. What if she'd forgotten about me? We'd had little contact since I'd replied to her email offering me a place to stay on her house. A lot could have happened in that time. What if she'd met someone else? A bullfighter? A burly Flamenco dancer? Another pilgrim? That Canadian DJ guy could have won her over with his prize French omelette. What if some local nuns had caught wind of what was happening and were standing outside her house with machineguns to protect her chastity? And how good was her English? Could she maintain a conversation on the phone or would it be a Tarzan and Jane type affair in person?

'Me Brad, you Natalia. You say, your house, me sleep on.'

No matter how many excuses I could invent not to call her, I knew I had to do it. And I knew the right time was now.

The words of Mildred in St-Jean-Pied-de-Port came back to spur me on: 'Every now and then you have to frighten yourself to feel alive.'

Reece raised his eyebrows and pointed to a payphone on the street visible through the wire fence.

'Wish me luck,' I said, digging into my wallet for some change.

With sweaty palms and trembling hands, I picked up the handset, fed some coins into the payphone and dialled her number. As the ringtone sounded, the butterflies in my stomach flapped frantically, and just as my nerves willed me to hang up, a husky female voice answered.

'¿Sí?'

'Er. Um. Natalia, *por favor*?' I asked tentatively.

'*Sí, soy Natalia* – yes, this is Natalia?' she confirmed with a quizzical final inflection.

'Natalia, it's Brad from England,' I said, praying she would remember who the hell I was.

'I've been expecting you, Essex hunk-boy! What are you wearing?'

Sadly, that's not what she said.

'Br-r-r-a-a-a-a-a-a-d! How are you? Where are you?' is what she really said, bursting with enthusiasm and warmth.

Though nowhere near the lustful opening line I'd been fantasising about, her animated response put me at ease. The ice wasn't broken, it was smashed to smithereens! I told her I'd be with her in Melide tomorrow and she told me to call as soon as I arrived. The big date was still well and truly on!

I now had twenty-four hours to prepare for the most important liaison of my life. I mulled over what I could do to make the transformation from pilgrim to pin-up. Should I get a slicked-back haircut, fake moustache and draw on some curly chest hair to make myself look more macho and Spanish? Learning some lingo might impress her too and I could add to the only chat-up line I knew from a 1970s Spanish soft-porno: '*Me has quebrado la ventana. Tenemos que hacer el amor.*'

I hasten to add I was taught that line by a Spanish-speaking friend of mine and have never actually watched the film, or used its English translation: 'You've broken my window. We must make love.' Honest!

On possibly the last evening of my life as a single man, I went into town to see what Portomarín had to offer. The answer was not a lot really, apart from wind, rain and noisy teenage girls. Outside a bar on the pedestrianised high street, taking cover from a fresh downpour, a large gathering of Italian girl scouts were clapping and singing in shrill voices. As I walked past, their guitar-strumming scout leader beckoned me over to join them, but I really wasn't in the mood. Unimpressed by my rejection of them, he made a derogatory comment, sending the girls into fits of high-pitched giggles. I had no idea what he'd said but could sense his words hadn't been very complimentary.

Further along the street, away from the campfire crew, I sat down at an outdoor café. Running Man Brad found me there and invited me to dine with him. At the restaurant next door, we grabbed a table by the window where the orange street-lights blushed in the rain lashing against the glass and feasted on various plates of tapas. I took the chance to quiz Brad on his life back home and he disclosed the turbulent tales of recent years. Before becoming a law lecturer, he was a high-flying lawyer, winning big cases but losing himself in countless expensive celebratory bottles of vodka. When he refused to pull out of the fast lane and slow down, his wife walked out and he hit the bottle even harder. In the years that followed, his greatest achievements were losing his job and playing dot-to-dot on his pet Dalmatian with a black marker pen after coming home blasted. From rock bottom, he picked himself up, diverted to a career in education that he found a lot more rewarding, and had recently married a yoga teacher. We clinked our glasses of water to better, happier times ahead for us both. After splitting the bill, I walked back through the rain to the albergue wondering if tomorrow's meeting with Natalia would lead to a similar happy ending for me.

27. DATE WITH DESTINY

The empty, magnolia-walled hall of more than a hundred black metal bunks was stripped bare of all pilgrims and their belongings. The bed sheets, once white but now a sickly cream, remained tousled on the recently vacated mattresses. A malodorous fusion of muscle sprays, suntan lotion, scented deodorants, sweaty socks and boots still lingered. Mournful skies and the rain pelting the windows completed the metamorphosis of the squalid albergue in Portomarín into a Soviet military hospital.

Remarkably, I'd slept through an evacuation of the entire building and had the whole place to myself while I readied to roll. Sitting on my bottom bunk, I pecked away at an apple and a banana while I studied the Camino's breakfast menu. Today's special serving was a fifteen-kilometre ladder into the clouds. Though not as steep as the recently defeated Cruz de Ferro and O Cebreiro, the abrupt incline would still be a cruel wake-up call in the rain.

Dense forest where dripping leaves quivered in the wind, desolate villages and swarms of plastic pilgrims were the main features on the way up. I encountered many large groups without backpacks, more often than not smoking, texting or blocking the path as they shouted and cheered for group photos. I routinely took a wide berth around them, muttering insults as I passed.

At the day's zenith in Sierra Ligonde, I was attracted to an albergue by some British accents and a 'Free Coffee!' sign. It was there I met Corwin and Kate, a lovely couple from Somerset. Compared to them, I was a plastic pilgrim too. They'd been on the road four months, which made my three and a half weeks seem like a warm-up.

'Yeah, we closed the front door behind us and just started walking,' Corwin said with West Country understatement as he tied his long brown hair into a ponytail.

Kate continued. 'France was very hard. We slept in some lovely campsites but mostly in church graveyards and it rained more or less every night. But we got through it together,' she purred, squeezing Corwin's hand a little tighter.

As we sat perched on a wall outside the albergue with our anoraks zipped up against the wind and rain, Kate filled in the gaps of their fairytale love while we sipped our tepid coffees. After quitting her job as a secondary school music teacher because of stress, she met Corwin at a Spanish evening class. Unbeknown to each other, they had both always wanted to walk to Santiago but had never quite found the right time. Then, four months ago, with the two of them unemployed, they took a bite out of their savings, packed their bags and fulfilled a shared ambition together. Their love had quite obviously blossomed and Corwin had recently popped the question at Cruz de Ferro. Down on one knee, he said he couldn't pass the highest point on the Camino without asking the woman who represented the highest point in his life to marry him. The dimples in Kate's plump, cherry-red cheeks deepened as she held up her hand to show off a sparkling ring.

'I hope you both live happily ever after,' I said sincerely.

Slipping the straps of my backpack over my shoulder, I left Corwin and his fiancée sitting on the wall and was immediately approached by two American girls. They'd made a beeline for me as they came out of the albergue and got straight to the point. They'd been sent by God from their church in the USA to volunteer on the Camino. In their hands were piles of leaflets. The title, in block capitals, read: 'GOD, JESUS AND THE TRUTH'. If my muscles weren't stiffening up after the toil of another uphill stretch, I might've stopped to chat but I had to stay nimble and get moving again. I made my polite apologies, plopped €2 into their collection box and bade them a pleasant stay.

Later on, a similar exchange took place with a Canadian girl and her German friend deep in the heart of a forest. I broke the ice by saying how I loved breathing in the invigorating scent of the ranks of eucalyptus and pine trees surrounding us. Shooting off at a wild tangent, they replied by saying how God had saved them from being torn to pieces by a wild dog – not quite the response I was anticipating. Then came the awkward questions.

'Are you a Christian? Are you thinking of becoming a Christian? Why walk to Santiago if you aren't a Christian?'

The tables had been turned on me. To them, I was the plastic pilgrim. A non-believer. A fake, hijacking their religion's sacred pilgrimage for a self-serving aesthetic voyage.

As we ambled on together through the fragrant woods, over a carpet of fallen branches, eucalyptus leaves and pine needles, attempts to convert me began. If I were ever to decide to hang a cross around my neck and become a devotee, it wouldn't be in a situation like that, with two self-righteous people condescending to me, judging me and treating me like I was inferior because I wasn't in their club. I would far more likely be inspired by an eccentric big-wave-surfing vicar, a message whispered to me by the trees, or a lyric in a song.

When it became obvious that we probably wouldn't be exchanging Christmas cards every year, the conversation dried up and we walked in uncomfortable silence. To get rid of me, they pretended they were tired and stopped for a break. I wasn't worthy of their company.

I tried to keep an open mind about their point of view regarding non-religious pilgrims, but from every angle it reeked of narrow-minded discrimination. As I raised before, my issue with plastic pilgrims was their bad manners, disrespect and lack of consideration for others. It had nothing to do with how far they were walking. Did they need to dine so late in the albergues and talk at shouting volume while others tried to sleep? Did they need to block the path unapologetically while talking on their mobiles, sometimes making us walk into bushes, nettles or perilously close to precipices to get past? Was it fair they got first dibs on limited beds and hot water when many of them were being driven around? And, was it right, that they were awarded a Compostela certificate for walking the last hundred kilometres, when someone who'd walked seven hundred kilometres in total on the Camino, but not *all* of the last hundred, wouldn't be granted one? That seemed very unfair and nonsensical to me and only encouraged the circus coming to town for the home straight into Santiago.

Measures also needed to be taken so that troopers like Corwin and Kate, German Gerald and Jean Raphael, all of whom had started out on foot from their home countries, got priority at the oversubscribed albergues. Maybe those who only had stamps from Galicia in their Credencial should have to wait an hour or two after opening before they could check in? Or in some kind of Camino initiation, they'd have to give a foot massage or back rub or be made to clean the boots of those who'd walked further? That simple measure could make them value their place a little more and bring to their attention that many among them had put their bodies through weeks and months of hell and deserved a little more respect.

Those on excursions, long weekend breaks and guided tours failed to appreciate that, for many, the Camino was a bucket-list item. For Corwin and Kate it was a once-in-a-lifetime odyssey. For Bob and Margaret, the Canadian couple I'd met on day one, it was a mammoth undertaking requiring two years of training and preparation. For people like Irish Peter and Tomer from Israel, who were mending their broken hearts, the Camino was a place to soul-search, heal and find inner peace. Was a little more sensitivity to people's personal quests too much to ask?

Back in town, at Palas de Rei, fifteen kilometres away from Natalia, any high hopes of meeting more congenial company were shot down by a testy waitress not keen on pilgrims of any kind. I meekly mumbled my order from the pilgrim menu options, which she begrudgingly jotted down with more grunts than words. Being eager to please, my first instinct was to say sorry for having the temerity to order food in a restaurant. But before I could beg her not to season my food with the toenails of a pilgrim she'd murdered earlier, a sharp prod in the arm got my attention.

Turning to my left, I saw that an old man had pulled up a stool at the bar next to me and was gesticulating and shouting. The object of his anger was the newsreader on the TV that was suspended on brackets in the corner of the room. Saliva in my face, a finger way too close to my nose and cigarette breath followed by more pokes in the arm made me migrate to a table away from the bar.

Refusing to let the morose waitress or the antics of the angry old man ruin my appetite, I sucked up the mountain of spaghetti bolognese in minutes. On a table opposite were some Germans I'd seen at the albergue in Acebo and I waved my fork and said hello with my mouth full. They nodded back in conservative silence, avoiding eye contact at all costs. The sour-faced waitress seemed to be bringing everyone down and smiles were at a premium in that glum establishment. Before my face turned the colour of the fading grey net curtains sagging in the windows, I finished my food, paid the bill and vowed never to come back.

Escaping outside, the weather mirrored the mood of the waitress and a storm threatened in demonic skies where gangs of black clouds had rounded on the sun. Trudging my way to the top of a long flight of stone steps leading back to the Camino, I heard a whistle from below. Santiago, José and the girls waved to me from way down at the bottom. I unleashed an imaginary rope which they all pretended to hold onto as they made their way up. Santiago gave me his trademark wink and thumbs-up combo, with big, happy blue eyes shining through his fuzzy auburn beard. They shouted up not to wait for them as they were stopping to eat, so I yelled down that I hoped to see them further on. Their smiles brought the first sunshine to a typically gloomy Galician day.

At the bottom of a hill, a brackish river convulsing in the rain as it passed beneath the five arches of a small Roman bridge signalled the town of Melide. Normally when I reached my final destination of the day, I'd seek out the albergue, grab a bed and go hunting for food. But in Melide, contacting Natalia took priority. With the rain getting heavier, I scoured the streets for a phone box, but every one I found took phonecards only. Seeking solace from the leaking clouds, I ducked into a bar and, where I least expected it, found a payphone hungry for coins. Competing with a TV at full volume and a handful of old men talking loudly, I stuck my finger in my ear and called her.

At first, when the phone rang and wasn't answered, I didn't worry. I figured she was expecting my call and was making her voice sound more seductive before picking up. But when the ringtone continued, on and on, I began to think she might have got cold feet. Unsuccessful in my initial attempts to contact her, I thought it best to reserve a place at the albergue just in case meeting Natalia didn't come off.

On my way through town to the albergue, I saw someone I hadn't seen since the very beginning. Even though this man had driven me insane with his snoring in St-Jean-Pied-de-Port, I was happy to reunite with Snore-kasaurus. He told me he'd covered an insane sixty-four kilometres since daybreak, trampling on my personal best of fifty-eight kilometres. For a man I estimated to be at least twenty years my senior, I considered his achievement nothing less then superhuman and would have sewed a badge of honour on his backpack if I'd had my mum's needle-and-cotton tin. I was really pleased to see a genuine, hardcore pilgrim among the plastics being driven around.

After puffing my cheeks through another cold shower at another austere municipal albergue, I returned to my belongings and saw my mobile flashing its light in the top pocket of my rucksack. Since this was the only way Natalia could contact me, I had it switched on for only the second time on the trip. I unzipped the pocket and saw she'd replied to a message I'd sent earlier.

> *Brad? I'm in San Cibrao until nine, more or less. When I'll arrive I'll phone you and one wine or beer or water jaja.*

It wasn't quite what I was hoping for. I wanted her to say she was coming to whisk me back to the family home, where all her relatives were around a big table waiting to meet me. Instead, the vague and slightly confusing message – I was dying to know what she meant by 'water jaja' – put me in something of a predicament. 'Nine, more or less' to fashionably late Spaniards could mean any time before midnight and I had no idea where or how far away San Cibrao was. She needed to know that meeting after the albergue's 10pm curfew for doors locked and lights out was going to be tricky. If she turned up later, I'd have no choice but to leave the albergue and sleep over at hers. Perhaps this could work out to my advantage after all? Or was this part of a grand plan to get me back to her place?

I shot back into town to the bar from where I'd called her earlier and tried getting in contact again. Left frustrated by the continuous ringtone, I sent a text explaining my dilemma and returned to the albergue for a power nap. I left my mobile on, hoping to be woken by a call or message from Natalia.

Proving to be as unreliable as she was mysterious, Natalia never called, and, totally bushed after another forty-kilometre day, I didn't wake up.

Come the next day, I had a dilemma: stay in Melide for another night in the hope that we'd finally get to meet, or leave and declare the dream well and truly over? It wasn't a hard decision to make. I had to keep the dream alive and give her one last chance to meet me.

After packing up and leaving the albergue, I breakfasted at a café last decorated when St James was still alive and choked on my croissant when my mobile vibrated in my bag. An unidentified Spanish number came up on the screen. It had to be her – at last! I pressed the green button. I heard cattle mooing, wind blowing into the headset, footsteps and heavy breathing.

'Bradsters!'

I recognised the voice immediately. It was my French friend Julien, calling on his work phone. The last time we'd spoken, he'd just returned from a business trip in Ghana, where a taxi driver had poked a gun in his ribs. For the princely sum of €20, his life had been saved. I was pleased to hear that he was still alive and well. Just about.

'Juuuuules! How are you, mate? What's with the cow noises?' I asked as more moos sounded in the background.

'Good news, Bradsters. I've been inspired by your emails and decided to come join you and the cows on the Camino!'

'What? Really? Why didn't you tell me? Where are you?' I grilled him as I gulped down my coffee to dislodge the croissant lodged in my windpipe.

'I'm in a field somewhere near Pamplona. I drove here from my place in Barcelona last night but fell asleep at the wheel and crashed my car.'

'That's crazy. Are you okay?'

'Yeah, I'm okay, but the car is wrecked. I left it on a pick-up truck and just walked from the highway. No big deal,' he said, playing down this latest brush with the Grim Reaper. 'I've only got a week off work, so I won't catch you up, but, listen, why not come visit me in Barcelona when you finish?'

Before I could accept the invitation, he interrupted and finished the conversation.

'Bradsters, I gotta go,' he said in a more urgent and serious tone. 'These cows are starting to surround me.'

A reprise from the bovine band came bellowing down the phone before the line abruptly went dead.

The surprise call from Julien and his invitation to Barcelona was the silver lining on a day the clouds came over my reveries of meeting, falling for and marrying Natalia. I tried on countless occasions throughout the day to reach her and went through a whirlwind of emotions in my failed attempts to make contact. Nervousness became frustration, dejection and then ear-steaming anger. How bloody rude! The least she could do was answer her phone, send a text or email me, saying, 'I'm really sorry but I didn't actually expect some stalker to track me down after I wrote my email address on a €20 note. Seek psychological help.'

I mean, how dare she! I'd conquered the Pyrenees. Spooned

Snore-kasaurus. Survived the Running of the Bulls. Had my nuts grabbed by a French girl. Taken a damn good bonking from an elephant. Soiled my pants in public. Got lost in the Spanish outback. Taken mysterious medicines. Walked more than fifty kilometres in one single day across the Iberian desert. Encountered shepherds, back-flipping punk rockers and hippies. Escaped the noble night silence. Walked by the light of a full moon with howling werewolves hunting me down. Braved the abandoned village of wild dogs. Advertised to a table of strangers that I would defecate on a windy mountainside. Slept in convents, underneath church bells and on stinky, bug-infested mattresses to the tune of a hundred snoring strangers honking their hairy hooters. Taken cold showers everyday for nearly a month. Donned my Cosmic Warrior cape. Claimed the misty Mountains of León. Refrained from murdering plastic pilgrims. Resisted strong urges to make advances on the Leah Army and Inke. Taken the long way up and down O Cebreiro to show Natalia how fit and strong I was. Seen a month of sunrises and actually gone one better than the spectacled Scottish songsmiths The Proclaimers. Instead of just singing about it, I had walked the five hundred miles to meet her. And I'd carried a Southend-on-Sea fridge magnet as a gift for letting me sleep on her house. The least she could do was reply to me.

Grrrrrrrrr!!!!

If Shirley MacLaine was right and the Camino did offer everyone a love affair, I had only fifty-three kilometres left to meet mine.

28. DANCING FANNIES

Determined not to let Natalia having stood me up crush my spirit, I focused on something more positive: my imminent arrival in Santiago de Compostela. Early evening I found an internet café in Melide and sent an email saying I'd be in Santiago in forty-eight hours. While I was there, I booked a room in a hotel in Santiago instead of at an albergue, to treat myself. That would mean having my own shower. A hot shower! My own bed in my own room. Nobody snoring apart from me. Maybe a TV and even air conditioning. All the little indulgences I'd not allowed myself even a sniff of along the way. I wasn't sure if I'd like it or hate it.

Softening the blow of not having met Natalia was an email sent to me by the Leah Army.

> *To: Brad Chermside*

> *From: Leah*

> *Subject: Road Runner*

Hey there good-looking!

We will call you the Road Runner cos you have just disappeared – beep beep!

Well, after our lovely forty-kilometre display, we had to take a rest day in Burgos cos Leah could hardly walk. It was perfect: we got so much done, took a leaf out of your book and threw some more things. Another five kilos. Now we are flying through.

Thanks again for the sleeping bag, it was absolutely freezing that night. But at least now we can say we slept under the stars.

We're going to Barcelona when we finish, so maybe see you there if you've got time? If not, hope to see you in London.

Leah 'n' Leah

Xxxx

I didn't want to get my hopes up again but couldn't help but think that perhaps things hadn't worked out with Natalia because I was supposed to get together with the Leah that didn't have a boyfriend. The Leah who'd just written to me and invited me to Barcelona the day after Julien had done so too. Had a new door been pushed slightly ajar now that the other one had slammed in my face?

Sifting further through my inbox, I had some heartening replies to my 'good news, bad news' email. These next two were from American families that had treated me like one of their own during my time working and studying across the pond.

> *To: Brad Chermside*

> *From: Nancy Y*

> *Subject: Re: Good News, Bad News, Good News*

Hey Amigo!

This was a really funny commentary! I know it was real and not always pleasant but very, very funny to read. Carry on and hope your rash has mended!!

Nancy, Ted & Sammy

> *To: Brad Chermside*

> *From: Ross G*

> *Subject: Re: Good News, Bad News, Good News*

We're loving your reports and we're with you in spirit. As they say in the USA:

Keep on truckin!

Ross, Marci, Brenton & Jackie

Clicking down the page, I was thrilled to see Ruth and Susan, two primary school teachers I'd worked with in the past, had been in touch as well.

>*To: Brad Chermside*

>*From: Ruth H*

>*Subject: Re: Good News, Bad News, Good News*

Bradley!

I'm sorry for not writing to you sooner but I'm so exhausted after reading your emails each day and hearing how far you have walked that I just have to go and lie down!!!! Please slow down, you are going to make yourself ill. Are you supposed to be walking that far each day? I'm worried – sorry, typical Jewish mother syndrome… lol! Anyway, it sounds like you are having a fab time and meeting some great people. I love reading your updates.

Be safe,

Ruthie x

>*To: Brad Chermside*

>*From: Susan P*

>*Subject: Re: Good News, Bad News, Good News*

Wow!

Not sure what else is appropriate to say.

Am stunned, moved and a little worried by your emails. Am loving every word of them. Really enjoy hearing of your travels. You are like Uncle Traveling Matt from **Fraggle Rock** *– do you remember that? He used to send postcards from his travels too.*

Well, best of luck for the next stage of your adventure, look forward to hearing all about it.

Keep safe and smiling,

Susan

x

PS Have heard that Vaseline is quite good for the chafing!

I saved the funniest till last and was really pleased to get an email from Jan telling me about his eventful journey from Logroño back to the Czech Republic.

> *To: Brad Chermside*

> *From: Jan A*

> *Subject: Re: Good News, Bad News, Good News*

> *Hola!*

> *It's great to hear that you are okay and still in good mood :-)*

> *I'm quite surprised but happy that you are having my mail! I don't believed that Slovakian girls would be fast enough to meet you and find you.*

> *Now I'm in Czech Republic, travelling a little, but I look forward for next year to finish Camino.*

> *Hitchhiking from Spain to Czech Rep was really big adventure – German police almost arrest me for smuggle drugs (it's impossible to explain for German policeman that it is TEA not a marijuana).*

> *If you meet that Australian guys tell them I send them best wishes!*

> *So Buen CAMINO amigo!*

> *Jan*

Everything Jan did seemed to land him in trouble, so I was happy to hear that he'd narrowly escaped German jail time for possession of tea. As for the 'Australian guys', I assumed he meant the Austrians, Sasha and Steffan, whom I hadn't seen since catching up with them on the Meseta.

As I signed out from my emails and began to think about plotting my penultimate day on the road, I was startled by my bag vibrating. My phone! I'd forgotten to turn it off after talking to Julien. I unzipped the top pocket of my backpack and saw a message from a Spanish number displayed on the screen. Surely not! It couldn't be – could it?

Hello Brad. Is me Natalia. ¿We see each other at six in the bar of my friend Dancing Fany's? Is very close to the albergue.

My initial reaction was one of self-righteousness. 'Too little, too late,' I spat back at the phone. She hadn't even had the decency to say sorry for making me wait around. What if I'd left town already? There wasn't even so much as an explanation for her delayed response.

Then I snapped out of it. I'd stayed an extra day just in case she got in touch. Natalia, after all, was the reason I was still in Melide. It would be a complete waste of a day if we didn't meet. I got down off my high horse and replied. It was only when I keyed in the words 'See you in Dancing Fany's' that the name of the bar tickled my funny bone. I imagined it didn't mean the same in Spanish as it did in English, but if anyone wanted to rival Peter Stringfellow, that would be a great name for a similarly sleazy establishment. I messaged Natalia back and told her I'd be wearing a light blue T-shirt and khaki combat shorts – the same things I'd worn every evening since arriving in Spain.

Dancing Fany's was a small bar on a pedestrianised side street of terraced buildings constructed from giant, sand-yellow bricks wedged together like Jenga pieces. On one side of the establishment was a tobacconist's, in and out of which shuffled a number of coughing old men, and on the other a sad and neglected stationery shop.

Outside the bar were six shiny metal tables and chairs reflecting the evening sun, and flimsy cardboard menus slotted into serviette holders flapping in the cool breeze. A slightly hunched old lady with straggly ginger hair was winding up red Coca-Cola parasols in preparation for the post-siesta rush. A student blowing into a saxophone in a music school at the end of the street provided some welcome and soothing background music.

I dragged a table into the sunlight, sat down, batted away the smoke left by a customer of the tobacconist's, ordered a fizzy water and felt surprisingly at ease. Natalia's mysteriousness, un-predictability and unreliability had made her seem less appealing as a future wife. We'd not even met and she'd already had my blood boiling. This wasn't how I'd imagined my fairytale romance would kick off. After the recent ups and downs, now I just wanted to meet her, more out of curiosity than in the hope of finding my half orange.

As I poured water into my glass, a shadow fell over my table.

'You are Brad?' asked a female voice.

I looked up from my book. The long and frizzy brown hair, olive skin and lithe body I remembered from the faceless photo had come to life.

'At last – Natalix_666!' I stood up and held out my hand.

Ignoring my offer of a handshake, she rested her hands on my shoulders and, Spanish style, pecked me on each cheek.

'*Gracias*,' I said, then immediately kicked myself. Why had I thanked her for that?

As I went to pull out a chair for her to sit down, another person arrived. A slightly camp, skinny, late-twenties man with short, dark, curly hair and gentle eyes.

'He is Carlos, my friend,' said Natalia.

We shook hands.

'Nice to meet you,' I said.

Why hadn't I said that to Natalia as well? I was still beating myself up for having thanked her.

A few seconds of awkward silence while we got comfortable in each other's presence seemed to make everyone a little tetchy. Natalia scratched her forearm. Carlos drummed the table with two beer mats. I peeled off the label on my water bottle. Racking my brains for something, anything, to say, I filled the silence with the first thing that came into my mind.

'Do you know what "dancing fannies" means in English?' I asked them.

Carlos, who said very little throughout but smiled a lot, didn't seem to understand. Natalia shook her head and pursed her lips, also none the wiser. Looking around to make sure no other English speakers were present, I whispered it to them as if sharing a secret. Natalia burst out laughing then translated for Carlos. He put a hand over his mouth and looked at me with a mixture of shock, amusement and disbelief.

'Fany,' Natalia explained, 'is another way for say the name "Estefanía". Of the day, this is a bar, and of night, the people come for dancing. For this, is called Dancing Fany's.'

The talk of dancing fannies did the trick. It lightened the atmosphere, and after they'd ordered small beers we relaxed into conversation. I cut to the chase and asked all about that €20 note. I was the only person, she said, who'd been crazy enough to send a message after she'd gone through a phase of writing her email address on banknotes when she was drunk. She apologised for not answering my calls and texts, explaining that she was scared to meet me because she was ashamed of her English. I told her she spoke really well and she explained that she'd been studying in her spare time to improve for our meeting. I thought that was charming of her. It was only when Carlos said he'd come along for support that she'd plucked up the courage to see me.

Just like I had my own soccer school, Natalia was a dance teacher with her own academy in town. She taught hundreds of kids weekly and occasionally took them to competitions all over Europe. She'd even won awards in her specialist discipline of salsa. Her idea that she might find love by writing her email on banknotes hadn't borne fruit and she'd been single for a couple of years.

Natalia and I got on great and had a lot in common. She was nice. She was approachable. Bubbly. Enthusiastic. Smiley. Talkative. She even taught me how to say 'dancing fannies' in Spanish, in case I wanted to open a sister bar for Spaniards to laugh at in England – 'los cho chos que bailan'. There was bad news though: there was no spark between us. Not in that way anyway.

After a very pleasant hour with Natalia and Carlos, we said our nice to meet yous, goodbyes, and good lucks. Though I felt slightly disappointed that the love I'd fantasised of hadn't materialised, I was glad that we'd at least got to meet. After two years, I finally had closure on the mysterious Natalia and there were no longer any what ifs to dwell on and eat me up. And though nothing came of our blind date, a sober, eye-opening realisation came to me from something so obvious but powerful she'd said to me that evening.

29. STICKING IT OUT

Before all the fannies came out for a dance, I migrated to a different café on my way back to the albergue. Inside, another big party of French plastics on a private tour had the two waiters run off their feet. After waiting patiently for half an hour I still hadn't had my order taken. As three of them broke off from the group and lit cigarettes by the entrance, selfishly letting the smoke diffuse inside, I ran out of tether. Enough was enough.

Walking into Santiago alongside fifty tourists wearing yellow caps and following a tour guide dressed in Rupert the Bear trousers holding aloft a pair of old knickers tied to a pole wasn't the grand finale I'd envisaged for myself. I recalled the best-loved saying of my favourite primary school teacher, Mr Manouvrier: 'I don't mind a laugh, I don't mind a joke, but this is a pantomime and I don't like pantomimes.' I didn't want my victorious last steps to be the current pantomime on show. I wanted them to be memorable for all the right reasons. I wanted my first distant sighting of Santiago Cathedral's spires to be like the first glimpse of Everest's peak for a freezing mountaineer. The palms of a paradise island for the starving castaway. The water source for the dying man in the desert.

Patting flat a wrinkle in my map, I calculated I could get to Santiago in one day instead of the two I wrote it would take in my last email. The remaining fifty-three kilometres would be hard but not mission impossible. I excitedly folded the map back into quarters, walked out the bar without ordering a drink and made up my mind. I'd get to Santiago de Compostela before the moon rose over the field of stars tomorrow night.

As if it was the first day of a long-awaited holiday, I darted through the albergue doors at 0704 the following morning and out into the beatific new-day rays flooding through the encircling pines. On either side of the waist-high drystone wall framing the steps up to the entrance, a group of cyclists were gearing up to get going. They clicked in helmet straps, pumped up tyres and dripped oil onto the chinks in their chains. At the bottom of the steps, sitting cross-legged in a circle on a plastic mat, were the Italian girl scouts happy-clapping a song, swaying to the waltz-like rhythm and its elegant rising and falling melody. The birds were chittering perfect backing vocals. Refreshingly, it was the first positive contribution I'd witnessed from the plastic pilgrim pantomime. The tune was enchanting, the atmosphere jovial and the air was cool and forest-fresh. That was until a big red van wheeled up and ruined the atmosphere.

While the van billowed diesel in the faces of everyone outside the albergue, the girl scouts tittered over and deposited their rucksacks on board. As the backpack chauffeur revved away in a low gear, leaving a dust cloud in his wake, the leader of the scout pack approached me.

'Do you 'ave a girlfriend?' he asked in an effeminate voice while pointing at me with a curled index finger.

The hordes of people present all stopped what they were doing. My cheeks began to sizzle with embarrassment while they awaited my answer. Even though I didn't have a girlfriend, I was about to say I had lots and that they were indeed all female, not a man among them.

'These girls' – he beat me to it, leaving me open-mouthed – 'want to know e-e-e-e-f you 'ave a girlfriend.' He gestured at the pack of giggling teenage girls in khaki scout uniforms accessorised with yellow neckties, all of whom were looking at me expectantly.

As I started slowly moonwalking backwards, he explained they were from Sicily, and the alarm bells began to ring even louder. One minute I thought a gay guy was chatting me up, the next I was being touted by a group of Mafioso teenage girls as their sugar daddy. With the chilling theme tune from the *Godfather* movies in my head, I swerved the question and took evasive action. Wearing a face like I'd just been caught trying on a petticoat by a fitting-room shop assistant, I waved an awkward and hurried goodbye.

With Santiago the objective before the lights in the star field began to flicker, and wanting to keep ahead of the gay scouts and Mafioso daughters, I powered through the sunny morning without stopping. Umbrous forest, glittering river valleys spanned by moss-smothered limestone bridges, wooded hills and comely villages were all easy on the eye, even as I was being hard on my body.

I paid for my territorial gains with the acute pain of returning shin splints, which nipped away at my energy from just above my right ankle. A solid five hours on foot resulted in me taking very deliberate, aching, pigeon steps, but I kept going, fired up by positive self-talk: 'One giant step towards Santiago,' I repeated over and over, Neil Armstrong style.

Early afternoon, as I waddled out of thick eucalyptus forest and on to the side of a single-lane carriageway, a roadside café called me in to recuperate. I ordered a large bottle of water and for the next five minutes slouched in my chair, closed my eyes and didn't move an inch. Whenever the commotion of the cars zooming past in both directions faded out, the sounds of the surrounding forest filled the fragile silence. The calls of the crows, the current of the nearby River Burgo serenading the woods, and the grinding of the tall trees tipping side to side made a soul-soothing ensemble. A sensual wind fondled my face, combed the hairs on my legs and crept down the back of my T-shirt, stroking my spine. Tingling with relaxation, my mind wandered back to my encounter with Natalia. More specifically, to something she'd said that had been playing on my mind.

After she'd answered my twenty questions about her, she asked all about me. Inevitably, my reasons for walking the Camino came up. Spinning the yarn about my career conundrum and how my choice of girlfriends had brought me nothing but trouble, she gave me some pertinent words of wisdom.

'The persons we love in our lifes we must to accept. Brothers, sisters, lovers, mothers, fathers. Not because of who they are. Not despite what they are.' She paused for effect and knocked a finger on the aluminium table. 'Brad. We must to accept them for everything they are.'

Her sage words resonated regarding my unjust treatment of certain ex-girlfriends. I don't mean the ones that forced me to change my locks, go into hiding or worry that I was being followed by a private detective; the Potty Dotties to whom I was foolishly attracted because they had long legs, just the right length hair or because the idea of dating someone from a certain country appealed. I'm referring to the lovely 'girls-next-door' who'd accepted my own imperfections – as a commitment-phobe, professional underachiever and person incapable of saving a penny, to name but a few. Though those patient, accepting ladies had ignored those gaping flaws in my personality, my irrational fear of the norm had made me blind to their virtues. I'd failed to appreciate them. I'd stupidly, heartlessly finished many relationships that had been going perfectly well.

Viewed from under the spell of the Camino's spirit of unconditional love, and having walked among its soldiers of acceptance, altruism and kindness, my reasons for breaking up now appeared ridiculous. Harsh. Judgemental. Arrogant. I used to comment to friends that a woman was too clingy because she wanted to spend all weekend with me; too pushy because she asked to introduce me to her friends after a positive start; too nosy if she was curious about my life. I mean, who the hell did I think I was? I was Bradley Chermside with skinny, chicken legs, big ears and a nose that stuck out like a hedgehog's, not Brad Pitt.

I cringed, recalling how I'd finished one promising short-term romance because her English, though very good, wasn't perfect and I was too impatient to speak slowly and clearly for her. If I'd taken that stinking attitude with me onto the Camino, I wouldn't have made friends with the many foreigners who'd enriched my experience. If I hadn't been puffed up with testosterone and an over-inflated sense of self-importance, that lovely young lady whose English far outshone my grasp of her language would most certainly have enriched my life too.

I remembered another shameful moment when I'd reduced one ex to tears by terminating an otherwise amazing partnership because she was void of opinions on issues I felt strongly about. Surely all that mattered was that we got on great, I really fancied her and we had so many other things in common like music, travelling and keeping fit? I mean, who did that? Who ended relationships that were going great because their better half wasn't interested in a mass debate on religion, politics and spirituality? If I carried on judging instead of accepting the imperfections of the women I met, I'd get what I deserved – a shallow, lonely existence spent masturbating instead of mass debating topical issues.

As they say, every saint has a past and every sinner a future. I saw clearly that I needed to stop sinning by focusing less on superficialities and more on personality, morals and strength of connection. It seemed so obvious, but I hadn't been putting it into practice. A quote I recalled from one of the many self-help books on my shelves at home summed up the whole Natalia story: 'Life has a habit of giving you what you need, not what you want.' I'd really wanted Natalia to be my Camino love affair. Turned out she was my teacher.

Pledging to change my immature ways I leafed through my guidebook and calculated how far I'd come and how far there was still to go. In my relentless morning march, I'd ticked off more than thirty kilometres and had just over twenty left. With around six hours of daylight remaining, the right time to go was now.

As I clicked the waist-belt of my backpack ready to depart, Snore-kasaurus came walking down the short slope from the forested roadside and took a seat. I tried explaining that I'd already paid the bill and was leaving, but my hand gestures and Fren-glish fell on deaf ears. He ordered a drink and, not wanting to be rude, I asked for another small water and stayed for a quick chat. He proceeded to speak at me in French and I '*oui*

oui'-ed everywhere possible to keep the interaction flowing. He proudly told me how, on reaching Santiago, he would have claimed nearly sixteen hundred kilometres from his starting point in Le Puy in central France. Just like when we'd bumped into each other on the streets of Melide twenty-four hours earlier, he seemed pleased to see me. So pleased, in fact, that he suggested we walk the last stretch to Santiago together. Grinning like I'd just offered him snails, Camembert, and a beret to wear while he ate them, he gazed at me in anticipation of a positive response.

As awful as I felt, I had to let him down and break the news that I wanted to walk by myself. Maintaining a conversation in a language I barely spoke was tiring enough as it was, let alone while traipsing 50 plus kilometres. I needed to be alone so I could absorb absolutely every detail of the crowning moment of the greatest adventure of my life.

The cheeriness drained from his face when I told him that, but he soon brushed off the disappointment. All had clearly been forgiven by the time he shook my hand, accepted my offer to pay for his drink and made his way back up to the roadside.

All was quiet when I ventured into the woods again. Thankfully, there was no sign of a matinee performance by the plastic pilgrim pantomime. Frustratingly, though, it wasn't long before the sharp, pinching ache of shin splints flared up again and plotted to foil my big plans. In defiance, I picked up a big stick from the sandy forest path, slammed it into the ground and stoically stomped on. What greater motivation could I have to smash through the pain barrier than Santiago and its field of stars? Emboldened by my new stick, I pretended I was a bloodthirsty hunter with a spear and pushed the unrelenting stabbing in my shins to the back of my mind. With or without shin splints, I would get to Santiago that evening.

When the seemingly interminable jungle of trees I'd trooped through for most of the day yielded to suburban streets, a skybound five-kilometre asphalt ascent took off. As I scaled the swelling tarmac, I looked down on the perimeter fence of Santiago airport, passed the high-security gates of a Galician TV channel's headquarters and clucked and mooed at the chickens and cows inhabiting the farmland in between. With no protection from the unforgiving sun and salty sweat stinging my eyes and gumming my soaked T-shirt to my backpack, I crested the toilsome incline and was rewarded with a sight for sore shins. Surrounded by rich, undulant countryside, a mass of terracotta rooftops kissing the feet of the imperial Santiago Cathedral towers!

'The Mountain of Joy', as the landmark Monte do Gozo translates, didn't even come close.

I ran down the hill towards a district of unsightly identical grey tower blocks lined up like dominos and forged ahead through characterless outskirts, the thwack of my stick jabbing into the ground, a warning shot that my invasion of the city was imminent. No matter how much pain I was in, I was going to arrive looking like a barbarian who'd conquered fifty-three kilometres since dawn and more than eight hundred kilometres in three and a half weeks, not like an old man hobbling to the shops to get his newspaper. Crossing the city limits, I snapped a beaming selfie by the roadside with a sign announcing 'Santiago' in the background. That photo captured me in the happiest few seconds of my life.

Advancing into the city centre, which was still coming to life after the siesta, I celebrated with public, unashamed fist pumps and cries of 'Yeeeeesssssss!' An elderly, suited gent smoking outside a café shared my elation and raised his cigar to me. I lifted my stick like a cricketer saluting a century and shouted '¡Gracias!' I liked him a lot.

For many pilgrims, reaching Santiago was a dispiriting anticlimax, but nothing and no one was going to ruin this for me. Not the waiters on the streets trying to cajole me into their restaurants, the fanfare of tacky souvenir shops or the locals harassing me to stay in their spare rooms. Striding into the Santiago Cathedral plaza like a warrior who'd just seized power and declared himself king, I simultaneously ejaculated happiness, ecstasy, satisfaction and pride. I'd done it! Fifty-three kilometres in twelve hours, fighting off the pain of my shin splints. Eight hundred and four kilometres in twenty-six days. I'd only gone and bloody done it!

The cobbled plaza was buzzing with jubilant pilgrims having their photos taken in front of the cathedral, its towers glowing gold in the evening sun, spires soaring in a speckless sky. Entering the cathedral, I was soon turfed back out again by a snappy security guard who refused me entry with my backpack. I was ordered to leave it in a luggage lock-up around the corner. Second time lucky, I was allowed in and joined the crowds of tourists left open-mouthed by its palatial interior.

I was determined to do what was customary for all pilgrims upon arrival. First I placed the fingers of my right hand into five indentations in a pillar called the Tree of Jesse. The pillar was topped with a seated figure of St James, to whom I said a silent prayer of thanks. Thanks for this incredible adventure. Thanks for this unparalleled feeling of contentment. Thanks for this smile hurting my face. Thanks for giving me the strength to walk through the pain of blisters and shin splints and for helping me refrain from twisting the bollocks off a plastic pilgrim. Thanks for helping me fight back the tears threatening to stream down my face any moment now.

On the other side of the pillar, facing the high altar, was a statue of Maestro Mateo, the twelfth-century creator of the cathedral's opulent main gate. It was said that by touching his head with yours, his genius would be transmitted to you. I needed all the help I could get on that front, so I head-butted him three times to make sure I didn't miss out.

Lastly, with watery eyes, blurred vision and a runny nose, I walked up the wide aisles to the high altar and the shrine of St James. Perched on a gilded, spectacularly ornamented podium overlooking the nave and countless rows of ochre pews, the statue of the apostle glittered with jewels and gold. Like the winning captain at Wembley going to lift the cup, I climbed the shrine steps and hugged that beautiful, hairy, saintly bugger and let it all out. I cried so loud, so long and so hard that my body shook and people came up the steps, put their arms around me and asked if I was okay.

I was better than okay. It was the apotheosis of my life. It beat my previous high of running the London Marathon in little over three hours. Topped getting first-class honours at university. Trumped crossing the line in the New York Triathlon in Central Park. Even outshone getting my twenty-five-metre swimming badge sewn onto my trunks at infant school.

Exiting the cathedral into the bright and glorious evening sunshine, wiping my eyes as I went, I immediately made for the pilgrim office to pick up my Certificate of Completion. When the man behind the desk signed and handed over the coveted Compostela, the clock on the wall behind him said 1904, which made it exactly twelve hours since I'd left Melide that morning, hell-bent on busting fifty-three kilometres to finally rid myself of the plastic pilgrim pantomime.

Though the feeling was electric, there was still something missing. I knew that this moment wouldn't be perfect unless I spoke to someone I hadn't heard from the whole time I'd been away – my dad.

As always, his Border collie Oliver answered the phone with an ear-splitting, phone-spooked bark before anyone could say hello. My lovely stepmother Ann calmed the dog down and said that Dad had popped round the corner to my nan's. Since my grandad had passed away, Dad had taken to visiting my nan daily, keeping her spirits up with countless cups of tea and biscuits. I was proud of him for that. I hung up and dialled the first phone number I'd memorised in my life – Nan and Grandad Chermside.

'Rather you than me,' Nan said when I told her I'd just walked five hundred miles across Spain. 'You be careful, darlin', they can be right sods, them Spanish,' she shouted over Ant and Dec's birdsong Geordie accents on the TV before passing the phone to Dad.

My nan, cute, dinky and loving as she was, saw in everyone

the potential to be a right sod. Not even her cat Fluffy was excluded. She was a 'bleedin' little sod' because she liked to spruce up Nan's flowerbed with faecal fertiliser.

Talking to Dad on the phone was a rare occurrence that neither of us had ever got comfortable with. He'd begin by asking if I was alright, then I'd ask him if he was alright, after which we'd repeat that a couple of times before filling the ensuing silence by agreeing that was indeed alright then, that we were both alright. Then he'd ask me if my car was running alright and I'd ask him if his dog Oliver was alright. Then I'd ask if Nan was alright and he'd ask if my band was going alright. Still stumped for things to say, I'd ask if Ann was alright and he'd enquire if business was alright. The subject of West Ham going down if they didn't buck up their ideas would often rescue the conversation when it was going far from alright. Invariably, he'd then tell me about a funny fart video on the internet, fill me in on who'd died or been taken ill recently in the neighbourhood I grew up in, and would then repeat the line about West Ham going down.

On this occasion, though, with my lack of coins limiting my time, I went off script and got to the point. I told him I was just calling to let him know I'd arrived safe and sound. He said he hoped I was alright after walking so far and that he'd pick me up from the airport when I got home.

By sharing this moment with my dad, after having warred with him for years, I felt we'd exorcised the ghosts of a painful past and made peace. Though it made me tearful, it made my day, my Camino, my trip of a lifetime, complete.

30. LAP OF HONOUR

After collapsing in one of Santiago's many albergues the evening I arrived, on my second night in the city, I lodged at the hotel I'd pre-booked from Melide. My room was a ghastly two-star throwback from the seventies that made Fawlty Towers look like the Savoy. A mahogany headboard and bedside drawers, beige bedcovers and matching nylon curtains waged an ugly colour war against mint-green walls. In the battle of the smells, mould and damp in the wardrobes competed to out-whiff a nauseating artificial vanilla room-spray. I much preferred the earthier scents of the albergues and my fellow pilgrims' armpits.

My room's interior-design horrors and unsettling odours were all forgiven when I turned the dials of the shower in the private bathroom. For the first time since day one in Roncesvalles, I had the sybaritic sensation of heavenly hot water racing down my head, neck and back like melting wax cascading down a candle. I took the longest shower of my life to rinse off the second skin of dust, dirt and sweat a month of cold showers hadn't shifted.

As the steam cleared in the bathroom, like an Amazonian tribesman taking tentative, maiden steps in the West, I cynically eyed up the embarrassment of luxuries at my disposal. Commodities that, for the last four weeks, had been out of reach. Shampoo. Conditioner. Shower gel. Hand wash. Large towels. Small towels. Hand towels. A bidet. In the room a small grey television hung on the wall over two single beds pushed together. The beds were buried beneath way more plump white pillows than I needed, especially since I'd got used to resting my head on my rain jacket rolled up in a ball. In the musty wardrobe were a trouser press and coat hangers. On a bedside table the remote dared me to click on the TV. Did I really need all this stuff, all this clutter, all these distractions I'd done without for the duration of my trip, when I'd never been happier, ever?

I sat on the bed wrapped in my towel with the TV redundant and my steaming feet on the cool laminate flooring, contemplating my next move. In the morning I could take a bus and go stay with Julien in Barcelona or I could walk three more days to Finisterre on the Atlantic coast. I pondered how disconcerting life without my backpack would be; stripped of my pilgrim status, access to discounted meals and cheap lodgings; no longer eligible to receive random acts of kindness from strangers; no longer sharing sleeping quarters with dozens of stinking snorers whom I'd thought I'd be happy to be rid of but now longed for in my lonely, characterless hotel room. I pictured walking the streets at home, a place full of memories but lacking the mysteries and marvels of the Camino. I dozed off, put to sleep by the hypnotising hum of the air conditioning, trusting a good night's rest would bring some clarity on my beautiful dilemma.

In the morning, I shot out of bed on autopilot and began packing my rucksack for another day's walking. Habit took the reins and made the decision for me. I checked out the hotel, bound for Finisterre. The Atlantic beckoned. A lap of honour to the ocean, I declared to the bathroom mirror, would be a fitting finale to a month that would shape the rest of my years. My thirst for freedom and my appetite for adventure were as insatiable as ever.

Before leaving the city, I stopped for breakfast, then treated myself to one last tour of Santiago on foot. I loved the place. Though it was a Monday morning, there was a carnival atmosphere in the air. Summer was in full swing. An enormous crowd had formed a circle in a plaza to the side of the cathedral. I jostled to get a view from the fringes as they cheered, whooped and clapped at a street performer's tricks.

Around the corner, tourists gathered in the main square and squinted in the morning sun as they looked up at the magnificence of Santiago Cathedral. An endless stream of pilgrims roamed the plaza, their hands gripping their rucksack straps, wearing proud expressions like kids who'd come first on school sports day. Even though they'd carried their backpacks for a million steps, none would release them from their shoulders because that would downgrade them to tourist status. With their rucksacks stuck to their backs like the shell of a tortoise, they remained part of the pilgrim aristocracy.

Airport-style reunions were taking place in all quarters of the city. Pilgrim pals who hadn't seen each other in days or possibly even weeks found each other and rejoiced with hugs, back pats and kisses on the cheek. Bearing witness to such moving scenes made me smile and on occasions the odd tear escaped as the emotion of such special moments became contagious.

In my forty-eight hours in Santiago, I was lucky enough to share similar moments with most of my favourite pilgrims: Crazy Frank, Sasha and Steffan; Peter, Tierra and Barefoot Bernard; the Leah Army and Tore. I relived the highs and lows with all of them over beer and tapas in the cluster of eateries under the bleached stone arches of Santiago's famous street, Rúa do Vilar. All of them apart from Crazy Frank were planning to take a day out and then walk on to Finisterre.

Boarding a bus to Madrid at Santiago bus station, Crazy Frank serenaded me for the last time. 'We meet again, I not know where, I not know when.'

I missed him already.

Tore and I had spotted each other through a sea of people in the cathedral square and embraced with a manly bear hug. He was with an attractive German woman he seemed fond of. She introduced herself but I quickly forgot her name, mesmerised by her piercing blue eyes as we came closer to shake hands. She was probably in her early forties and I was sure she'd tear Tore to pieces given half the chance. I shot Tore a quizzical look, seeking confirmation that Danish and German ties were indeed being warmed and strengthened. He winked back. I guessed she was yet to see his feet.

Tore was a great guy. So serious, yet so much fun. So geeky but oozing cool. So stereotypically Nordic with his ginger hair, pale skin and blue eyes, yet so English in his dry sense of humour. Not wanting to be the third wheel any longer, I left Tore with the German lady. 'You might want to wear socks,' I whispered in his ear, pointing to the toenails sprouting from his sandals, which were painted in various shades of blistery black and blue.

Having soaked up as many sights, sounds and memories of Santiago as possible, it was now time to head out of town. As I made my way to the yellow arrows leading back to the Camino, I heard the meditative tones of a busker playing the bagpipes. The sound drew me through some shady backstreets to the top of a flight of steps descending into a dark alley in the grounds of the cathedral. I sat at the top of the steps, closed my eyes and felt the music freeze my spine, every plaintive note sending goosebumps up my vertebrae. I was vibrating with a pleasure that defied belief. I had never felt more open to love, positivity and a divine energy than in that moment.

On that unassailable high, humming the melody of the bagpipes, I left Santiago in red-hot, late-afternoon sunshine and headed deep into the verdant Galician countryside. Thankfully, most of the twenty-two kilometres to my next stop, Negreira, were in the shade of handsome woods. Having my backpack on, with my boots beating on the turf beneath them and the wind of adventure behind me once more was invigorating. I felt like a retired boxer with his gloves back on; like a castrated dog given back the fire in his balls. I was ecstatic. Singing and jumping while I ambled through mint-effusing eucalyptus forest, whacking trees with big sticks and throwing stones at imaginary targets, I chased the butterflies, communicated with the cows and so loved being alive. The highlight of the day's walk was a limestone bridge over a crystal-clear river where a glimmering mini-waterfall framed by trees and vegetation made rainbows in the sun's refracting rays. It was the picture of an exquisite artist. The artist was Mother Nature.

With darkness chasing me down, I couldn't stay for long applauding such natural beauty and made it to Negreira just before the moon sang the sun a lullaby. The albergue was nowhere to be found until a Spanish couple I'd seen numerous times that day waved me to follow them. In the nick of time, they got me there before the doors were locked for the night. Though the albergue was *completo*, I was allowed to sleep on the floor. I had come to prefer that instead of a bed.

In the small dining area surrounded by vending machines, I squeezed around a wooden table with four Danish guys, Alex, Christian, Jonas and another whose name I had no chance of pronouncing correctly. I just called him Lennon because he was wearing an Abbey Road T-shirt. He said he preferred his new name.

They offered to spice up the bland pasta and vegetables I'd conjured up in the kitchen with some mincemeat they had left over. Soon to join us was an elderly Swedish woman whose positive energy, shining blue eyes and enthusiasm seemed at odds with her long, unkempt grey hair. All of them spoke fluent English and we got on famously. The Danes offered me a shot of super-strength Spanish liquor to wash down my dinner. I took one sip, which blew my head off and set the back of my throat on fire.

My head still spinning, they suggested we have a press-up competition on the lawn outside the back door. Christian, a sickeningly handsome lad who looked more like a *Baywatch* lifeguard than a pilgrim, beat me easily. Only after I'd belly-flopped onto the grass with my arms shaking did he tell me he'd just left the army. Hardly fair competition, I argued, as they all laughed at my expense.

Before bedtime I got to know more about someone I'd seen many times but with whom I'd never had the chance to speak properly. German Gerald, who'd been one of the many pilgrims at the table on that unforgettable night in Grañón, shared the story of his arrival in Santiago. After walking for four months and an astonishing 2,300 kilometres from his home in Munich, he fell to his knees at the altar in the cathedral and, just like me, sobbed uncontrollably. He cried again as he told me, and I squeezed my eyes, trying to fight back my own tears.

Manning up and pulling himself together, he randomly launched into a cockney accent. 'The raaaaay-ne in Spaaaaaay-ne falls maaaaaayn-ly on the plaaaaaaay-ns,' he repeated over and over. Each time he said it, he went up a few decibels as if that would make it funnier.

Even though he continued for an amount of time that exhausted my supply of forced laughter, I liked him a lot. Now in his mid-fifties, Gerald had been a high-ranking member of the German army. You could tell, too, because his naturally authoritative tone made you stop, listen and instantly give him your undivided attention. For having walked what would almost be the distance from London to Moscow, he would always have my respect too.

The following day wasn't all rainbows, waterfalls and minty fairytale forest like the day before. It was, as Luís would have described it, thirty-seven kilometres of 'bing bong, bing bong', up and down all the way. The conditions didn't help either. The weather just couldn't make up its mind. It was uncomfortably hot, then uncomfortably cold. Sometimes desert dry, then flash-flood wet. You never knew whether to wear your T-shirt or your jumper, slip on shades or zip up your waterproof.

After walking through four seasons in a long and laboured day, I met Davíd, a quietly spoken but chatty Spaniard who I'd last seen way back on the Meseta. He and I walked together a good few hours and the conversation kept us alert when we were both tiring.

Just before we stopped for the day in Olveiroa, we plodded along a long asphalt road, straight as an airport runway and hugging a swampy stream. Frightened frogs sprang from one bank to the other when they felt the vibrations of our footsteps. From the undergrowth I grabbed a stick and tapped the banks, causing dozens of them to jump across to the opposite side. It was extremely entertaining watching them leap from one side to the other, crossing in mid-air, and a welcome diversion from our tiredness.

Olveiroa was a small village of nothing more than a steep hill, an albergue, and a barmaid with bosoms that bounced around just as much as the frogs. On her T-shirt the words 'Show me the world' were emblazoned across her lively chest. In her bar, Davíd, the Danish boys and I sank a few beers without saying much as we stared at her with our jaws on the table. In such a tiny, remote little village, we agreed she must be the girl all the guys were vying for. She knew it too and strutted about with her breasts stuck out straight and true. Such an unexpected sexual stimulus from Titsolina Bumsquirt as my mum would've named her, was almost too much to deal with after having lived like a monk for a month.

We ate like sharks later on at the rustic albergue. Once again, the generosity bestowed upon us was incredible. A very attentive hospitalera and waitress explained the local specialities of the three -course meal we were being served. *Caldo gallego* – Galician broth – was a delicious hot starter of cabbage, potatoes, white beans, fatty pork and chorizo. The main dish, *empanadas gallegas*, the hospitalera said, was a pasty-type pastry loaded with beef and 'kitchen'. I was sure she meant to say 'chicken', not 'kitchen', but didn't want to stop her in full flow. The *tarta de Santiago* was an almond cake with a lemony zest dusted in icing sugar.

The one sour point of a sweet mealtime was the English guy sitting next to me. What a spiky asshole. Seizing on her 'kitchen' for 'chicken' error, he played smart-arse by pointing out her mistake then proceeding to ask questions in Spanish. No doubt, he was just doing this to show off that he spoke Spanish. The waitress raked her eyes over him and in retaliation replied to him in Gallego – the language of Galicia. He soon shut up, firmly put in his place. He tried to save face by whispering insults about her in my ear. I just ignored him and couldn't wait to get away from the table and his negative presence. After meeting so many brilliant, inspiring people, mixing with a such dark heart made me feel uncomfortable. I'd forgotten people like that actually existed. But sadly they did and it reminded me the world wasn't as perfect as four weeks on the Camino had made me believe.

Olveiroa sticks in my memory for one other notable thing – the whole village reeked of cowpat from surrounding farms and fields. The pungent dung constantly kicked you in the nostrils. Every now and then the wind would pick up and intensify the stench so badly, I'd taste it in the back of my throat.

On my third and final day westward, the promise of the Atlantic got me out of there before dawn. The Camino started out roving through lush green fields, winding round yet more dense forest and chasing gushing rivers. Mid-morn, as it dawdled up a blustery hillside, the cry of a seagull overhead was the first clue of a treat that would be hard to beat. From the top of that grassy, plump escarpment I caught my first glimpse of Spanish sea. The land fell away between the green hills, revealing a triangle of dark blue Atlantic on the curtain of grey horizon. I'd pounded the turf for nearly nine hundred kilometres from France to see the white-capping ocean bubbling with excitement to greet me. I laughed and cried tears of happiness and screamed my gratitude to the heavens. I wanted to hug someone but as usual was alone. Instead, I took a picture and tried to bottle the moment and remember that view forever.

The last part of the day, I walked side by side with the sea, breathing her salty brine into my lungs. She danced and swayed and hissed and boomed as the tide rushed in to welcome me. In the highest of spirits, I bounced along white sandy trails through knee-high grass, over a wooden boardwalk taking in fleets of boats bobbing in a marina, then strode down a long seaside promenade into Finisterre. The three-day lap of honour had featured some of the Camino's toughest terrain, but the spectacular scenery, people I'd met and ocean vistas made it all worthwhile.

I was relieved to find that the albergue reserved its beds exclusively for those who'd walked from Santiago. Pilgrims arriving by bus were told to look elsewhere. An Irish guy, another

Peter, was hospitalero and signed my second Certificate of Completion in a week. I'd now completed el Camino de Fisterra as well as the Road to Santiago and had two pieces of paper to frame and impress my future in-laws.

Before the Americas were discovered, and when McDonald's was just an old man's farm, the Romans mapped Finisterre as the furthest point west in Europe. Unaware that Portugal's Azores existed, they believed it to be the end of the world as they knew it and christened the area '*finis terrae*' – the end of the earth.

Tradition tells that the earliest pilgrims burnt their clothes on the cape at sunset to signify the end of their old life and the beginning of their new one. Following this sacred custom, Davíd and I hiked the three kilometres up to the lighthouse atop the promontory of Cape Finisterre, where we met Gerald and the Danes. Using their walking staffs, they'd erected a tripod for burning our walking clothes. It was probably the best outcome possible for my Camino clobber. I'd worn the same single T-shirt and pair of shorts for the last month and they were now beginning to smell like I'd found them in the bins.

Davíd and I contributed some pizza we'd cooked back at the albergue and a bottle of red wine for our last supper at sunset on the cliff edge. The Danes brought the all-important beers. Joining the party was Fabrizzio, an Italian with a wild afro and John Lennon glasses, two quiet and pensive German women, and a friendly American guy from Arizona.

The Danish boys had the fire ready to go and we waited for sunset. I climbed a rock and looked out to the infinite, vast swathe of ocean with a ferocious wind, screaming and shouting in my ears. Beyond the breakers, the sea seemed as flat as a table, like I could roll a marble across it. At the bottom of the cliffs, swelling waves unleashed their fury, thundering against the cliffs, creating mini-waterfalls where the sea poured back into the ocean. If I'd fallen from my lofty perch into that whirlpool below, I'd have been tossed around like an old sock in a washing machine.

The sun soon began to slide, and here, at the second most

westerly point in Europe, the ball of fire was as big as the sky. Its blinding reflection lit a blazing path across the sea, like a UFO shining a light inviting us to walk on water and come aboard. We all sat in our own little spaces in silence, paralysed with peace and pleasure, each of us alone with our thoughts. I vibrated with a skin-tingling happiness and an unparalleled, elevated state of consciousness I had never known in my life: a divine and pure love for myself and all these strangers on the rocks with whom I was sharing this special moment but whom I'd probably never see again.

The Danes burst into a melancholic but soothing a capella song in the deep and dark tones of their native tongue. Though I understood nothing, the melody was as pretty as the surroundings. We cheered the boys when they finished, then Gerald picked up the baton and sang a similarly mournful tune in German. Hearing a lone, elegiac voice with the symphony of the sea made me tearful and blurred my view of the sun setting fire to the ocean.

After pouring out the red wine into plastic cups, we lit the fire, threw on our clothing and watched the flames lick them to death, reducing them to smouldering ashes. This was the official beginning of our new lives and a beyond perfect ending to my Camino.

Fabrizzio followed another tradition and sent his two walking staffs tumbling down the rocks to be gobbled up by the sea. Gerald went off to sleep somewhere on the cliffs below and when the sun finally melted into the ocean, three of the Danes and Davíd went back to the albergue. Jonas and I, unable to tear ourselves away from the zillion stars overhead, decided the Milky Way would be our roof for the night. We slept on the rocks under the lighthouse, its searchlight beaming across the Atlantic. We lay on our backs, cocooned in our sleeping bags, wearing all our clothes to protect against the bite of a wild and bitterly cold wind. We stared in wonderment at the shooting stars whizzing across the sky like fireworks.

Though our position on the clifftop was precarious, we forgot those worries by telling jokes, pissing off the rocks into the ocean and singing Beatles tunes. Monty Python's 'Lumberjack Song' also got several renditions:

'I'm a Lumberjack and I'm okay, I sleep all night and I work all day

He cuts down trees, he wears high heels, suspendies and a bra

I wish I was a girlie just like my dear papa!'

We played the fool until tiredness beat us and we fell asleep, trusting the stars would protect us from the elements and the tide wouldn't climb the cliffs and the ocean swallow us.

The next morning, back at the albergue, it was time to say goodbye to the Danish boys, Gerald and Davíd. I thought it was time for me to up sticks too, until I had an unexpected reunion with Tore. I was in a café on a payphone to Mum when I saw him hobbling past. I said a hasty goodbye, slammed the phone down and ran down the street to catch him up.

Tore's plan was to rough it and sleep on the beach for a few nights. I couldn't think of anything better and had the perfect excuse to delay my reluctant journey home.

After dumping our backpacks on the blonde sands, we collected rocks for a fire pit and wood from the trees at the top of the dunes, then made the acquaintance of the others living on the beach. First we met John, a seventy-one-year-old who lived in South Africa but was originally from Liverpool. Sitting cross-legged against a rock in his red beanie hat, he stroked his long white beard and told us about his years running marathons. 'I had a heart attack last year, so I've stopped doing the 42k and now I'm just doing 10k!' he complained.

There was also a dreadlocked Swiss guy who'd walked from Switzerland and, like a true pilgrim, was planning to walk back. Our other neighbours were some Spaniards who'd been camping on the beach the whole summer and a Swedish girl who caught everyone's attention with her dramatic arrival. Approaching the shore, she threw down her backpack, flung out her arms and span around in circles. She soon became so dizzy, she fell into the breakers fully clothed, then lay in the sand laughing wildly. She had the true spirit of a freedom-worshipping pilgrim.

In total I spent five nights sleeping on the sand and got to reunite and reminisce with most of my favourite shell-mates. The lovely Leahs; Irish Pete, Barefoot Bernard, American Tierra; Steffan and Sasha, Arthur (the fed-up German I'd met at the albergue in Astorga); Austrian Elizabeth, Inke, Bence and Luís – they all came rolling into town and slept on the beach for at least one night. It was an extra-special treat to spend time with Steffan and Sasha again, who I hadn't seen since the day I walked fifty-eight kilometres to Carrión de los Condes.

Luís's arrival at the beach was typically comical and memorable. From a distance I saw a mystery guy drop his rucksack, strip naked, then run into the sea like a puppy seeing water for the first time. When he returned to his belongings with his big grey beard dripping wet, I recognised him as Luís. He shouted over for me to come join him swimming naked in the sea. I politely refused.

'*Más tarde* – later,' I replied. I was getting good at this Spanish stuff.

'*Esta noche con la luna* – tonight with the moon!' he suggested, pointing to the sky. This was so Luís – entertaining, energetic and childlike.

To keep ourselves amused on those lazy beach days, Tore and I created the Pilgrim Olympics. We used walking sticks as javelins and did sprint races across the sand. When Tore told me he was a black belt in Karate, I told him I'd still be able to beat him in a wrestling match. I was wrong. He floored me in seconds.

Following Luís's example, we too swam naked in the sea, to keep cool in the intense heat. When we weren't playing stupid boy games, we did our best to stay out of the fierce sun by cowering in the precious patch of shade the cliffs threw on the white sands.

At night the small congregation of pilgrims sleeping on the beach came together around a fire and shared food and drink. A quiet Spaniard strummed a guitar. Acoustic versions of 'Redemption Song', 'Knockin' on Heaven's Door' and 'Wish You Were Here' were just some of the many songs on a set list that lasted the whole evening. Jesús, another Spaniard who'd been living on the beach all summer, played token bushman and fed the fire, disappearing every now and then, before returning with bundles of wood. One night, a Polish guy turned up, threw his backpack down and began breathing into a harmonica.

It was how I imagined a Californian beach would have been in the sixties with the same ambience of peace, love and brotherhood. Scouse John said we were a perfect example of how the world should be - the Pilgrims Party of United Nations, twelve nationalities side by side around that beach fire, every one of us accepting each other, just like Natalia had said, for everything that we were.

31. PILGRIM FOR LIFE

Just like Finisterre was the end of the world for the Romans, coming back to England was the end of my world. Though I'd only been on the Camino for a month, that had given me ample time to sample an alternative way of life that I found far more gratifying and sustainable. A life of minimal consumption for maximum satisfaction; of sharing what little you had with others; of loving unconditionally; of trusting in strangers, with random acts of kindness, non-judgement and acceptance being the norm not the exception. It was the sort of utopia I'd always dreamt about, a supreme civilisation where the assumption was that people had positive intentions rather than clandestine, ulterior motives, which was what living in south-east England had conditioned me to suspect. It was like I'd time-travelled to a golden age in humanity's history, where the most serious social problems were snoring, body odour and blisters.

With my heart still pining for the Camino, I struggled to adjust back to normal life and did all I could to keep the pilgrim in me alive. For the first few weeks after my return I refused to sleep in my bed and curled up on the floor next to it. I took long weekend walks with my rucksack packed exactly as it had been on the Camino and got abused by gangs of youths calling me a 'gyppo'. After getting stared at by teachers, kids and parents during football-coaching sessions, I reluctantly shaved off my goatee. I was so attached to everything related to my Camino, I kept the hair in a sealed plastic bag as a souvenir. I filled four-pint milk cartons with water and went running with them in my rucksack because I felt like a cheat moving without weight on my back. I was so determined to continue living like a pilgrim, I even moved out of my rented flat, lived out of my backpack and stayed for short periods in friends' spare rooms in an attempt to replicate albergue life. Living this way was my downfall and led to a period of depression and disillusion with life in general.

Another reason for my post-Camino blues was the bold move I'd made soon after touching down in the UK. I agonised over leaving my band but realised it had become a straitjacket constricting my personal and professional development. I'd outgrown the lifestyle that supported my ambition to be the singer in the world's biggest band – the weekly routine at an insufferable, unfulfilling day job, nightly rehearsals, weekend gigs, hangover, then repeat. The juice just wasn't worth the squeeze any more. Quite simply, wanting to become the next Bono was the mission of the person that went to Spain but not the person that returned. Where once I fretted over every little detail regarding songwriting, gig bookings and online promo, I had become vacant. Aloof. Indifferent. As Martin Luther King Jr once said: you don't have to see the whole staircase to take the first step. The musical and social divorce after a five-year marriage to my bandmates was that first step. Though it was painful, it was absolutely necessary.

The next step on that staircase to a new life was closing down my soccer school. Since I'd started the business to fit around band commitments that I'd now relinquished, there was no reason to proceed with such a stressful and deeply unsatisfying job. Within four months of my return, my ten-year football-coaching career was over.

Seeking a stable income while I dreamt up a new dream, I got a full-time job working as a personal adviser to college students. It was an office-bound post that became my prison. After six months of pen-pushing, paper-shuffling, email-chasing, meeting-evading, coffee-sipping, biscuit-dipping, doughnut-scoffing, time-wasting, office-gossiping hell, I embarrassingly broke down during an appraisal with my boss.

'Take two weeks off,' she said, avoiding eye contact while shuffling uncomfortably in her seat at my unexpected, blubbering meltdown. 'Think about what you want to do,' she suggested, ushering me out of her office as quickly as possible.

The first thing I thought to do to raise my spirits was return to the Camino. To the place where I'd resuscitated the wandering wonderer, the inquisitive, fearless boy inside the bored man that had first set out for Santiago a year earlier. Even if I had to walk it backwards, on my hands, or skip it, I just needed to be back there to revive that part of me I'd lost touch with since coming home.

I missed the Camino's inexhaustible supply of little pleasures terribly. Eating lunch slumped against a wall or the stump of a shady tree. The quirky characters like Crazy Frank, the Italian flower lady and Marcelino the man with the big white beard who gifted me a walking staff and wine near Logroño. Cutting through the small-talk and getting straight to the deep and meaningfuls with people to whom I'd normally never even say hello. The magnificent scenery, charming towns and splendid cities. The awe-inspiring sunrises and sunsets. The little buzz of excitement at seeing a yellow arrow when I thought I was lost. The groupie grannies chasing the Bread Man's hooting van down the street. The jubilation at seeing a shop or bar actually open for business after an eight-hour, shadeless, thirty-degree day. The discounted three-course menus for pilgrims. The release of inner peace from exchanging hearty 'Hola's and 'Buen Camino's with natives and nomads alike. Food I'd normally leave out for racoons tasting like a gourmet meal. The relief of kicking off my boots and giving my feet a fresh-air pedicure. Entering shops in rural shanty towns that turned out to be an elderly person's kitchen with an array of goods spread out on the table like a school tuck-shop. Watching close-knit Spanish families and friends walking, talking, drinking and linking arms together on the streets. Pushing through the pain barrier and breaking through physical and mental boundaries I'd thought were beyond me.

I'd never felt better about myself than I did on the Camino. Stronger. Wiser. More confident. Indestructible. Free from all worry and the psychological self-harm that was now consuming me.

Before going back to Spain, I got in contact with my pilgrim mates to see how they were faring. Crazy Frank offered me some time out, inviting me to Budapest for a weekend. He'd just got his forklift-truck licence and had started a new job. Life had taken a new and calmer course, and he and Szilvi were living in domestic bliss. We hurdled the language barrier by YouTubing Depeche Mode concerts, eating delicious Hungarian food and knocking back *pálinka*, a vicious spirit that fools you into believing you could beat Arnold Schwarzenegger in an arm wrestle. In his studio flat poked into a suburban high-rise, he was so relaxed in my company, he even kissed his girlfriend's backside in front of me. She was, you'll be relieved to hear, wearing pyjamas at the time. There was no taming Crazy Frank's wild side, even with Szilvi around.

Irish Peter replied saying he was in South Korea teaching English and was head over heels with a local girl. Closer to home, the Leah Army had parted ways in London but remained best friends. Little Leah had gone back to Australia to be with her boyfriend after a bout of love sickness, and Big Leah was working and loving living south of the Thames. Big Leah and I had met in Barcelona after the Camino and in London a few times, and got on really well, but nothing else developed and we remained friends. She showed no signs of the post-trip comedown that was crippling my happiness. Tierra, like me, had loved the Camino so much that she'd gone back there at the earliest opportunity and stayed a while, volunteering in an albergue. She'd found a place where her New Age soul felt at home. Sadly, I never heard again from Barefoot Bernard or Sasha and Steffan. Tore, and Davíd, the affable, loquacious Spaniard I met between Santiago and Finisterre, were regular correspondents and uploaded lots of photos from the trail. Both were soon to graduate as civil engineers and were looking forward to starting their careers. All my shell-mates seemed to be doing mighty fine, which left me even more perplexed as to why I'd gone off the rails.

Focusing on the positive, I undertook some research that

shed a little light and logic on why the Camino had given me such unassailable highs. In the orbits of academia, I uncovered a plethora of studies suggesting that sunlight increases secretions of serotonin, the body's natural, mood-lifting, anti-depressant neurotransmitter. With one month on the Camino arguably bringing more sunshine than a whole year in England that was a lot of love and light to make for a happier soul.

Light is also a major player in our body's circadian rhythms – our internal twenty-four-hour clock. Humans have evolved over thousands of years to operate at our physical and mental optimums between sunrise and sunset. Sunlight wakes our bodies in the morning, and when it gets dark, our eyes send a signal to the brain that it's time to feel tired. Our brain, in turn, sends a signal for our body to release melatonin, a sleep-inducing hormone. That's one of many reasons why it's so hard for melatonin-deficient night-shift workers to sleep during the day. Only since the invention of the lightbulb in 1879 have we been able to operate after dark with such ease. My Camino body-clock, synchronised with dawn and dusk, had therefore been reset to the way of living for which our bodies are actually wired, which was another possible explanation for my surge in mood and elevated energy levels. Moreover, out-of-synch circadian rhythms are a well-documented behaviour in patients fighting depression.

Another important ingredient in the Camino's happiness cocktail was the chemical dopamine. Every time we accomplish something that contributes to an end goal, our brain's intricate reward mechanism, installed for achieving objectives, is triggered. The mood-elevating chemical dopamine is released, creating a sense of pleasure that keeps us focused and motivated when we're taking steps towards our goals. Perhaps this was why seeing those progress-affirming yellow arrows, ripping pages from my guidebook once I'd walked a section, and beating my daily records was so gratifying.

There are also countless studies championing the merits of walking. One such study in the *Journal of Mental Health and Phys-*

icalActivity concluded that it may be just as effective as pharmaceutical drugs for helping patients suffering from mild depression. The body produces stress-reducing, happiness-boosting endorphins and enkephalins during exercise, and walking also activates the parasympathetic nervous system, which helps our bodies shift from 'fight or flight' mode into a more relaxed, peaceful state.

More analysis published in the *Public Library of Science and Medicine* postulates that walking for just eleven minutes a day is enough to extend your lifespan by two years. Multiply that by an average of eight hours, or 480 minutes on foot every day on the Camino, and you can go get a frame for that telegram from the Queen. Take your cat with you and it may well end up with a lot more than nine lives.

So there you have it, hard scientific evidence that catching the early worm and walking can make you happier, less stressed and actually put years on your life. Was it any wonder I felt like Superman, fusing all those physiological rewards with the mental benefits of pulling over from the rat race to slip into the fast lane of adventure.

I only had two weeks back on the Camino, walking from Pamplona to Burgos, but it lifted me out the doldrums, just as the research suggested it would. My first time as a pilgrim, I went from feeling good about getting started to thinking I was Captain Invincible when I finished. The second, I went from the brink of depression to a more elevated, positive and empowered mindset. From broken down on the wrong side of the road to heading in the right direction in third gear. Having my walking boots on again gave me time to reflect on a year of self-sabotage and personal anguish and to see the error of my ways. Instead of trying to live a civilian life like a pilgrim, I realised I had another, better choice: to use everything the Camino had taught me to improve my day-to-day existence.

Though I didn't see it at the time, from the moment I first decided to walk the Camino, I was motivated by two things: meaning and purpose. Even though I wasn't enjoying coaching anymore, having the goal of walking to Santiago on the horizon gave meaning and purpose to a job that wasn't challenging for me anymore. Knowing it would pay for me to walk the Camino was the motivation I needed to get up and go every day.

My new task after my two-week time out from work would be to map out a new Santiago to wake up for in my post-Camino life. Financial, professional, creative, familial, friendship and relationship Santiagos. New, highly motivating targets on the horizon to give me renewed meaning and purpose. Goals where the journey towards the final destination would be just as enjoyable as the prize at the end. A journey that required growth, learning and evolution. I realised it was my duty. My obligation. My debt to myself. To use my pilgrim spirit to guide me and stitch the discipline and good habits I learned on the way to Santiago into my post-Camino days.

I went back to my office job having set myself a professional Santiago. I resolved to make sure all the youngsters in my caseload were in a better place personally and academically than when I first met them. While doing so, my financial Santiago was to save enough money to move permanently to Spain. In Julien I had a best friend in Barcelona and a place to stay and get started. With no personal or long-term professional ties left in England, there was nothing stopping me.

The prospect of immersing myself in a culture I'd fallen in love with on the Camino was very appealing. I looked forward to socialising over a meal instead of indulging in the UK's number-one pastime of binge drinking; to outdoor sports in the sunshine instead of being locked indoors with Noel Edmonds on the TV, and the rain and wind beating on the windows; to having every day decorated with new discoveries rather than the scripted, routine banalities that now described my life in England; to learning a new language, having the Camino just a train journey away, and talking to old men on benches.

Touching down in Barcelona, my first goal was to get working on my next professional Santiago: find a job I actually enjoyed. I had no clue what that was going to be and suffered a soul-destroying period of trial and error. I taught English for a few months to Spanish school kids. It was adorable hearing them pronounce biscuits as 'bee-skew-eets,' fruits 'frew-eeets,' and apple 'app-lay.' The novelty soon wore off though and it felt like a step backwards from coaching soccer, which is what I was trained to do. I taxied tourists on a rickshaw for a week but thought better of it when I realised that my competitors touting for business on the streets were prostitutes, drug dealers and vendors of fake designer watches. I worked as a telephone operator for a British hotel chain in their Catalan HQ but soon reasoned that the €800 monthly salary wasn't worth the daily shift of nine draining hours.

During those early, character-building days in Barcelona as I struggled to find my vocation, I had to have some strong words with myself. I would talk myself out of returning home by re-writing affirmations into my journal.

> *If you can walk fifty-eight kilometres in a day. If you can cross the Meseta. If you can overcome the distress of shin splints and blisters. If you can take a bonking but still get up and go again. If you can scale two peaks higher than Ben Nevis, walk the equivalent of three marathons on three separate days and nine hundred kilometres in a month. You can get through the growing pains of settling down overseas.*

Without those Camino experiences, which had sharpened the saw of my life skills, I'm not sure I would have persisted. The words in the email from Chappers that I'd opened that beautiful night in Burgos had come true: 'You will never be the same when you come home. You are going to have this new resilience that will stand you in such good stead.'

It was that same resilience that got me through those overworked and underpaid early days in Barcelona. Luck, as they say, is where effort meets opportunity. And without that resolve and effort, born on the Camino, I wouldn't have found my vocation.

Back in England I had uploaded some headshots, vocal demos

and a promo video onto a musicians casting website. I was hoping to find paid work in some capacity as a singer but had heard nothing. Until now. I was invited to audition for a position working as a professional vocalist in a nearby tourist resort. Not only did I get the job, I was to have my accommodation provided and would receive much more money than a pilgrim needed. So I hadn't fulfilled my abandoned ambition to become the next Bono, but getting paid for singing covers was definitely the next best thing. It was also much more fun than being caged in an office, like I'd been in England.

Though it was never easy finding my feet in Spain, I came out the other side. I evolved from confused young adult sleeping on Julien's floor to home-owning, breadwinning, bilingual man. I no longer battled an irrational fear of the norm. After my post-Camino ups and down, I craved the norm.

With my newfound personal and professional stability, I was ready for the one thing the Camino had promised but failed to give me – love. Thanks to my past love-life traumas, I'd become an expert at recognising the early-warning signs of trouble and steered well clear of the crazy Maisies. Neither did I place all my bets on the email address of a woman I'd never met. As romantic and exhilarating as it was crossing a whole country for a blind date, in hindsight, I was highly unlikely to meet the right woman while I was still that painfully immature version of myself.

Flashing back to my post-Natalia epiphany that life gives you what you need, not what you want, I met someone who blessed me with so much more than that. Someone prepared to accept me for all that I was – a late developer, a former pilgrim with his Santiago goatee in a bag, a man that made her walk to Santiago with him for a third and fourth time. A woman with a big, gentle heart who can't walk past a homeless person without feeling the need to buy them a hot drink and a sandwich. My Yoko Ono. My soul bride. My wife. Rachel. I love you.

Need a rest and a laugh after walking all that way?

Why not go to my website where I'll tell you how you can listen to some songs and see some funny photos from my band days.

Beware!

My shirts were so loud, you couldn't hear the music.

www.bradleychermside.com

See you there!

ACKNOWLEDGEMENTS

A thousand thanks to fellow author Joe Cawley, who helped keep my book writing ship on course and always responded to my SOS calls.

Joe is the author of the best-selling, *More Ketchup Than Salsa* book trilogy. Sample an audio dollop of his books at: www.joecawley.co.uk

To my dear friend Ruth Farrier, for scrutinising every detail of my myriad drafts and pushing me to smooth off a piece of work that was very rough around the edges. Ruby Tubes, you're an angel.

To my editor Lucy Ridout, for her expert assistance in turning my emails, journals and dictaphone recordings into a story.

To all the pilgrims with whom I was lucky enough to share such a magical time on the trail. I'll treasure all the lessons, laughs and memories you gifted me everyday for the rest of my life.

Lastly, but certainly not in the least, to you, for buying my book. I really hope you enjoyed the true story of the greatest month of my life.

Printed in Great Britain
by Amazon

15382227R00150